The Twenty-Year Phenomenon

Men and Women Talk About the
Breakup of Their Long-term Marriages

Jean Brody and
Gail Beswick Osborne

SIMON AND SCHUSTER

NEW YORK

Copyright © 1980 by Jean Brody and Gail Beswick Osborne
All rights reserved
including the right of reproduction
in whole or in part in any form
Published by Simon and Schuster
A Division of Gulf & Western Corporation
Simon & Schuster Building
Rockefeller Center
1230 Avenue of the Americas
New York, New York 10020

SIMON AND SCHUSTER and colophon are
trademarks of Simon & Schuster

Designed by Eve Kirch
Manufactured in the United States of America

1   2   3   4   5   6   7   8   9   10

Library of Congress Cataloging in Publication Data

Brody, Jean.
The twenty-year phenomenon.

1. Marriage—Case studies.   2. Divorce—Case
studies.   3. Middle age—Case studies.   I. Osborne,
Gail Beswick, joint author.   II. Title.
HQ734.B839   306.8'9   80-10313
ISBN 0-671-25042-6

Our grateful thanks to our researcher and all-purpose assistant, Kay Walker. And to Sumner Shapiro, M.D., for invaluable direction and consultation. And to others, too numerous to list, for insights, advice and support.

To the tellers of these tales

Contents

Introduction

In the past decade our society has witnessed a steady drift away from monogamy, dramatically expressed in rising sexual infidelity and a divorce rate of almost epidemic proportions. A relatively new phenomenon is the dissolution of long-term marriages, those that had survived intact to and beyond the twentieth anniversary and were regarded as stable and secure. It is logical to ask, What is happening?

And if we look to nature on this point, the response is not encouraging. "Well, what did you expect? You've raised your children to sexual maturity and that's all we bargained for, all that evolution requires of you. You've outlived your usefulness. By fooling around in your laboratories and extending your life beyond its natural span, you are now substantially outlasting your reproductive period."

If we turn from nature to more empathic experts for suggestions as to why these seasoned unions fall apart, we encounter numerous possibilities. Imagine an informal gathering of professionals from various disciplines in the social sciences: The sociologist might offer that the situation is a predictable result of the changing function of the family unit. In times past, the close ties of the extended family reflected mutual reliance in terms of such basic needs as food, shelter and nursing care. Today, those needs are serviced, though not met, by a plethora of social agencies that not only allow but encourage the shifting of caretaking responsibilities from the individual to the state. What is lost is the sense of shared accomplishment and interdependence that can bind people together.

The psychohistorian could argue that our present dilemma is a culmination of the kind of intense self-examination that began with Freud; that while self-awareness and self-criticism can be valuable tools for self-knowledge, they can also spiral inward to become self-absorption, producing a generation of zealous narcissists wholly devoted to "doing their own thing."

One of the psychologists would submit that the middle-aged blossoming of women—returning to school or to an earlier abandoned career—is a healthy, natural response to the easing of nesting activities that occupied her earlier years, but that it comes inaptly at a time in her mate's life when he begins to feel the need for a more intimate, more dependent relationship. He resents the loss of her attention and searches for closeness elsewhere.

The Eriksonian psychiatrist would readily agree that there are indeed stages or seasons in a man's life, and that somewhere around age forty, a kind of cosmic itch begins to plague him wherein he reevaluates his accomplishments and associations. These inevitably pale in the light of his own recently acknowledged mortality, and the revisions that result can include change of job, life style and mate.

The physiologist might propose—hesitantly—the unpopular notion that men, like women, experience midlife hormonal changes and that these errant chemicals can plunge a stable, responsible husband/father into anything from a full-blown revival of juvenile misbehavior to psychotic breakdown and suicide.

And finally, there is the man in the corner who wandered into the wrong meeting and has been listening attentively. He is without professional credentials. He has been married for twenty-one years. He announces, "You guys are drowning in your own jargon. It's really very simple. It's just that sex with the same old person gets dull and boring after all those years."

There is no consensus; there are probably seeds of truth in all of the above. You will find these kinds of answers in the magazines you pick up at the newsstand as well as in highly respected psychological journals. And at this point, in all humility, we must admit that we do not have *the* answer. You cannot turn to the last page of this book and find it triumphantly writ: "This is the Cause and this is the Cure." We are not even certain there is a disease, let alone a patient. It may simply be that we live too long, that the genetic blueprint for our behavior runs out at forty or thereabouts and we must blunder willy-nilly through the second half of life with no help from the coded experience of our forebears.

Further, the current, exaggerated interest in all phases of midlife behavior, including divorce, may be a passing fad that will go the way of society's obsession with the developmental psychology of children so popular a few years ago. This often happens with psychosocial concepts; they emerge, are tried on, polarized, solved and then reexamined until finally they are sufficiently explained and accepted, and thus cease to be a novelty. Perhaps in the next century, with this feat accomplished, people will live through midlife without the benefit of public outcry and dissection. Perhaps the cataloguing of the characteristic and catastrophic conflicts of the passage will be returned to the hands of aging novelists, philosophers and poets.

But meanwhile, this particular epidemic has touched everyone. Surely no one who picks up this book has not experienced the collapse of an old marriage, either personally or through close friends and relatives. The "well-married" couple is in trouble, and whether this is an expression of a normal developmental stage of life or a pathological side effect of a cultural revolution in a sickly society, it is nonetheless bewildering, threatening and painful to those who live through it.

It occurred to us that it could be enlightening and valuable to go directly to the protagonists themselves, to ask *them* what happened—how they explained it, how they reacted, how they behaved, how they felt, how they adjusted or failed to adjust to the loss of a twenty-year emotional investment.

We elected to restrict our investigation to the so-called middle to upper-middle class. Our rationale was that these relatively well-educated, affluent people would have significant factors in common. Their resources, both financial and social, allow them a certain luxury of dissatisfaction, and the means to explore it.

We talked with many people, professionals in the behavioral sciences and potential subjects, and from the latter selected eleven individuals—six men and five women—who agreed to tell us their stories. We feel particularly fortunate that we were allowed into the lives of three ex-couples— thus, through Kate and William, Ellen and Stefan, and Julia and Gabriel, the reader can view both sides of the marital coin.

All of the subjects were married for at least twenty years, were in their forties at the time of separation, are the parents of adolescent or young adult children, and in each case it was the husband who physically left the home. As you will see in the coming pages, the issue of who left whom is not a simple one.

The interviews were conducted over a ten-month period in 1978–79. They varied in length and involved from one to four sessions. They were taped, transcribed and edited for chronology and clarity. Conversational grammar and punctuation were retained where possible. Names and identifying details were changed.

Although we worked from a set of questions, the sessions were unstructured; people were encouraged to speak of whatever they wished and to dwell on those aspects of their marital and personal histories that seemed important to them. Thus, interviewer and interviewee met as peers and together attempted to solve a puzzling mystery.

Given is the notion that the mated pair forms the closest, most demanding of all human relationships. The mystery is not only what caused the death of the marriage, but also what caused it to survive for over two decades.

The following chapters are the data, the people themselves—the heart of the matter.

JEAN BRODY
GAIL BESWICK OSBORNE

The Interviews

There were good years together,
One has to remember that towards the end, surely—
moondazzle, peach weather,

brilliant noons, eloquent storms, sweet
new spears of tenderness,
all the lovely things, natural and trite,
one has to believe, I guess,

make life worth living, made it worth our while
to have come to middle age
with such brutal knowledge of one another.

MONA VAN DUYN

Kate

Kate separated from her husband, William, less than a month after they celebrated—with old friends—their twentieth wedding anniversary. They are the parents of two boys, nineteen and eighteen. Kate is a forty-six-year-old writer with a B.A. in journalism. Her interview took place nine months after the separation.

"How can something that starts out so fresh and new and full of hope get to the point where you just let it die . . . let it die without even saying some words over it?"

WE'VE BEEN SEPARATED a little less than nine months; actually, it's eight months, two weeks and six days since he moved out of the house, but in a way it began long before that. We've been separated, been distant from each other, for much longer than that.

As I look back on it, there was a steady going downhill for the last six or seven years. It was gradual, subtle even, with small chunks falling off . . . less and less closeness all the time. We were still functioning as a couple, particularly as parents, but we were moving away from each other.

A lot happened to us all at once. We turned forty. Bill had two serious illnesses that were very hard for both of us, although then I didn't realize just how hard. He changed jobs. And there were so many deaths—his father, his sister, his oldest friend—so much loss and sickness and change within a relatively short period. So it wasn't just *one* thing; it was many things and we couldn't handle them. We flunked disaster.

Soon after his father's death, a dentist discovered a white spot on Bill's tongue and recommended a biopsy. There was an awful period of not knowing, maybe three weeks in all. It seemed like forever.

I went with him to the doctor for the results of the biopsy. It was malignant. The doctor said something to Bill about taking a couple of weeks to get his life in order. It was really scary, like "Get things in order so you can die." I looked at Bill—he was pale—so I interrupted the doctor and said it would be better if he did the surgery as soon as possible. It was as if I took over. Bill said later he was glad I did that, but it kind of set a tone. I felt like I couldn't show I was afraid— felt I couldn't admit I was terrified because I had to take care of things, had to be strong.

Afterward we went to have a drink. We sat there in the bar holding hands but we didn't talk about it. I *wanted* to talk about it. I kept forming sentences in my mind but they wouldn't come out. The problem was, I thought I had to be someone to lean on—it was ridiculous! But that was the role I took on, have always taken on. It was never assigned to me, but all my life whenever there was an opening for a tower of strength or a pioneer woman, I tried out and usually got the part.

And there was another thing—maybe more important. He was going to his hour, his analytic hour, and it was nearly time to leave. My thought was that he would tell his analyst how he felt about it, and in a way that was fine. I thought, "That's her role and this is mine." God, how dumb! So I left him and went home and I started to cry. I really cried . . . and I prayed. I hardly ever pray, but this time I prayed that if it was bad he would die from cardiac arrest or complications during surgery—just don't let him lose his face bit by bit, be eaten up a little at a time.

I don't remember what happened when he came home. We didn't talk about it, how we felt about it, and I guess we went back to being whatever we thought we had to be.

In the hospital the doctor said Bill would need a private nurse because of the danger of suffocation from swelling in a tongue operation. I wanted to stay but they wouldn't let me, so I spent the night in the waiting room and kept peeking in the room to make sure the nurse was awake. She really got irritated and I don't blame her. If only I could have said, "It's not *you*, it's *me*. I'm so worried." And she could have said, "Yes, I know, but I'll take good care of him." (I guess I want to rewrite the dialogue of the last six years.) Anyway, it was okay—and tongues heal quickly. But he wasn't able to quit smoking and that bothered him.

He left his private practice in psychiatry and took a staff job at the hospital shortly after that. That was hard for him too. He's always had trouble being around a lot of people, he's not the friendly, easygoing sort, never has been. At the beginning he complained that he wasn't getting along with anybody. He'd been eating lunch at his desk so I suggested he go to lunch with people, shoot the breeze with them, have them over. I even suggested he take the *secretaries* to lunch. Honest to God, sometimes I think I'm not very bright.

Then he started having trouble with his neck and back. He'd had that trouble on and off for several years, but it started to get worse on this job, and one morning he woke up in terrible pain.

He went to the orthopedist and they really did a number on him—said it was all in his head. Finally they put him in traction in the hospital for a couple of weeks and then ordered complete bed rest with a traction setup for the rest of the summer. It was about three months at home, with him in *bed*, and it was just terrible for both of us.

He's a lousy patient and I'm not the world's greatest nurse, which was something I didn't really understand until much later. I'm very good at maintenance, at making sure everything is done. I ran up and down stairs extremely well, saw to creature comforts, fixed trays, rubbed his back, changed the sheets, bought books and crossword puzzles—all that. But I don't think I was available for what he really needed and wasn't able to ask for.

I was aware of it, that we were in a bad situation, and I wanted to do something about it. I talked to a friend of mine, which was very hard. Normally I never talked about our problems because I had some nutty idea that I would be betraying him—that it was disloyal.

But my friend is a very wise woman and I needed some wisdom. She said how hard it is, particularly for men, to be sick, because they're so ashamed to be helpless. If you do too much, they think you're treating them like children and they resent that—but if you don't do enough they feel abandoned. So she said it was really important for Bill and me to *talk* about it—to admit to each other how difficult it was. I tried to talk to him but he thought I was just complaining. And I tried just being there—reading to him or talking—but he was away someplace in his head.

Part of the problem was that I had some resentment which I wasn't aware of at the time—some stuff left over from growing up—and I'm sure it showed. When I'm sick (and maybe in my whole life I've spent a week or two in bed so I don't even know what it *is* to be sick) I like to be alone. I'm the cat that crawls off by itself. But who wants to be alone for three months?

Anyway, I guess it got to the point where I was just doing my job. Coffee, tea and milk. Cheerful and dutiful without much understanding of how awful it is to be completely dependent, to have to rely on someone for everything.

We would talk about it in an intellectual way: "It's difficult to be incapacitated, degrading to get paid for being disabled . . ." but not "Christ, it is *hell* . . . I feel shitty . . . I'm embarrassed . . . I feel like a four-year-old with Miss Cheerful Dutiful waiting on me hand and foot and resenting it." And which hand do we bite? The one that feeds us, of course.

Much later he said he felt I hadn't taken good care of him when he was sick. That came as quite a shock and I had to think about it a lot, really hold it up to the light and examine it. As I said, I think it had something to do with the way I grew up. Maybe I'm just rationalizing but I wasn't sick and I wasn't around anyone who was. In our family you went to bed to sleep or to die, so I really had to be in bad shape, not able to *move*, before I'd lie down and admit there was something wrong with me.

And, over the years Bill had called himself a hypochondriac. There were times when I felt, Yeah, you're right, you *are* a hypochondriac. Now are you really sick this time? Oh, come on, you're not *that* sick. Just pull yourself together and you'll be fine. It's just a little cold, it'll go away . . . It's just a virus going around . . . it'll be gone in twenty-four hours . . . it's just a little cancer, my dear . . . it'll be fine after they cut your tongue out . . . it's just that you've broken your back supporting us all these years . . . a couple of months and you'll be swell!

It wasn't like that—I didn't *say* anything like that but I'm sure that attitude came over. But I honestly don't think I was aware of it at the time.

He didn't talk about how he was feeling, and although I wanted to, I had pretty much given up trying to get through and around and over the wall he built when he didn't want to talk. I had accepted that those were the things he talked about to his analyst—private, mysterious things that were solved on the couch. I thought that one marvelous day when the analysis was over, a miracle would happen, and everything would be all right, and he would talk to *me* again.

Toward the end of this illness, just before the doctor finally diagnosed the problem and recommended surgery, we were close for a little while. It was a "you and me against the world" thing. The orthopedist was still dragging his feet and Bill was getting worse. I said the doctor didn't know what the hell he was doing and that Bill should get an outside consultation. He was concerned about doing that because he hadn't been at the hospital very long and he didn't want to make waves.

But I bugged him, encouraged him, supported him, ran back and forth with X rays, went with him to the orthopedist and asked a lot of questions and interfered and glared a lot. And finally, after a lot of manipulation, they did a myelogram, which showed a ruptured disc so they did the surgery. It was a kind of triumph. We had beat the system and we'd done it together. Maybe married people need more mutual enemies.

We talked during the early years of our marriage. We were very close in the beginning. His internship was a marvelous time. We were poor but rich in each other. I suppose that everyone has that first-married glow for some time. The years in New York were good. But there were a couple of incidents that weren't dealt with very well, harbingers of doom, maybe. When he would find fault with something I did I became aloof, above reproach. And he would clam up when I criticized him. But all in all, it was a warm, loving time and we kept the magic intact for quite a while especially considering we had children too soon and too close together.

Our first child was born when we'd been married less than two years, and the second fourteen months later. Just the same, we kept the skyrockets going off for a long time, and that was very important to him. He still hasn't learned that even skyrockets get dull if you have them every morning for breakfast—that love has different ways of expressing itself at different stages. Not sure I've learned it either.

Our first big failure in communication was when we left New York and came back to San Francisco. We had originally planned to spend only two years in New York and then to come home for the third year of his residency. As it turned out, we really loved New York but he thought I wanted to come back and I thought he wanted to come back and somehow we never got around to discussing it.

Maybe that's when we started assuming too much about

each other—about what the other felt, or wanted, or needed —instead of going through the pain of finding out what really was going on. We did and still do have an almost spooky kind of telepathy, but I don't think it will ever take the place of something spoken like "I love you" or "Please tell me where it hurts."

Things were bad when we first came back to San Francisco. He had to work in a state hospital for six months before he got into the residency he wanted. I was pregnant again and big as a barn, feeling ugly and tired and depressed. We had a gloomy apartment, weren't having much fun, he was driving a long way to a job he hated.

I had a very difficult time with the second birth. It was a cesarean after a couple days of ineffectual labor. He was with me all the time for those two days and was very tender, very loving. I couldn't get comfortable—couldn't lie down, stand up, sit up—I was just miserable. He'd drive me around in the car, lie on the floor with me, put his hands on my belly —a lot of holding and touching and caring. We kept going to the hospital and they kept sending me home because I hadn't dilated. It turned out I was in labor without dilating. Afterward, there were complications, an infection; I had a postpartum depression, not very serious, but I didn't realize why I felt so awful. Josh, our first, had been so easy, the whole thing such a pleasure. I thought, This mothering number is a real snap—you just pop 'em out, feed them and change them and love them. Easy! But with Rand I was so sick I could hardly drag myself around to take care of him. And I think Bill was irritated with me. I think he was afraid I wasn't going to be a good mother, like his own mother wasn't a good mother. He didn't say so, but I felt it, I felt judged somehow.

But all that passed—passed into our heads, where you

store those unresolved things until your head won't hold any more. We moved and got some help in the house and things were good. We started to go out and to entertain, we had more money—had a pretty good time. We were in our early thirties and were so busy we didn't know what we thought anyway.

Then I decided to go to work part time. I had some vague idea of a career. I wasn't sure what I wanted, but I wanted to do something. I'd been a copywriter so I went back to that and I thought it would work out well because it was part time. So I was with the kids a lot but not that twenty-four-hour-a-day thing that can be so deadly.

Also, I was helping Bill, transcribing notes and doing letters and some bookkeeping, so in a way we were working together.

But then it was decided—and I'm not quite sure who decided it—that I should be home with the children full time. Bill's clinic was into a lot of theoretical and practical stuff on raising kids, and a woman he worked with who had quite a bit of influence over him really took exception to my working. When I pointed out to her that *she* was a mother and *she* was working, she answered that her work was really important. God, I was so *dumb!* Why didn't I just tell her to get the hell out of my life?

Anyway, I did a lot of thinking and decided, "Yeah, we do have these kids and they're the most important thing right now so I'll do that." As a matter of fact, I did enjoy it, but I managed to do other things anyway. It was never enough for me to be just wife and mother. I had to have other interests. So I wrote commercials at home and that worked out fine.

I didn't hear any more from that woman unless she was responsible for the "don't be too affectionate with the kids" routine I got from Bill once. I know now that he was concerned I would be seductive with them—a lot of mothers are —you know, sleeping with them and showering with them and being a little girl with them—and that can really screw them up. But I just liked to hold them and hug them and touch them, to be warm with them—that's the way I felt. But he was the expert, so I accepted it without question. I don't hold much with experts any more. But I had to become an expert myself before I learned that.

We settled into our mid-thirties. The kids were in school, we bought a house, we were busy. He was feeling good about his work most of the time. We were involved in causes . . . saving the world . . . doing group things with friends . . . tennis . . . volleyball . . . vacations . . . just moving along. Sure there were bad times, but who doesn't have bad times?

As I said, I don't know exactly when we started talking to each other less—started growing apart. Some people can point a finger at an incident and say, "This is when it all turned sour," but I think in our case we just stopped tending the garden as carefully as we used to and the weeds started to take over. But, if I had to choose something as a turning point, it would be my mother's death. She and I had never been close; she left when I was five and my father raised me. I didn't love her but she was my mother and when she died I felt a lot of guilt.

I started writing fiction—wrote a novel that should have been cathartic, but I didn't understand I was writing about myself. It's a pretty good novel. I had a lot of insight into the characters. It was just that I had no insight into the author. I was really troubled by what I was writing and I started drinking too much. I'd start at five o'clock and was on my third drink by the time Bill got home, so that by bedtime I was a zombie. Who wants to make love to a zombie?

I can look at those books now—I wrote three—and I see I wrote down a lot of what was going on between us, but I didn't know it at the time. If I had been more perceptive I might have gotten into therapy, which I really needed. But I wasn't, and I didn't.

At one point after I had made an ass of myself—falling down, spilling wine all over my new dress—I felt bad enough about myself to ask Bill for help. He said he would ask his analyst for a name, and I couldn't take that. As it was, I felt she was keeping him away from me. I wanted to talk to *him* about it and I guess he couldn't handle it. So I just picked myself up, had another drink, and went on.

This was just before the sky started to fall—just before all the deaths and illnesses and changes. There's no question we didn't or couldn't share our feelings about all the bad things that were happening. We did talk some, but it was mostly on an intellectual level—like, This is the way people behave during a loss, this is what they do or think or feel. We talked about the dynamics of it—it was almost clinical.

When his sister died, I did a lot of carrying and fetching, helped make the arrangements, took care of the food, details, the maintenance of death. I was a shoulder for everyone to cry on, except for him. Later he said he should have appreciated my taking care of his family but he had really wanted me to take care of *him*. He was angry, I was hurt, it went nowhere. Maybe I was trying to punish him, like "Get rid of your goddam analyst and maybe I can be a wife." Or maybe it was the crazy notion that it was his therapist's job to take care of his problems.

There was *always* a therapist of some sort right from the beginning, and I never got over resenting it. I felt, "Why do we need this third person in our lives?"

He had told me early in our marriage that analysis was very important to him—the thing he wanted more than anything else. That he hoped it would fix those things he didn't like about himself, make him warmer, more giving, less narcissistic. So I tried to accept it and I read a lot of books, but

I think it was still an embarrassment to me and it made me feel I had failed him.

We had one very ugly conversation, I think during the time of his friend's illness. His friend was dying of cancer and Bill was very depressed. One afternoon we sat in the living room and talked about Our Sex Life. He said that I was cold and ungiving and I said that he was too demanding—that it had gotten to the point where the only time he ever held me or touched me was when he was horny. You know, the old complaint of old marriages: You don't bring me roses any more.

Then he said that we were both cripples—that he had a small penis (was there ever a man alive who was satisfied with the size of his penis?)—and that I had small breasts. It took me forever to get over that. I don't know why it was so devastating, but for a long time I *felt* like a cripple. I would look in the mirror and I would hate my body because it hadn't grown big boobs.

Then there was another time, I'm not sure when, but I think after all the deaths and shortly before he stopped smoking. I don't know what started it but at some point he said maybe he should just find an apartment. I said something like "Fine. Do whatever you want, I don't care . . ." but then I backtracked and said, "This is not a very good time, the kids are too young—we probably ought to talk about it later."

We both backed off, afraid to do anything that drastic, I guess. But he had *tried* to talk about how bad things were, and I had treated it like so much garbage. I guess by that time I had erected my own walls. They certainly were not all his doing—I'm a good builder of walls myself.

During this time I was not physically attracted to him. He was getting seedy, he looked old, acted old—he'd grown a beard which I never liked and he wore those terrible glasses.

It all made him look like a rabbi and it really turned me off. What happened to the handsome man I married? Same thing that happened to the pretty girl he married, I guess. They were both getting older.

Anyway, we lived together and we functioned together, and in some ways it was comfortable because we counted on each other for certain things. And I was busy, going to school full time, taking biology, learning about LIFE. I had no time to look at how my own life was going. Since I couldn't do anything about my body, at least I could have a voluptuous mind. How silly!

So sex became a pretty mechanical thing for me—"Okay, let's get it over with." I didn't say it, but I'm sure I acted that way. And it was terribly important to him that I enjoy it— that it be lustful and fun and satisfying. I understand this somewhat now, but it's still hard for me to talk about it. Like a lot of women my age I had been subjected to that wonderful piece of scientific information that there was something wrong with you if you didn't have a vaginal orgasm. I didn't have orgasms during intercourse. I had so-called "immature clitoral orgasms" before, with digital or oral stimulation. . . . Jesus, I sound like some goddam sex manual!

But I was very ashamed of it because I thought I was weird or perverted. Funny, a lot of women complain because they don't get this—and I had it all those years and couldn't accept that it was okay to feel good from that sort of loving. Someone said to me recently, "If it feels good and the book says it shouldn't, throw the book away, not the partner." But I was hung up and I couldn't talk to anyone about it. We'd have intercourse and I'd think, Oh, God, there's something wrong with me that I don't get it this way—and the dumb thing was that I enjoyed the intercourse itself—I mean the feeling of being united, being joined, being one—it was really enough but I didn't know it. So I would pretend to have an orgasm, and later, I didn't even bother to pretend at all. I just lay there like some long-suffering lump. I *was* a cripple, I couldn't talk . . . I had a crippled tongue.

After his sister died, Bill had a lot of trouble with sore throats and colds, and once he spit up blood, which was the thing that finally convinced him he *had* to quit smoking. So he arranged to go to a place out of town where you can kick all kinds of bad habits, or at least exchange them for something else. He asked me to go with him, but I was absolutely terrified at the idea of having to give up cigarettes. I'd given up booze and I figured that was all I could manage without losing my mind.

Now I wish I had gone. I wish we had talked about it because the smoking thing has some awesome importance for him which I still don't understand. He came back all cured and reformed. I didn't smoke around him but he complained about how I smelled—so I tried not smoking from three o'clock on so I wouldn't smell like cigarettes when he came home, but he still complained. I tried to quit and I couldn't do it and I was furious with him for wanting me to.

Anyway, bad smell or not, we continued to make so-called love. Then we went to a meeting about pornography. This was the Sex Era—it seemed like every other scientific meeting was showing stag films and calling it education. It was a *very* stimulating evening. He didn't say a word all the way home. I was feeling pretty heated up and I imagine we were the only couple from the meeting who didn't have a party that night.

After that evening we did not have intercourse for a little over three years, and as unbelievable as it sounds, it was never mentioned. I was more or less content with this arrangement. It didn't affect our relationship very much— which was pretty superficial by this time anyway. We dealt with domestic things, with the children . . . just went along like nothing had happened.

Soon after that we bought a large house with lovely grounds and a pool. The boys were in high school. Bill was getting along better at work, I was busy lecturing and writing . . . God's in his Heaven and all's right with the world. We slept in the same bed and never touched each other. How can something that starts out so fresh and new and full of hope get to the point where you just let it die . . . let it die without even saying some words over it?

Then one night—he came home late, from being on call, I thought. He moved over to my side of the bed and I said something like "What brought this on?" He mentioned about our anniversary coming up in a couple of weeks and said we ought to see if we could get to know each other better. It wasn't any good. I didn't have anything in the house, and he used a rubber, which I don't like. It didn't occur to me to wonder why he had them. Then we tried again a few days later and that was much better except I said something about his being greedy, which was dumb—I think I was trying to be flirtatious and had forgotten how, but it touched off something and he was angry for days.

The next morning he followed me out of the bedroom and said, "What happens to romance between married people?" I turned around, and his face was full of such pain and bewilderment and unhappiness. I said, "Something else replaces it." There at the eleventh hour was a chance to talk—but we didn't. I just kept on walking.

I didn't see it coming. I should have—it was all there for me to see. But there was this thing, this timetable in my head. We hadn't reached the end of his analysis, when everything would be okay—when we would, like two brand-new people, start to pick up all the pieces, collect all the loose ends, take care of all the dead nerves. I was sure this would happen, like some sort of miracle, once he got rid of his analyst. I know it sounds naive, terribly unsophisticated. It was my own private fairy tale.

I hadn't seen any big changes in him. There were changes,

yes, but I thought they were normal for a man in his forties who's worried about his health and is having to face up to his own mortality. He was running and swimming a lot but that didn't seem unusual. At some point it occurred to me that he was on call quite a bit. It was supposed to be one night a week, but it began to be more than that. I said something about the boss not liking him, but I didn't think much about it. For the past three years when he'd been on call, he had stayed at a motel close to the hospital. But he stopped that. He would come home late when I thought he was on call, but then he wouldn't get any calls and I thought, Isn't that nice. I have a strange way of protecting myself from the truth.

Then one evening he came home early. He fixed a drink, then went off to his study and put on some old Frank Sinatra records, goodby songs, and he came back in a while and made another drink. At some point I asked him if he wanted to eat and he said no. I went about my business, Rand and I ate, I cleaned up the kitchen. Later I went in to say goodnight. He was in his office sitting at the desk with another drink. He was crying. I went to him, took him in my arms and said, "I can't bear to see you this unhappy—what's wrong?" He was really weeping and part of it was the booze but so much was desperation.

He said he couldn't talk about it, that he wanted to protect me. Then he asked if I was feeling strong. Then he said he'd been seeing another woman for three and a half years. I don't know how long I stood there not saying anything. Finally I said, "I thought it was something serious—I thought you were dying." And he said, "I am dying—can't you see I'm dying?"

It's hard to remember what happened. I'd been lying to myself for so long, it wasn't possible for me to believe what I was hearing. I kept saying to myself, "This is a nightmare and I'm going to wake up in a minute."

Then he started talking. I've read since that this is what a crisis is like—the words just tumble out all jumbled and all on top of each other. He had to say it all, and with all the little details—a rambling effort to say everything. I just listened. It was like a bad movie or a soap opera—I mean things like that don't *really* happen. It was like listening to somebody else's story—not this man I had known for twenty-three years.

He said she was a secretary at work, and he had asked her out the week after he came back from the smoking place. He said he had realized even before he went to the smoking place that he was going to have to have another addiction to take the place of smoking. Does that make sense?

He said he hadn't meant for anything to come of it. They went to dinner and then to the motel where he stayed when he was on call and that's what they did once a week for three years—and a couple of times she met him on out-of-town trips.

He said that it wasn't really serious until she developed some odd symptoms which he diagnosed as a very debilitating illness, a crippling illness. God! Another cripple—and that by that time he had formed "an attachment." "You become attached to people," he said.

I started thinking about the kinds of records he'd been listening to and the books he'd been reading. Dying females and impossible love, all the way from La Bohème to Scott and Zelda. Then he gave me a rundown of the poor dear's problems—her ovaries, her cervix, her hysteria—she sounded like a real winner. But he said he felt she had made him well and he had made her sick. Where was his fucking analyst when he was on *this* power trip?

Finally she told him she was tired of being his mistress and that if he didn't leave me she wouldn't sleep with him any more. However, she did say it was okay for him to take her to dinner and play handsies and footsies, and that's what the extra nights on call were about.

Then he told me about her involvement with other men—
that he'd gone to her house and another man was there, and
she talked about how it was sexually with other men, and
he'd written a lot of letters and he didn't know why he felt
this way and she was not that attractive. She was sick . . . she
was crazy . . . she wasn't very smart . . . but he was hooked
. . . it was an attachment and she looked like his sister and
acted like his mother . . . she was young . . . and he was the
father and the doctor. . . . So much, all jumbled together.

Finally I just couldn't stand it any more. I went to bed. I
guess I went to sleep. I guess I got up the next morning and
went to work. Everything is a total blank until the next evening. We sat in the living room and talked. I was very angry
by that time. The paralysis had worn off.

He told me that the people at work knew about the affair
and that a couple of our friends also knew. He said that for a
time he had felt really crazy and had talked to people about
it—he'd been unable to help himself. I said something about
it being so undignified. My life was falling apart and I was
worried about dignity. Anyway, I said a lot of things like
"How could you do this to me? . . . How could you let us
have a twentieth-anniversary party and invite all those people? . . . You've made a fool of me, humiliated me, hurt
me. . . ."

I was really troubled about his taking something as personal and private as our life together and hanging it out on
the line for everybody to see. Like he had acted in bad faith,
betrayed a trust, violated something.

I think I overreacted about all of this so I wouldn't have to
confront what was really on my mind—the other woman.
That's the hardest thing—that's the hardest thing of all.

The next day we talked again—we were cool and aloof and
civilized. He said he thought there was nothing left between
us; I didn't challenge that. He said that either he should
move or if he stayed he would want to have more freedom.

That was like waving a red flag in front of me. He couldn't do it himself—couldn't come right out and say he wanted to leave me—but he presented it in such a way that I would tell him to go. Sure enough I did.

He found an apartment. I helped him pack, packed him some dishes and linens, even some pictures—Miss Cheerful Dutiful to the end. Then we went out to dinner. We should have gotten an award—it was a brilliant performance.

Sunday morning he got a U-Haul trailer. Our youngest, Rand, and a couple of his friends helped load it and they left.

A little later I went out to lunch with a friend, that good, wise lady who is one of the treasures of my life. Then I came home. Rand wasn't back yet. I wandered around through the house—just wandered around. Then I picked up a book of poetry he had given me before we were married. The inscription referred to a poem called "Epithalamion," which was about the raw materials of love and how you have to carefully and patiently and constantly fashion them into a work of art.

He wrote, "I never did figure out what an epithalamion is but I've never before been so overwhelmed by such an abundance of raw materials and such a challenge and desire to sculpt and create, and such a vision of power and wisdom. Goin' my way?"

On our tenth anniversary I returned it to him with another inscription: "An epithalamion is a nuptial love song or poem. P.S. I think we're making progress."

That Sunday I made another entry: "On this gray morning —just twenty-five days after we celebrated our twentieth— we laid down the chisel, mallet and stone, and admitted that we had failed to make a work of art. That is not to say that there was not still tenderness and liking but the passion simply did not survive the years. Does it ever?"

And I think at that point I realized that I had lost something very important to me, and that I had lost it a long time ago, That day I began a long journey back. It's been a very painful one, full of detours and cul-de-sacs and dark alleys. An old friend described me as a brick wall that had been bulldozed. I think that's a good analogy.

Now I'm looking at all the bricks in this pile and trying to figure out how to make a wall that has some give in it. I've even gone into therapy—that old enemy—and I'm finding it's not all that mysterious. It's a way of getting help when you need it—and I need it.

I've done a lot of reading on separation, loss, attachment, depression and everything I can find on the Male Midlife Crisis. Bill says that's what he's going through. But I don't think that's all of it. Maybe I'm simpleminded, but I think that if our sexual relationship had been good in those last years we would have worked out the other problems. I think that distance in bed leads to and feeds other kinds of distance. I know sex isn't everything, but it sure can mess up everything if it's in bad trouble.

Bill came back the following Saturday to pick up some things and we went to dinner. He asked if I wanted to see his apartment, but I didn't. Then he brought me home and a little while later I called him and told him that for the first time in several years I really wanted him. I went out there —we behaved like people on a date. It was very exciting, very sensual, very eighteen-years-old—very skyrockets. We made love—*really* made love. And for the first time in the twenty-three years I've been working at it I had an orgasm *during* intercourse. When I thought about it afterward, it wasn't much different. But I felt, "Okay, you finally passed Orgasm 101, you are no longer weird and perverted—now you are mature." Goddam experts! Fuck the experts! An orgasm is an orgasm is an orgasm! What really matters is how you feel about that person next to you—wanting to merge somehow and knowing you can't. It goes a long way beyond skyrockets. Before and during can be wonderfully exciting because of the erotic feelings you're having, but it's afterward that tells the tale. Sometimes there's a kind of unbearable tenderness—is there such a thing as a joyous sadness? I don't know—it's not really describable. It's maybe that you're so alive and at the same time knowing you're going to die. But you can't have that all the time either. Mostly it's just warm and so comfortable and nice and good and trusting —that's a lot. That's an awful lot. . . .

Over the past months I've spent one or two nights a week at his apartment, and once we went away for a couple of days. We've probably talked more during this time than we had in years—talked about ourselves, about how we feel: "Allow me to introduce myself. You haven't really looked at me for years. I'm the girl on the rock, the student, the daughter, the wife, the mother, the bag of bones, the reluctant matron, the reformed drunk, the other woman, the thorn in your side, and protein in your brain. . . ."

Since we separated I've felt more comfortable saying things to him that I wouldn't have said in the past. Maybe then I didn't want to rock the boat—but once the boat has sunk . . . ?

And then there was his analysis—*always* his analysis! But from the moment he left, I felt, "What's happening here? You're not through with that yet—oh, shit, come back—this is not the way the script goes."

So, after three years of not caring much one way or the other, I realized that I was in love with my husband. I know it's not that simple. It probably has to do with a lot of things —not wanting to be alone, fear of being old, loss of self-esteem, rejection, habit—a whole lot of complex things. But I began to compete with the Other Woman and then with Other Women.

One of the things that had happened when everything

went downhill was that *I* went downhill. Before, I had always been concerned with how I looked. I did the tennis number and the ballet number and the exercise number, wore nice clothes, had my hair done, my nails done—all that. I was attractive to other men and Bill liked that. I wonder if men measure a woman's worth in terms of how many of their brethren want to take her to bed?

When we met, I was divorced, I was working in television, drove a red convertible—was kind of glamorous and sophisticated in a homegrown way. But he fell in love with the girl who read poetry. He was always pleased and surprised that I knew as much as I did, that I had read so much, that I was —he said—wise and warm and understanding. That's the description of the good mother, right? I should have been smart enough to realize that he wanted the girl in the red convertible around too. I think a lot of us forget that.

But, at some point I lost interest. I was having a love affair with my brain and I didn't care if he found me attractive or not. I didn't care what other men thought either. I was a little disgusted with men at that time. Some of our friends were making passes—obviously the natives were getting restless —and I remember thinking the old farts should act their age. Humm, I guess they *were* acting their age. Anyway, like a lot of women, I became a little dowdy. I didn't get fat or wear printed housedresses, but I wasn't taking bubble baths either.

'So, after Bill left the house I dropped from 130 to 115 almost overnight and I looked pretty good. I bought some new clothes, including some ridiculously tight pants, bought new makeup, had my hair done—bought a lot of bottled promises to make me young. I even had an eye-lift—to make me young or cure my blindness? I also dug out all the rusty provocativeness, the femininity, flirtatiousness—all that stuff I had packed away and forgotten about.

In a way I put myself in the position of being the aging

filly in his stable. It's hard for me to believe I would do that
—that I was willing to risk the humiliation of competing with
women who were new, exciting, available, on the prowl, and
younger—mostly *younger*. I don't do that any more—I mean
there isn't that terrible desperation. I feel more like me now,
but I did discover that I *like* being skinny, I like putting on
a face, I like wearing nice clothes—I like being a classy
broad.

To begin with it was for him, and also there was a brief
period when I had to prove I was still desirable to men. I
think most women in my position go through this. Strange
that we need to prove it by leaping into bed, but we have to
assure ourselves somehow that we're not old bags. It doesn't
solve anything and it's sad to watch. I'm glad I realized that
early in the experiment.

Our relationship changes as it goes along, and it bounces
back and forth. Sometimes it's very affectionate, sometimes
kind of comfortable old-married—and sometimes there's a
lot of hostility. The good thing about the hostility is that it's
usually out in the open now instead of being hidden in a
sulk. We've had some really good evenings when we've
talked about painful things and didn't get angry or hurt or
have to give up.

How things go with us seems to depend on whatever else
is happening in his life, how his work is going; I don't think
he's had much satisfaction from his work since he left private
practice. And how things are going with Her.

When he left me, he did not walk into loving, welcoming,
open arms—or thighs. It's been an on-and-off thing for
months, and from what he says he's taken a beating in the
oldest way in the world. Hard to believe that he has a "sexual
problem" again. They used to call them ball-busters; now
they call them liberated women.

For a while he was burning up the bed with a lot of different women. He had the candles, the music, the theater pro-

grams, the match covers. Maybe it was because he hadn't had a lot of experience with women when he was young and was trying to make up for lost time—to experience Woman. Or maybe it's a part of that race against getting old—the race you can't win. But during most of this time he was also seeing me. We'd go out to dinner or to the theater—but usually he would just call and say, "I'm lonesome," or "I've got some scallops," or "You want to come over?"

The answer is always yes. Against some very good advice, the answer is always yes. If my grandmother could hear me she'd say, "Have you no shame, Katie?" And I would have to answer her, "No, gramma, I have no shame."

SHE is thirty-two. The other women he was seeing were all in their early thirties. For the most part he sought out younger women, just like it says in the book. We've talked about it and I think it's a serious thing—immature, maybe, but serious. He's terrified of getting old, of being old and infirm and impotent—all those things some men—all men? —worry about. We've talked about being the same age, and I read something recently about seeing your own age in the faces of the friends of your youth. So that's part of it—he sees me getting older and he has to run away from it. I'm the most lasting friend of his youth, and if I have lines in my face and my veins are showing and my skin is beginning to pucker, that must mean it's happening to him too.

It would have helped if he'd known some old people who had good lives. There are such people, you know. People who make it into their eighties with their health and their brain cells and their potency—all kinds of potency—still intact.

We *all* get older—it's a biological truth. Our bodies get older and some of the parts wear out and the finish isn't new any more—but damn it, that's what *happens,* and if you can't accept that, you end up acting like a fool and not liking yourself very much.

The children? What do you do about the children? You try so hard and you make a whole lot of mistakes, that's what you do. Both Bill and I wrote Josh about it—he was away at college. Bill told Rand when I was sitting there. I don't think I said anything. I think we've handled it reasonably well, given our weaknesses. I know Bill's terribly concerned about how it affects them, that they be as unwounded as possible.

Rand's response when Bill told him was pretty typical. His attitude was "That's the way it is . . . I understand . . . it's between you . . . it's none of my business." He pretended that's just the way life is—it falls down and goes boom. He's certainly his mother's child. But he *was* affected—his grades went down—he graduated from high school Magna instead of Summa, which is not too tacky. He was irresponsible about some things, which was unusual; was cranky, which was unusual; did some atypical things, for him, but they were all pretty minor and to be expected.

But he was forced from time to time to deal with me when I fell apart. I'm sure it was frightening for him. Once I went into my room and stayed there for two days in the pits. I couldn't get out; I just dug in deeper. Then sometimes I would just burst into tears, or wander around in a daze, or not eat.

He was worried and bewildered. He'd never seen me come apart at the seams before. But for the most part he was accepting and he kept the whole thing at a distance, although there were a couple of times when he wanted to talk about it. Once he and Bill got back from a weekend trip where he had "caught" his Dad with a woman. They were both upset when they got back and Bill told me what had happened, said Rand wouldn't talk about it—wouldn't talk at all.

After he left, Rand said to me, "When are you going to sell the house?" We sat down and talked for a couple of hours and he was able to bring up some things that troubled him. He said, "When are you going out and see the world?" And he was curious about the two extremes of behavior—his dad running around acting crazy and his mother holed up in a cocoon.

I told him his dad was on an odyssey and I reminded him of how Ulysses was delayed by Circe with the promise of eternal youth; how he had to have all those adventures before he came home; how Penelope waited for him while weaving a shroud by day and unraveling her work by night. We talked in abstractions but we knew what we were saying. Then I told him I'd already been out in the world, if he meant knowing men—that before I married his dad I spent a lot of time out there and found it a bit wanting. But that his dad hadn't—hadn't had that chance. He'd never been really free and irresponsible and silly—had never been young, really—and he'd never had any glories except for that ecstasy when you first fall in love. That's a pretty big glory, but you can't hold onto it, because the fantasy person becomes the real person after a while.

I read to Rand from *East of Eden,* where Steinbeck describes what a "glory" is—that exquisite feeling of being so unbelievably alive—it just wells up and you think you'll die of it. I've had it sometimes, working; once when I was with Bill at Mount Whitney; once on a mountain by myself; several times just looking at my kids. You can't will it. It just happens—if you're lucky.

It was a good talk—really good—and then Bill called and asked me to come out. Rand stood there listening to the conversation, and when I hung up, he said, "Is this weaving or unraveling?"

Another time when I was down, sad, he said, "I thought you said your depression would be gone in six months." I nodded. Very like me to put a time limit on something. He said, "Well, you're three days overdue."

When Josh came home from college in June, he wanted to

know what this nonsense was all about and he was very open and very angry about it. He had the impression that I had kicked Bill out—that it was all my doing somehow. He got the story in bits and pieces, from Bill, from Rand, from me. At one point, when I was depressed, he put his arm around me and said, "I love you, Mom." He hadn't done that for a long time and it really got to me. I thought, Here are these three people I love more than anybody, more than anything, and I can't even get the words out—I of the crippled tongue.

So we tried to learn to talk—all of us. Bill really wanted them to understand, and he was so frustrated that it didn't seem to come out right. He said some things he would rather not have said—too heavy, too much detail—but he wanted them to know he was human, that he wasn't breaking up the family on a fly-by-night, spur-of-the-moment thing—that it was something he couldn't help and that he felt helpless. . . .

Once when Bill was talking on the telephone to Josh about Her—something about her illness and how she was treating him—I heard Josh say, "I sure wouldn't let a woman treat *me* that way." He was furious when he hung up—said something about his dad acting like he was the kid and the kid was the father. He said, "He sounds so silly!" It's awful when your parents, your gods, show up too often in their clay feet. Anyway, he stormed around and said he was going to go over there and punch her lights out . . . he was going to tell that bitch to leave his dad alone, to go pick on some other family. . . . He didn't do it, of course, but he felt better.

All in all I think Josh is better off because he's been able to be angry—to talk to us about it. For the most part Rand has swept it off in some corner in his head; I expect it'll come back to haunt him some day. Those things do.

My own anger is something else. I am so painfully aware of how much I contributed to this—to this—well, a marriage is community property, it takes two to make it <u>fail</u>. At least two. I think we had more than our share of outside help. But anyway I have tremendous anger for myself, and I guess that's why I'm so depressed. I'm angry with him too and sometimes I've been able to get it out in a fairly straightforward way, but there's no good healthy cleansing rage—if there is such a thing.

My rage is for Her, and for his analyst, and for some peripheral women who were his advisers, I guess you'd call them. All through his life these women have cropped up—older, or his age, associates of some sort usually—social worker types who became confidantes—mother figures, maybe? They never seemed to last very long. He doesn't seem to sustain relationships for long periods and he hasn't had a good friendship with another man, but come to think of it, I don't know many men who have.

I think it's the same with his friendships as with the sexual thing. He wants skyrockets all the time, and God knows there are times when your friends are dull and tiresome. My wise lady once said, "That's what friends are—people who put up with you when you drag ass."

There's a woman at the hospital—someone he was close to. This bitch *encouraged* him to leave me, then later encouraged him in the affair with Her. She's what we used to call an old maid and it probably isn't possible for this new breed of people who never committed themselves to anybody to understand the things that can be between two people after twenty years together. They couldn't possibly understand and at the same time say, "Well, it's obvious *that's* not working—why don't you just dump it and try something else?"

My feeling toward her is, Goddammit, lady—that's my life you're fucking around with—that's hands on my belly and my kid's concussion and "The Night before Christmas" and real days and real nights and magic and good times and so-so times and awful times. . . . You can't even *begin* to know what goes into twenty years.

And the analyst. Bill said *she* had encouraged the affair for the first two years. So I wanted to see her, to talk to her, but she wouldn't see me—said it was unprofessional and it would interfere with her objectivity about him. There *are* people who feel it is not a good thing to treat the person in analysis as a separate entity, without taking into consideration what effect the process has on the other people close to them. So I really felt betrayed by her and the process that's supposed to make people better or warmer or more giving or whatever is missing . . . God, it's complicated. I hope *her* husband is screwing every thirty-year-old secretary he meets, and I hope she knows it, and I hope it hurts her all the way to the bone. . . .

Then there's Her—the Other Woman—I don't know why I can't say her name today. It's the same as my middle name and I have a lot of trouble with it. It's like, You took everything—you took my songs and my poetry and my restaurant and my Egyptian period—you even took my goddam name.

She didn't play fair. Why should I expect her to? I don't know. Some sort of outdated code. She knew he was married, knew he had a family. I've seen so many women manipulate men who were sexually interested in them and I've done it myself, so it's easy for me to make her the heavy—believe it was all her doing. A lot of "liberated women" today, when they get to be thirty, look at themselves in the mirror one morning and it's Jesus, where did those lines come from? Is this a gray hair? What is this around my middle? And they look around and they begin to think this being alone stuff is not what it's cracked up to be and they start thinking about babies and mortgages and white living-room furniture. I don't know if that's what happened with her, but it happens a lot.

Soon after we moved to the new house, she rented an apartment close by. That's not fair. When he transferred to another clinic, she followed him there too. That's not fair either. Then she insisted he leave me—used the oldest club in the world: "No leavee, no nookie." And she did a weird thing—told him she was coming by our house at Christmas . . . and that she was coming to our anniversary party. Weird.

I wonder if I symbolize her mother or some kind of Freudian thing—taking Daddy away from Mommy? She's getting a little long in the tooth to be doing the Daddy number.

After Bill left I decided I had to meet this Superwoman—this Supermonster. He was describing her in such a negative way, it was hard to believe he cared anything about her.

I fully realize that there is no way in this world she can be anything but a whore in my eyes. There is no way I can be objective about her—impossible.

I am the old alpha wolf, the dominant female, and this is my territory. A stray bitch in heat came slinking in and she pissed on all my trees and stole my old man. It's that primitive. What I really wanted to do was to kill her, but I'm not capable of it. So I called her, she came to my house, and I didn't kill her—I gave her tea and behaved like the civilized person I am.

I was surprised—no, shocked—at the way she looked. Ordinary, I mean cheap-looking. Cute in a Kewpie Doll way, a face with no bones in it, and she'll be fat in a couple of years. I'm expecting the young Elizabeth Taylor, and this waitress walks in. (The old alpha wolf is snarling and doing a little pissing of her own.)

The essence that came over was one of helplessness and I was a bit disarmed by that—I always am. *That's* a good brick to get rid of. She said she didn't know how it started—that he was ready for something and she didn't know where she was coming from. . . . There was a lot of psychojargon: "Where I'm coming from . . . my space . . . the place I'm in . . . relating to . . . looking for myself. . . ." She said she didn't know where we lived when she moved into her apartment. There was no evidence of guilt, of being sorry about anything—just total self-absorption.

Then she said it was all over between them, that she cared
for him but it would never work—that he was too emotionally dependent on her, that he should find himself, be his
own person—all that bullshit you hear at cocktail parties
nowadays. Ten years ago he wouldn't have given a woman
like her the time of day. Funny . . .

She asked me how I felt about him now and I made the
disastrous mistake of being honest with her. I said that I still
loved him and that I wanted him to come back.

She called him a couple of days later and allowed as how
they could try again. Old alpha bombed out.

The thing of it is—I *do* love him. I even like him. Why do
we like people? It's a whole other thing than loving or
"being in love." There are more requirements somehow.
You really get down to basics and he is basically a very decent man—that's one of the reasons he's having so much
trouble through all of this. If he was a son of a bitch he
wouldn't worry about it. But he's not. He's not cruel or ma-
licious. He does what he says he'll do. You can count on him
—trust him. I have a great deal of respect for him—I really
do.

He has a lot of the qualities that are important to me—a
sense of humor, intelligence, a social conscience, a desire to
do good work and a feeling of the importance of that work. I
think he's having a problem with that right now. He's having
to give up the dream of being President, of winning the
Nobel prize, of going down in history for doing something
revolutionary in his field. It comes to that for most of us who
long to do something special, and you feel almost naked
when you have to let it go. When I realized I wasn't going to
be a great writer, I mourned for a long time—but I got over
it. There are other things besides big tits and great
novels. . . .

Since Bill and I separated, I've been depressed most of the time, so I've lost interest in things that were exciting for me. Work, animals, writing, lecturing—things that kept the fires burning. Also, I haven't functioned all that well in practical ways like going to the market and doing laundry and paying bills and having things fixed. It's much better now, but for a few months I simply wasn't reliable. In a way it was good— the boys learned to cook and shop and do their own laundry —their dad didn't learn those things until he was forty-six. It was just such a tremendous effort to do *anything* but that was the depression and that's getting better.

I've learned some very valuable things. I've learned that I am not a pioneer woman—that I am not required to be a pillar of strength or a Rock of Gibraltar. Not only am I not required to, but I'm not qualified. So I don't have to apply for that job any more—I am a reformed rock. I can be weak and the world's not going to fall apart. I can be vulnerable with people who matter and not be done in.

There's been a rather painful reassessment of myself—taking stock, gathering up those bricks and trying to figure out which ones need to go. Belated certainly, but I suppose it should be welcome whenever it comes.

I get along better with my kids. There were things I was rigid about with them that no longer seem necessary or important. I've been more honest with them. It was as if I didn't have the energy to be less than honest. I think we're going through some difficult changes and I've made some mistakes and will probably make a lot more—but they've had a very good look at the down side of me and I think we've ended up caring about each other more than just as parent and child, and that's good.

And with friends. I am fortunate—no, maybe it was by design—I have some very good, very old friends. In the past I had played my part with them too, all decked out in my bootstraps and stiff upper lip. Well, it turned out they still loved me as a wet noodle.

You find out a lot about friends and would-be friends during such a time. Friends, *real* friends—or at least this was my experience—do *not* judge or lecture or tell you all about the much worse thing that happened to them in 1965. They're simply very available, loving sounding boards or laps or shoulders or ears—whatever you need. They *know* they can't fix it for you and they don't have to take any power trips at your expense.

Acquaintances, people who aren't close, or new people—I find I don't have to bother pleasing them. I've spent a lot of energy during my life in pleasing people who didn't really matter all that much. I'm still friendly, outgoing, relatively considerate because—well, because that's the way I am. But I'm not so concerned about making sure that people like me.

And about Bill—in many ways that's positive too. Being able to talk with him, being able to feel good about sex after all these years, being more like real people somehow . . . I do hope—I'm not sure it's realistic—but I hope we can try to be together. It all feels so unfinished. When things went bad we didn't even *try* to do anything about it, but even so there's still something very special there, something there. . . .

I haven't thought much about the future—I'm so stuck in the present. I am working on a couple of projects. I suppose I could become totally engrossed in work—I've done that before. I'm not interested in having anything with another man—perhaps I will be later. It isn't that this has ruined men for me or anything like that—its just that I think I may be that anachronism, a one-man woman.

My feelings about being supported vacillate. There were

times when I felt like I'd put in my twenty years and deserve my pension. But then I think, I *do* want to be financially independent—nobody likes to be an unwelcome burden. Then there have been times when I thought that as long as he has to support me, maybe he won't take on another commitment.

I don't know which is the real feeling—it's like so many other things: "Will the real way I feel about this please stand up?" I don't think the answer is in "finding yourself" or "being independent." We are dependent creatures—that's the kind of animal we are and we need to depend on each other. I want to need—and to be needed. I want to rely on and be relied on. I want to love—and be loved. There's all this talk nowadays about personal growth and change, but there must be some way to grow without having to grow apart.

I know we all die alone, but I think it must be much easier if someone you love is holding your hand when you go.

William

William was faithful to Kate for seventeen years before a barrage of personal illnesses and family deaths forced him to recognize his own fragile and limited life span. He is a forty-seven-year-old psychiatrist with two sons, now eighteen and nineteen. He was interviewed nine months after separating from Kate.

"You know, when your life is all screwed up and nothing is going right, you just throw all the cards up in the air and see if you can reshuffle. That's what I was doing and I was aware of it. . . . I didn't care about anything—except changing."

THE LAST FEW YEARS of my married life were unreal. There was a tremendous distance between us which was denied on her part—at least, I thought she was denying it. I think it began when I was sick in 1972–73. There were a lot of fall-aparts when I turned forty. My dad died, my sister died, my best friend died—all within one or two years. Also, I had a diagnosis of cancer and had surgery for that. I changed my whole job situation—ran into some heavy adjustments at work—and then I started to have problems with my neck. I just wasn't well in any way.

The way the illnesses began—with all the stress from my dad's death I was smoking a lot and I shouldn't have. I have a bit of bronchitis and nose trouble and I was smoking these cigars—Schimmelpenninck, the brand Freud smoked—not the big fat juicy ones but the little dry stems. They cost more but it looks like you're being less indulgent. And, like Freud, I had the beard. Anyway, the dentist said I had a white spot on my tongue and sent me to a doctor right away and the doctor said, Quit smoking and tomorrow you've got to go into the hospital and have a piece of your tongue taken out. And it was cancer. It took me years before I was able to read the biopsy report from the surgery. But he got it all, there was nothing left.

Then my neck started bothering me and I would get tired and have backaches and shoulder aches. I was trying to figure out in my analysis what was wrong and my analyst said it was physical so I went to several orthopedists—I know now how they are, they don't know any more than I do, but one of them, who was trying to be friendly and nice, showed me my X rays and said I had degeneration of a disc. I remember I went out and just sat in the park and I felt like it was the end of the world and I was never going to be able to work or do anything.

So after the cancer surgery and the first troubles with my neck my practice was down the tubes and I decided to change to a job that was more secure. I went to work at the hospital and the new situation turned out to be shaky and a little crazy and ungratifying in many ways. Anyway, after I'd been working at the hospital for six months my neck got really bad, and one day I woke up with very bad pains—the disc was pushing on a nerve and it was like a toothache all the way down my arm.

In all the medical commotion that followed, the internist said, "Oh, by the way, those tests we took show you have something wrong with your thyroid and you have rheumatoid arthritis." On top of everything else it was like some bad joke! I'm still being treated for the arthritis—the blood tests get better all the time. The thyroid problem was treated for a while and seemed to go away.

So I was disabled for six months, home in bed, in and out of the hospital, and I had to have surgery for the disc, and I guess I just got so mad at Kate because she couldn't take care of it somehow. She couldn't make it well—I don't know—some dumb fantasy. I was depressed. I was irritable. She was annoyed that she had to take care of the kids, be the daddy, as she said—and I was terribly lacking in confidence. I was sick, couldn't do anything. She would make lunch, change the bed. She had said before she really didn't like that kind of thing. I don't know, I just—I know I felt very disappointed. And I was embarrassed, ashamed, humiliated. I couldn't really be with the kids because I was sick. I'm not sure I did a very good job even before that. And I was on disability. I was worried—how long could *that* go on?—and I wasn't really earning a living, just making money by being in bed. I was annoyed that Kate didn't run out and get a job or something and take over. I wanted her to do more. You know, it was crazy—I wanted her to go out and take my place and at the same time be there and comfort me, and then I'd be annoyed, and it was—very, very difficult. Being sick—it ruins things.

When *I* was a burden I thought that everyone else was a burden—such an awful burden, to try to be a family person and keep the family together. I was too frightened to be frightened—I was angry. The disability was cause for tremendous resentment. Needing to depend more, the idea of disability rather than dying, of being unable to function— that was *bad.* It's like the future became very short and unwelcome.

I thought about how I only have so much life left—I'm on the downhill part and what do I want to do for the end? All the things I've done seem to have been for other people and what is the thing in life that seems the most valuable and rewarding, and how can I pursue it? Some thoughts about health, and about some kind of an affair, and with a younger woman. I don't know if I consciously thought about that then, but it turned out that's what it was.

Even though I had the surgery and even though I got better and could do more, for a long time it bothered me to sit, and it was hard to be at work. My back will still get pretty sore all of a sudden. Now what does this have to do with anything? Well, when you're in bed with somebody you like to snuggle. I can't because I get all stiff. It really interferes. And I'm still using a heating pad and crawling back into my hospital bed when I'm feeling bad, and I'm hard to comfort and it's hard to find it within me to comfort other people. You want to sleep alone—that's still a factor, not as bad as it was. And the other thing—one thing leads to another—Kate and I had this excuse about why we weren't having sex for the three years up until last January—because of poor William's back, you know? Which was really ridiculous. She says she didn't think about sex that much but after I began the affair with Betty I thought, Well, with Kate I can use my back as an excuse.

I was angry with Kate, stopped liking her during the time I was sick. Even now I'm still angry. If things didn't go right I would blame her. Or blame the relationship. Or blame myself. You can do all three, you have a choice. But yes, I'd blame her because she'd allowed that for all those years—allowed herself to be blind to the fact that we weren't having sex. I tried a couple times to bring it up but she didn't react so I gave up and thought, I can't possibly talk to this person —she's so blind and stiff.

I consciously felt at the time of my illness and afterward that I didn't want to stay with Kate after the kids grew up. I wanted something else. The marriage was nearing its end and I felt ... well ... I've put in my years, paid my dues, served my time, and now I want to do something else. Sometimes I'd feel, Oh sure, that makes sense, why not? That's the way you do it these days and to think it should be any other way is just silly.

Kate says she had no idea that this was going on in my mind, and that's another thing that still makes me angry. Just like when we have pretty good sex now I think, Where the hell were you all those years, you stupid shit? Where were you when I needed you?

Then, the whole smoking issue is important. I really

needed to quit smoking, and after the cancer operation I stopped for about two or three months and then started again and continued for about a year. Then two things happened —my sister died and I started coughing up blood. That was enough—I knew I had to quit, so I went up north to a special five-day program and it worked. Kate had read something about this and she put the ashtrays away all over the house and she didn't smoke in my presence any more, but I knew she was still smoking. It angered me, and the smell was really bad. I said her smoking didn't tempt me but it must have because I thought it had to be harder for me if she was smoking and I had to stop all by myself. Unreal . . . silly . . . childish.

But there was another issue which was, Look at me, I'm trying so hard to be healthy and she's not—not taking her Geritol, you know? She didn't take care of her teeth and was just letting herself go to pot. It bothered me. I'm sure I must have told her about the teeth because she finally went to a dentist, but I guess I was pretty hostile, didn't tell her most of these things—scared.

Before we were married and shortly after, I sometimes complained about a few things and it seemed to make her so mean that I stopped, got cowardly, decided it wasn't worth it. I remember one time during my residency in New York —I was on call and she went out drinking with a lady friend. She got home at three in the morning and I was standing on the stairs like some outraged parent or husband or child, and her response was, "Why, I didn't do anything wrong! How could anybody think anything of what I do?" Kind of omnipotent. It looked like she felt she couldn't do anything wrong and shouldn't be criticized. I know she didn't feel that way but that was the way she presented it to me: "Who are you to . . . ?" It wasn't a hostile kind of "Who are you to . . . ?" It was more above it all, like "I'm an only child and I don't operate on those principles."

So early in our marriage I stopped telling her when I was angry at her. And it was really ridiculous—sometimes I would come out with a half-brained disguised complaint or bitchiness, and she would accept that. She would make *me* omnipotent, would take that for the rule of the house. She wouldn't question it—really crazy. And I tried to caution her about being too affectionate with the kids—that's how you ruin kids. She overdid that, became too distant and formal. She's much less like that now.

Then there was the business of the analysis all those years, beginning about three or four years after we were married, after the kids were born. The usual complaint—when I went into treatment, it was, I'm unhappy with my wife or I'm depressed and I don't know which. And I still don't. Is it that I'm unhappy with her and therefore depressed or is it that I'm depressed and therefore unhappy with her? About the sexual adjustment, she says it started turning bad when we got married. Before that we spent weekends together—people didn't *really* live together then, that was the good old days. But I think things went wrong after the second kid was born because I was so unsympathetic to her. She had Rand fourteen months after Josh and she wasn't quite ready and I didn't realize what kind of adjustment it was for her. She was depressed and I didn't recognize it—I'm such a great clinician! And so I got mad at her because she didn't seem to be Supermother, and after that . . . I don't know, maybe that's why I went into child psychiatry—to figure out what was the right thing.

After the birth of Rand—I'm having trouble remembering —I suppose we both just got more inhibited in some ways. Maybe I'm borrowing her memory, but it seemed at the beginning of the marriage there was something more magical about it all. But it got to be trite. In adolescence I had concerns about my sexual ability and they seemed to go away about the time we were married, and then after a while, about six or seven years ago, they came back. So of course I blamed Kate for being an unsuitable partner and she says she was, that she wasn't that interested any more. Before that time it was okay enough that I thought it could be perfected —there was still hope, somehow.

After my illness we talked about mundane things like how bad it was at work and about her going to school or her volunteer job. I could tell that there was a distance between us because I didn't really integrate her into my new crowd at the hospital—maybe I didn't want to get into it myself. And I didn't get much involved with her crowd—I was really nasty about that—you know, I can always hide behind "I'm busy" and all that garbage.

There's a psychologist I work with, Madeline, and for about a year before I quit smoking I leaned on her, confided in her. We almost got to be a romantic couple. We talked about my leaving home and getting an apartment. We would go for walks at lunch, and in talking to her I realized how dissatisfied I was with Kate. Madeline said, "You shouldn't stay in a marriage when you're unhappy and you have a sore back because you're unhappy and all." Finally, I was daring enough to mention some of these things to Kate—the terrible way we were getting along, the coldness—how it's just not working so let's forget it. She said, "Okay, if you want to do that. Screw you, I'll be all right, I'll manage." I was kind of annoyed—I thought, She's just waiting for me to leave, isn't she?

At that time Kate was a pretty heavy drinker. It wasn't quite as bad as taking her home in a wheelbarrow, as I did for years—that had leveled off—but I think she was still drinking quite a bit and I objected to that. I felt helpless, hopeless—felt I had done a lot to try to correct that, and it still reflected on me. I wasn't being good to her, I wasn't making her happy—was ineffectual in changing that. The complaining I did—you can only do it so much. What good did it do? Anyway, within weeks, maybe within days of telling her I was thinking of moving out, we went to a psychiatric meeting on a Saturday afternoon and she had these strange symptoms. It happened about three times—like her head would explode and she'd become disoriented. Maybe it was a stroke.

I said, "Why don't you get psychiatric treatment? Because there's something wrong with you, it's not all me." That was another way I had of complaining, and she said no. She had a checkup and the internist told her it was stress, but even so, she quit drinking hard liquor, started drinking only white wine, and the problem went away. Also, I didn't talk about leaving any more. Such a chicken! I didn't want her to start drinking again, which she's apparently done. When she comes over to my place now I give her all kinds of booze and I don't care . . . I do care . . . I don't know. When I get her drunk I think what I'm operating on is, It's okay, she won't become a sick drinker again because she doesn't have to live with me any more, so she can do it once a week. Just like sex with me won't destroy her either because it's only once a week.

Anyway, Betty was a secretary at the hospital and Madeline and I were accustomed to meet in Betty's office because it was halfway between our offices, so I got involved with her, just as friends. Then Madeline got married while I was up north quitting smoking. I didn't know in advance this was going to happen—it was kind of short notice. She'd been fooling around for twenty years and hadn't been married till the age of forty. So that was that. I'm not sure how attached I'd become to her but I had to switch attachments, plus my sister had just died, and I remember being in Betty's office and Betty and Madeline both consoling me.

When I was up north I knew that I was going to be looking for some kind of liaison because I figured that if I stopped smoking it would unmask some kind of basic frustration, drive, need—probably it would be sex. Either that or I'd be angry at everybody. So I came back and I said to Betty, "It's really great to quit smoking—you want to do it? I've learned how." And she said, "Yeah." And I said, "I'm on call tonight, you want to go to dinner?" She said, "No, but we can have dinner next week." We did go to dinner and it became a very important weekly thing. She quit smoking but she went back to it and wouldn't tell me for a couple of months.

Of course, Betty could afford to do all the things in the way of being supportive and affectionate that Kate couldn't do— because she didn't have to live with me. I know that now. And Betty's young—thirty-two. We went through stages. It got notorious and we had to pretend it was not happening. But within three or four months I stopped sleeping with Kate altogether and was faithful to Betty, and I was thinking I really had a good deal here because I didn't have to leave home or break up the family, didn't have to worry about divorce. Put it on the back burner.

About a year and a half later, Betty had some funny physical symptoms, and after talking about it for a couple of months my analyst and I decided she had lupus. I think I started making some clumsy responses to her that she didn't understand because she's still denying her illness even now. But very shortly afterwards—that summer—she decided that she didn't want to continue on in the same way and when was I going to leave Kate and if I wasn't going to do it this month, then forget it. As they say down at the Jacuzzi, she closed her legs. She said she just wanted me to leave Kate. It was kind of muddy what it was she really wanted and what she was really saying. I think she was still worried about her sickness and was disappointed that I couldn't help her somehow.

So I got increasingly depressed. A couple of months later I went through the difficult experience of dropping in on Betty and somebody else was there. I asked her about it the next day and she told me and it was like the end of the world! I really was crazy depressed—got increasingly crazy—and I decided to have this twentieth-wedding anniversary party. I figured that Kate and I weren't going to last much longer and I wanted a big thing before the end. It was just like when I decided to buy that new house—if they're not going to have *me,* then at least they'll have a nice house.

There's a whole other configuration there with Kate. It's obvious that she's getting older and she's not as attractive as she was, and I'm really very simpleminded or primitive or narcissistic or something, but I can't stand it. And I spent thousands of dollars trying to work that out in treatment and didn't get anywhere. Or maybe I did get somewhere—I left. And it's kind of ignoble that I didn't leave her sooner.

The way it all came out was like a bad movie. After Betty's suggestion that I leave Kate—her pressure, her neglect—I started talking to a few people about divorce and I started trying to find people to sleep with. I wasn't sleeping with Betty very often at that time, maybe once a month. I guess this was part of her pressure for me to leave Kate.

Anyhow, it was a Thursday and on Thursdays I had to go uptown to the hospital annex where Betty had been transferred and I was terribly upset and anxious, troubled, and I can't remember exactly what I did, whether I said hello to her or tried not to see her. But all week I'd been very aware that our relationship was not working, and I just felt so bad —and guilty for worrying about that relationship when I was in another relationship with Kate. The whole thing was falling apart. And so I went to the analyst and then I was on my way to the hospital and my car broke down. Just one of those days. I had to leave it in a gas station and rent another car and it was too late to see the rest of my patients so I went home. I got home early after a nasty day and around 4:30 I started drinking. Bourbon and ginger ale. And I started making some tapes, I don't know for what—for the car, perhaps.

It was Frank Sinatra, Rod McKuen and nostalgia up to here. And depression. And I started crying. Kate was in the kitchen—it will be funny next year, it's half funny now. She came in and said, "You want to have dinner?" I said, "No. No, I'll have another drink." A month before I had gone through a similar thing and she'd come in while I was taping a song like "It's Time to Say Goodby" and I was crying and she didn't even notice, I swear, which just crystallized my resolve that our marriage was too crazy, why should I stay here and . . . ?

So I just got more and more sloppy, really started crying, and finally she came in and she said, "What's the matter?" and I said, "I'm weak, I'm weak, I just can't do it." Even though I was drunk and even though I was maudlin it was really like the end of everything—a total pouring out of all the despair. At first she became extremely comforting, which I hadn't seen for a long time. She kind of held me, asked what's the matter. And I told her about Betty.

Every sentence made her step further away. She said, "How can this be? How come I didn't know?" And I said, "Well, you just weren't looking and there was this, this, and this." And she said, "Oh, was *that* what that was?" Like that medallion. I bought a present for Betty that got charged on the wrong account—I'm sure that always happens—and I had to give it to Kate for her birthday. Well, she gave it back to me the day after I told her. That was an example of how she could have known if she had been thinking straight. And when she said, "Why didn't you tell me before instead of letting it go on for three years?" I answered, "I didn't think there was any resolution other than leaving and I wasn't ready to leave until the kids were both in college." It had been a very tolerable arrangement as long as Betty was available.

After awhile she went to bed and I went out walking, then drove around. I went over to see an old friend of ours. Kate had thought I'd gone to see Betty but it had been quite a while since I'd just drop in on her.

The next day we didn't talk about it and Saturday I said, "I think we ought to start thinking about some plans to separate." I was thinking of staying in the house while having some kind of legal separation or starting to file for divorce— something real crazy. Anyway, she said, "Well, if you're going to be seeing her or anybody else, you can't do it here. There's nothing to think about, you just go." So I did.

I had seen this apartment while I was driving by. I figured I needed a place close to the hospital and under four hundred dollars, and the apartment met all the criteria. I sat out in the garden after I looked at it and decided, and the next day Rand helped me move some furniture over. Kate seemed very helpful, as I recall. It was like she was making my lunch so I could run out for an hour, something like that. She got the dishes together—it confirmed my idea that she was just waiting to get rid of me.

Kate was sitting right there when I told Rand. I said, "I'm going to move," and he said, "Well, okay." He didn't really understand what it was all about at the time. Maybe he does now. I'm not terribly surprised at the boys' reactions—you know, there's supposed to be a lot of hostility and some depression and some goofing up, and they've done all that. Some of it I think they would have done anyway. Rand deals with me by just ignoring me or forgetting I'm around or forgetting our appointments, and I guess he wouldn't have done that if I hadn't left. But the other thing that is troublesome is that it's hard for me to talk with either of them, and it's probably worse than it was before I moved out. It's been bad ever since they became teenagers.

I sent Josh a letter at school to tell him I was leaving. It was after his letter about how badly he was doing. Josh is better with me than Rand is. He tries. He's very sociable in a one-to-one way. When I can talk to him casually, about nothing in particular, sometimes about important things, it's okay, but when I am forced into the parental role—guide dog or cop—I don't like it and they don't like it. I feel uncomfortable telling them, Don't waste money, comb your hair and get new clothes . . . all that stuff. Kate doesn't like to do it either but she does it better. Anyway, I think it's a little worse than it would have been without the breakup, but it's always been a problem relating to them. Really, I care about them and I respect them a lot, but there's this terrible distance. I try to do the externals and keep things stable and keep up a sort of relationship with them, but I couldn't be close with either of them after a while. Maybe I'm getting the comeuppance of my own childhood and maybe none of it could be analyzed away. I had a lousy relationship with my parents and I can't do very well as a father.

My parents were divorced when I was two and my father married my stepmother when I was four. When I was six, my mother—I was living with her—suddenly decided that she couldn't take it, which is an unfair abbreviation, and she left. My sister and my brother and I went to live with my dad, whom I didn't know, and my stepmother. My brother is dead —he died when I was eighteen. I was the youngest until I was fifteen and then I was the oldest because the two older ones were gone. I had a lot of thoughts about I'm not going to do like he did, not going to get a divorce, at least not until the kids are grown up, because it was hard in those days. I don't want to remember the resentment and yearning, but I can remember the embarrassment. In those days it was unusual—it was like we were orphans. We didn't talk about it at school. The good old days.

I felt pretty high when I moved out—elated. And scared about simple things, about existing—like a little kid wondering if he can make it away at camp. But from what I can recall and from what people tell me I was pretty crazy for a few months. I would invite women over and I would have to tell my life story and they got scared off. Old friends don't seem to be scared off, but they aren't calling me every week either. For a while I was crazy from the infatuation with Betty, I guess, more than from the separation. Betty still wasn't available, not until recently. We would go out once or twice and then all of a sudden she wouldn't want to see me. Then I would say I wouldn't see her and she would call me and we went around like that three or four times. She was unable to tolerate what she called my craziness—when I would idealize her or get too romantic or need her too much. That's when she would cut it off—in more ways than one.

I went through that big drinking thing and trying to find somebody to sleep with every night and it was terrible! Everybody said it would be terrible and it was, but I had to do it. I was outrageously flirtatious. I tried not to be and it was worse. I don't think it's really sex—that compulsive flirting that comes right after a breakup. It's more the "getting old" business and needing to prove something. And like adolescence, it's finding out what you're like. Maybe you don't find out, but you make the attempt. That swinging single thing, the desperation—it was so confused. I was thinking about Betty then, and since she's been available I haven't been seeing too many other people—a few, when I get annoyed with her.

Then my fourth anniversary with Betty came around— fourth anniversary is better than the twentieth, you know— and I simply sent her some flowers and said that she'd always be very important to me. Somehow that made a difference and she stopped being so hard to get, in the old parlance, and started to become a problem the other way. She got terribly dependent and couldn't seem to put one foot in front of the other unless I told her what to do, and then she accused me of being too dependent on her. I don't know if *she* knows whether she wants to move in and live with me, but she spends time over here, doing nothing . . . we play cards . . . or maybe she just doesn't want to go home and clean the house . . . or she's tired. That's what it is usually—she's tired and sick and wants to sleep. That's another way I feel totally inadequate, because I can't tell how much is physical and how much is emotional for her, let alone myself. And either way, what can I do about it?

I told her six months ago I thought she had lupus and she really wouldn't listen. The closer you get the less open you get. In fantasy, what is so appealing about Betty is that her disability would be brief and then the disease would be fatal. Although that's not even true, it's just a fantasy, because there could be a lot of disability. There's a whole vampire thing here. That's why I'm so guilty and depressed now. If I'm going to take in youth by being close to a youthful person —stay forever young, like a vampire—what's that going to do to my victim? So it turns out that this person has this awful disease and she comes around wanting to lean on me and—that's hard. You know, I can't say, Go away, don't bother me. I care about her and I'm also stuck.

I can't see that she is the one for the next twenty years. But who knows? I guess I feel responsible for her illness—guess I still have the fantasy, but on a little less primitive level, that it's a hot-potato thing—that I'm her last partner before she has to sit down. If she's sick and she has been with me, then she doesn't have the strength to go out and find another relationship. I don't think she wants another relationship— maybe she just wants me to be her mother, who knows? But the way I see it, if somebody gets disabled while—I almost said while they're in my employ—well, I'm stuck with them. That's depressing, but I've always been depressed and I'm still depressed and I really don't know how much the current situation with Betty is a factor.

She's sometimes outrageously neurotic. A while ago she called to tell me her cat is sick. I think it's got an abscess and it's going to get better, but she's been off work on account of it. She has symptoms of a lot of things, there's always some kind of dumb crisis—a very needy person. If she's got a sick cat and she's totally depressed over it I can't say to her, You're silly, there are more important things in life.

There's nobody I can express everything to, nobody I'm really close to. I think early in a marriage the women can easily become very—dependent doesn't quite cover it—but it's like needing approval from the husband. And somewhere around middle age it all shifts and men find that they need all that too, dependence or a noncompetitive belonging, and I don't know—that frightens me and maybe that's why I don't have anybody to talk to.

There's been running this year—I'm really running away, and one thing to run away from is dependence on somebody. Whether they come through or whether they bomb—there's still a dependence. It's funny, because when you get old I guess you need to depend on someone. I don't know what the hell I want. Does anybody know what they want? I guess I want some corny things like meaning in life and pursuit of health and for a while I thought the thing with Betty was what life's all about—to have some kind of fancy love affair and if it doesn't last to find another one. I'm not so sure about that any more, but it seemed that to be loved, or to have somebody that you really like in bed, was the king of experiences in life, which is true, but you can't have that all the time.

I'm interested now in yoga classes and jogging and—a new hobby. It's funny, you try to find new hobbies and you keep going back to the old ones. Like wine—that lasted a month. I'm still looking for something to capture my fascination. I frequently comment that I'm feeling old and yet in some ways I am healthier. But I feel old politically—much less liberal. I feel old interpersonally. Really, if I had the nerve, there's so much crap I wouldn't put up with from people. I feel old in the sense of having done a lot of things—so I did them and so what? I don't really want to do them and they're not that much fun. But I don't know what is.

Sometimes, like when I think of moving to another city and I start to clean out my files, I think of canceling out my life insurance or I think of getting the kids situated with a $30,000 trust fund and then I won't have to worry about continuing to be responsible for them day to day, set it up so they can coast for another five years. Or when I stopped seeing the analyst and stopped calling friends—when I think of closing out the past, throwing away a lot of old papers—I think I'm getting ready to suicide. I'm not, really, but sometimes it occurs to me. I've had enough experience with my self-loathing and my emotional incapacity to know the impasses, so I think the only way I would be suicidal is if I had some nasty physical disease that would leave me totally incapable and crippled. Then I think of getting a gun, or air in the veins, or an overdose of potassium, whatever—I've made no plans. My father comes to mind—he was sick with cancer and the last year of his life was so miserable for him and everyone else. I think that was another instance where I felt I didn't want to be like him—and I am—distant, sarcastic, cynical, sometimes a workaholic, burdened.

There are some patient files—I used to keep pretty decent process notes, still do—but there would be four or five years of notes from two or three visits a week and I suppose I had a dream somewhere along that I'd write a paper, I'd write a book, I'd do some research, review things. I won't cure the person but I can find a new theory, you know? I've got papers all over the place—I just want to throw them out. I don't want to be burdened by that ambition because I'm never going to do it. But it's kind of sad. I mean, that's the end of a dream—to be significant in my field and really do something

wonderful, and—well, I'm just a hack. Terribly unimagina-
tive and stodgy—the same complaint I have about the place
where I work. Every once in a while I try to do a little bit
more, but I'm just worn down, worn out, haven't found the
initiative or whatever it is that I suppose I used to have. I
don't feel much good at anything—I'm confused. Perhaps
I'm looking for what might come along from the outside, day
by day, looking for whatever will motivate me.

Maybe at the hospital—I could be in charge of it and do
something useful, be a chief instead of an Indian along with
all the social workers. There's a lot of rankle at what I'm
doing—occasional satisfaction, but there are better things to
be doing. Occasionally you get some pleasure that you really
helped someone, but I definitely don't get pleasure over . . .
at . . . I'm getting my prepositions all mixed up—it shows
I'm disoriented—I don't get pleasure in the hand-holding
treatment that a lot of people seem to need, and I needed, for
about one hundred years. It really drives me up the wall if
somebody's missing somebody from their family and I'm
supposed to be the surrogate, and that's what often happens.
Really, it annoys me, it angers me, makes me feel put upon.
Or similarly, if somebody is just so nastily not taking care of
themselves—"Here I am, take care of me!"—it infuriates
me. I suppose I have a right to have those feelings but there's
something about that whole constellation of helplessness,
particularly when it's contrived or when it's a device or when
it's improper. Maybe that's an aspect of the work because I
get most of those cases when I'm on emergency duty, and
people who have emergencies, usually that's the way they
operate. So you can be annoyed at them because they're
immoral—aren't conducting their lives properly and get into
problems like that, right?

About the future—I see a new job, a new relationship with
somebody. I wouldn't have any kids. For a while I was really
trying to be more open with everybody—and something's

happened. I do run into feeling guilty or depressed and that's not too good for relationships. I don't know how Kate lived with me all that time. Lately it seems like I am getting out of these feelings quicker and trying not to burden others with them—just staying away, not bringing guilt and depression with me. I don't know if it can work this way—actually living with somebody—but maybe. Hiding parts of myself in a relationship—I guess that's no change.

But I think I'm still changing rapidly. In any week I'll have all kinds of mental states and experiences. It's like being a little bit more alive. There certainly is some pain with that, but as I mentioned before, it's something I can get over more quickly. And as far as enjoyment, people say I look happier and healthier. I think I'm living more in the present. I may be acting out the past all over again, but I feel more in the present. For a while I've had fewer highs—this thing with Betty is oppressive.

It's hard to say how important sex has been—sex serves so many purposes—I mentioned the vampire fantasy. And if Kate and I had continued to please each other I wouldn't have needed something outside. Sex has to be important in marriage.

With Kate—I feel competitive with her and would want her to believe that I'm doing wonderfully and that I'm thriving without her and that I know what I'm doing and where I'm going. I don't want her to think that I'm hurting, because it was such—in many ways—such a terrible thing I did. So I should have good reason for it and it should somehow be the right thing. I should come out right in order to make it worth all the pain that everybody's going through. I should be happy—rich and successful, and not have any back pain at all—which in no way is true. Then I could say it was all her fault and I'll do wonderfully without her, right? Get rid of *the problem*. And, in fact, I've already got another *problem* that I can't get rid of.

Sometimes I think, Okay, Kate and I have to go through this and it's natural. But sometimes I'm still terrified about what she might do in retaliation—vague things—we joke about it. Putting curses on people and stuff—like a sore back, or impotence—that's a pretty good one. I've had that a little bit. It could have been I was getting the flu or something. It happened about three times a few months ago and three times over the past two weeks—actually only a couple of days altogether. Still, it was embarrassing. But also, I wondered, Do I hate everybody? I don't know, maybe I do.

At the moment I don't feel right about anything. When I have considered all the things I could consider and tried to come to a conclusion, the separation was a good thing—not necessarily for the boys, but for Kate and me. It'll take a while for the boys to get over it but they seem to be functioning better. Kate will probably find herself professionally. She said she didn't want to get married again. I guess she'll have a few friends and another cat and—I don't know. I think I have mixed feelings about her finding herself—her working —and lately, well, this may be a lot of crap like she says, but I feel like I've emancipated her, and I think it's important. I'm sure I was guilty for tying *her* down, even though she says she likes it and doesn't want me to go. I really feel like she's going to blossom out of this and find herself better. I think I was definitely dragging her down, if she had to be so defensive and blind about what was really going on. She seems a real person more frequently now than she did.

I guess I do like Kate now. She's a very—impressive person, very easy to talk to, and has a lot of interesting things to say. Most people I meet don't. It's amazing that I lived with her all those years and either she wasn't doing it or it was oppressive to me to hear her babble. She has definitely changed—is a more interesting person, and I think it's the separateness that does it. Not the separation, but the separateness.

She's much more overtly hostile to me occasionally and I'm able to be that way with her. My feelings about her change rapidly. Last week I was convinced I shouldn't see her at all—we were both feeling too much hostility. I'm not much good at fighting—have raised my voice a little bit and walked out a couple of times. Kate gets on a tear a little bit, but I just passively sit by and discover that if I let her go through it then she'll feel better and she'll be nice. But generally we can be friends and we can even have sex, which sometimes seems to be affectionate and at other times I don't know what the hell it is. It's a lot more comfortable now, pleasant, there's even more lust, but there's not that romance and fascination and all those things that may be carried over from adolescence but that I had been needing for a long time. Still, it's better than it was for years so I won't complain.

Once I told Kate she was second best, number two, and that's pretty hostile. There was a time when there were a bunch of people and I said she was really good compared to all the others except one—Betty. Kate and I have a pact— she wants me to call her when I want to see her. For a while she was calling me. The pact is, we can certainly do this without any commitment. What's lacking is, well—I wish I could wax poetic—I call it sparkle, romance—I got that from Betty for a while. But I think that when people get close they mix their problems up together and that can ruin a lot of things. You just keep bouncing back and forth between closeness and distance. I feel—I really feel frequently that I don't know what the hell I'm doing. And it's another concern that I'll find out I don't know what the hell I'm talking about —like right now.

Probably a few times a month I think about going back to Kate—because she's so easy to talk to and she certainly cares and she told me and that's worth a lot. But it's similar to the first year or two after I quit smoking and I would think, How nice it would be to have a cigarette. And then I would remind myself, it makes you sick, it smells bad and you can't exercise and you look like a nasty person—and then I wouldn't want a cigarette any more. It's called aversive conditioning. So when I think about going back to Kate I think of all the painful problems and I don't do it. She's better now at communicating. I *was* doing well—I was for a while. But I think it would happen again like it happened before if I went back. Incidentally—about smoking—Betty has quit again and she gained fourteen pounds. That's not very good. I really did like her skinny, when she looked about fifteen years old.

I'm sure that resentment over giving Kate money will come—it's maybe bubbling. I don't really want to buy a boat or go to Alaska yet. Next year I might. It's still at the point where she can say, "You didn't take me out to dinner as much as you took her out to dinner so you still owe me"— you know, all that garbage. And I can still afford indulgences, so I don't notice that I'm supporting those people. But I comment on it, so I must have some feelings about it.

Kate said, "You don't have to worry about supporting me because I'm going to expect twelve hundred dollars a month for the rest of my life." I said, "Oh, you've had your twenty years and now you want your pension." Then I talked to some other people and I found out that her demands were a bit unrealistic and I told her so. You know, it was good I could tell her so, and she said something like, "Well, you can't blame me for trying." It might be that I will be supporting her for twenty years but I don't think so. The point is, it's the same as with Betty—Kate did some things for me so I'm obligated. The obligation is pretty big.

The fall-aparts—you know, when your life is all screwed up and nothing is going right, you just throw all the cards up in the air and see if you can reshuffle. That's what I was doing and I was aware of it. I didn't care about anything—except changing. That's why I think it's the midlife crisis, why I think there is something biological about it. Oh, sure, there's the neurosis on top of it, but it just built up to such a peak, such confusion, such adolescent revival—it was so compelling—unbelievable. And judgment is probably so poor—but it was like you just *got* to do it. And that's frightening too, because you have so little control over it—like, what are my innards doing to me now?

Fran

Fran is forty-nine years old and had been married for twenty-two years when her husband left a note telling her he was going to live with another woman. Although she has a college degree, her life was primarily devoted to homemaking until she opened a small business a year before the separation. She has three children—boys, twenty-two, twenty, and seventeen, the youngest still living at home. At the time of her interview she had been legally separated for three years.

*"He was always what you would call a
family man, and we were thought of as a
kind of storybook family. . . . He spent
time with his kids, we played tennis, we
went to church, we saw our friends—it
was a normal family life."*

WE ALWAYS TOOK THE KIDS to Catalina in the summer. We'd
done that for ten years. We'd spend a couple of weeks and
the kids would invite friends along so we always had a gang.
It was a ball. Then when we'd come home, we'd leave the
boys with my folks and Larry and I would go on our summer
junket up the coast.

Well, that last summer on Catalina, things were different.
Larry spent an awful lot of time reading. He'd always read a
lot but this time he seemed more interested in reading and
in being alone than in participating in the things we had
always done together. Just before we left there I said something about our trip—our junket—and he said we couldn't
do that because he had to go to a convention in San Diego.

When we got home he went out and bought a new travel
bag and new undershorts and new socks. He'd always had
good clothes but he made such a point of doing this and he
was so particular about the way he packed his coat and
slacks. I began to smell a rat. . . .

After he left I called the hotel in San Diego and said I
understood there was a convention for such and such a
group, and they said there was no convention and I said
thank you very much.

My next thought was, I bet he went to Santa Barbara, because that was always our first stop. So a couple of days later I called the motel and asked for Mr. So-and-So. The clerk said that Mr. and Mrs. So-and-So had just checked out. In the next few days I called the different places where we would go and I found three places where they'd been. I thought, To hell with it. I know what he's doing.

I couldn't ever figure out why he would want to take her to those places. They weren't big splashy places—they were just the places where we always went together. If I was going to go away with somebody I wouldn't want to go to the places where I had always gone with Larry. Why did he do that?

When he got home, I said, "I hope you had a nice trip." And he said, "Oh, I did." Then I said, "Well, there's not going to be any more of *that*—it's one or the other." We had been through this before and he had always given up the girlfriend. He said, "It's all over—I had to do it." He had to take her on this trip so he could make up his mind. I said, "If it's over, that's fine, but if it's not, don't think you can play this game because I won't put up with it."

He really wouldn't talk about it much beyond that. He was never the kind who could really communicate. He couldn't sit down and say, Okay, let's really lay our cards on the table and what are you going to do and what do you think about this? . . . He was always evasive about things. I said, "What are you trying to prove? Are you afraid to be fifty?" And he said, "I just know that I'm not happy. I've put up with a lot all these years and I just don't think I want it that way any more. . . ."

That was in September, and after this confrontation I thought he had given her up. I thought things had blown over—I thought everything was getting better.

Then just before Thanksgiving—the Friday before—he had to go out of town but he said he'd be back that evening. We had an appointment with the photographer to have a family portrait taken the next day. I kissed him goodbye and I went to work, but I had a very strange feeling all day long.

I sensed something—I don't know what—when I got home from work. I walked in the front door and went straight back to our bedroom. The note was on the dresser. I read it and I read it again. "Dear Fran—I'll be back Monday to pick up the rest of my things. It's all over and I'm moving in with Gloria." That was it. That was the note.

Well, I just fell apart, but I felt like I had to put myself back together because of the family portrait. I had wanted that portrait. I'd been thinking about it for a couple of years —that the boys were getting older and that it would be such a nice thing to have. I thought, I'm going to go through with it. I'm going to have that picture taken. So I told the kids Dad was called out of town and we went, me with tears in my eyes, and had the picture taken. Sometimes I look at it now and—you know?—but it was something that seemed impor-tant at the time.

When we got home, I said, "Okay, kids, I've got something to tell you." Well, all three of them were completely dumbfounded. They couldn't understand why their father had done that because in their minds we had always been happy. If we had been arguing parents, then they probably would have figured . . . well, I can understand it. They just couldn't believe their father would do that to their mother. But they were great, they really were. It was, Mom, don't worry, and Mom, everything will be fine. . . .

Monday morning I called the shop and told Lorraine (she's the girl who works for me) I wouldn't be in. I told her what had happened and I said, "I want to be here and confront him." She said, "Oh, don't do that—it will only make it worse." I said, "No, I've got to face that man and talk to him."

So I stayed around all day but he didn't show up. Tuesday I went to work and he came about six o'clock that evening.

He told the boys to go to the garage and get all the empty
cartons they could find. Then he just started going through
the closets and drawers and dumping everything into boxes.
He told the boys to help him take everything to the car. They
didn't want to do it but he insisted. I tried to talk to him but
he said he'd talk to me later. We didn't really have a conversation. He just gathered up his junk and took off.

After he left I saw him maybe five or six times. And a
couple of times he came by and took us all out to dinner. It
was an awful situation but I thought, Well maybe if we're all
together he'll realize what has happened. It was a disaster
each time we went. He'd start tearing me down and complaining about the boys—about their grades or something.
He'd just blow in and say his piece and blow out. Greg, the
oldest, said, "Mom, do we have to do that again?" I said,
"Well, I thought it would help Daddy." So maybe we did it
once more after that and then decided to forget it.

Then he'd want to talk to me alone. He'd call and ask me
to have dinner with him—he'd say he really needed to talk
to me. I'd say, "Sure," but it was very hard because I was so
miserable and all I wanted to do was cry. He'd have too
much to drink and start ripping up a storm. He told me he
had never really loved me—that it was a marriage of convenience. Mind you, we had gone together for five years before
we were married. I could never understand how it was a
marriage of convenience.

He said that I had never helped him in business, had never
been an asset to his career . . . that I was either too fat or too
skinny . . . that he couldn't love a girl who wore glasses. I
had *always* worn glasses. And one time he said, "I'd really
like for you and Gloria to meet each other, to go out to lunch
together, because if you met her then you'd understand why
I've never been happy with you."

I look back on it now and the whole thing was so stupid,
but at the time it hurt and I don't know whether he knew

how much it hurt. I kept going back to it because I felt something was terribly wrong and that if we could just talk about it or if he could go get some help—I mean after that many years of being happy together—oh, not completely happy, but I just didn't feel that he was doing the right thing. I mean he was so different than he'd ever been—he had always been good to me. I don't know what made him change. It was like Dr. Jekyll and Mr. Hyde. But after a while I couldn't take it any more. After one of these dinners I'd be upset for two or three days and I could hardly pull myself together.

Larry was never a secure person. From the time he was a little boy he was just moved from one boarding school to another. He was never close to his family and that was why he wanted *his* family to be close, because he had missed that as a child. I think the first time he felt any real security was when we got married. He was always very fond of my parents and my sisters. He wanted them around a lot. After all this happened, my father said, "You know, Frannie, Larry hasn't even called me, and he and I always got along so well." I said, "Dad, I think he wants to divorce all of us from his life."

Larry and I met in college and went out off and on for a couple of years. Then I came home and he'd fly over on weekends and one weekend we decided to get married. I was the kind of girl who liked to have a good time—parties, dancing—I love being with people. Larry was not like that and I knew that before I married him. I knew I was giving up the kind of social life which I really enjoyed. And yet he had other things—qualities I must have seen in him at the time that overshadowed this. I guess I figured I had been around long enough, had been footloose and fancy free long enough so maybe it was time to settle down. We weren't kids —we were twenty-five and twenty-six when we got married.

We'd been married almost two years when the first baby was born. They were good years. When I was pregnant the second time, seventeen months later, Larry had his first girl-friend. The same thing happened during the third pregnancy. You don't know about it for a while, especially when a man has the kind of job where he has appointments in the evening—has to entertain at night. I was busy with babies and when he'd call and say, "I won't be home," I didn't question it. I suppose there were others through the years—one-night stands—how do you know about those things? But I knew about the two when I was pregnant and we talked about it. He said he wouldn't do it any more. When it came down to the nitty gritty he gave up the girlfriend. It wasn't that I was repulsive or ugly or cranky or disinterested when I was pregnant. I felt great—I was never sick. I gained a few pounds but it was all sitting right here, and I kept myself looking nice. I just don't know what it was.

It wasn't sex. Sex was always good with us. Now he says it was a problem, but I know better—I was there. There wasn't a problem until the last year we were together. You see, he was never what you would call a warm, loving individual. That just wasn't his nature. He was demanding—he was the big man, the big football player, the athlete. "I'm Larry—I'm strong." And he was the kind that when he wanted his sex he wanted it—and when he didn't want it, he didn't want it. It was never—there was never any romance. He just wasn't the lovey-kissy type. He was never a demonstrative person at all. When he wanted fun and games, we had fun and games, and that was fine with me. In the last year, of course, it was less, because he was being satisfied by his girlfriend. I complained about it but, you know, he was tired or he had worked too hard—the old story. But that wasn't until the last year.

He was always what you would call a family man, and we were thought of as a kind of storybook family. He wanted his family all there together—doing things together. He spent time with his kids, we played tennis, we went to church, we saw our friends—it was a normal family life.

His work was a problem for a while but there were never any big financial worries. In the first ten years or so that we were married, he went from one job to another, not really knowing what he wanted to do. Before we were married, his parents footed all the bills, and when they died they left him a trust fund. But in between it was kind of a blow to him that he had to go out and earn a living. Then he got into a business he really enjoyed. He got along well with his partner. They started the business from nothing and it grew and did very well and he got a lot of satisfaction from it. I thought he'd fussed around for so long and finally found his niche. He had proven himself and I was proud of him. He'd put it together and I thought that would give him the security he needed as a person. Apparently it didn't.

It took me a year and a half to get over him. It actually did. It was that long before I could go out with another man. Oh, I went out with friends. They were really good about saying "Let's go out to dinner tonight" or "Come on, we're going to so-and-so's house and they want you to come along. . . ." That kind of thing. I have a good friend and she and I would go to shows together and out to dinner. We went to San Francisco and Palm Springs for weekends. That was good for me at that time—a little social life—no man-woman relationships but it was at least getting out of the house.

I *wanted* to go out—or I felt that I had to. I wanted to and I didn't want to—it was a very difficult situation. I just couldn't believe that after that many years you couldn't talk about a problem and iron it out and have it all be fine again. If our marriage had been five years or even ten years I think I could have accepted it a lot easier—but twenty-two years?

That's almost half my life. So it was a gradual kind of getting over. I finally had to get mad and to realize what he had done.

I had other things to worry about too. I had opened a boutique about a year before he left. At one of our "dinner meetings" he asked me how long I thought it would take me before I could be on my own, and he said if I wanted to go into a different business or back to school or whatever, he would help me. But I decided to stay with the boutique and see if I could make a go of it.

Then I had some problems with Tad, my youngest boy, not serious problems but serious enough that I had to do something about them. Tad was fourteen when this happened, and that's a lousy age to be without a father. He was very hurt—he just couldn't believe that his father would walk out on him—so he took his hurt out on me. I tried taking him to therapy but he said he wouldn't go and that it was dumb to spend the money. He was doing anything to get in trouble and to see how far he could push me.

He started selling marijuana. I think he did that so he could be the big cheese at school—get some attention. It was a hard period for Tad and it was a hard period for me. It's over. I'm sure he smokes a little now and then like most of them do, but I can't let that bother me. Larry had very little communication with the boys after he left, and that was strange because he had always wanted them around—was always interested in them and what they were doing. I don't know when is the last time any of the kids have seen him. It's been a long time.

Greg is back East, working—he has no contact with his father. Greg's always been a very conscientious kid, a good student—the whole bit. It bothered him that he lost his relationship with his father, but he said in the beginning he had lost respect for him and didn't want to have anything to do with him. He still feels that way.

Robby, the middle one, worked for Larry for a while but he really hated it. I didn't talk to him about it because I didn't want it to seem like I was pumping him about what his father was doing, but he'd make comments. Larry hired Gloria's son too but he just fooled around and Robby had to do all the dirty work. Finally Robby just got fed up and said, "I don't need this," and he quit. I don't think he's seen Larry since, unless maybe they've played tennis a couple of times.

There was one incident a couple of years ago when Larry and Gloria had a party and invited the boys. Greg would have no part of it, but I encouraged Robby and Tad to go. Robby took his girlfriend along and she said Larry was insulting to her—that he ordered her around—you know, Go get the spatula . . . Clean the table. The kids left early. It bothered me—their going to the party. I didn't want them to like her—Gloria—but at the same time I felt they should go because he's their father and that's what he's doing now. All the same I was relieved when they didn't like her—said she was bossy. Robby said she had a big mouth. That was good to hear.

I've never met her and I have no desire to. I've seen a picture of her but I've never seen the whole Gloria. She's in advertising and Larry met her through work somehow. She's just a couple of years younger than I am. I mean she isn't any young chick. She's apparently been married three or four times and has children by different fathers, and I don't know how many men she's lived with. There was one child at home when Larry moved in with her, but I guess that didn't work out and the girl went to live with her father.

Soon after he moved out, Larry told me that she was just marvelous—that she was helping him so much and had a lot of contacts. Somehow through her he was going to lots of parties and conventions. I couldn't understand that because he had never liked big parties, never liked to be around a lot of people. That was another way in which he changed.

Some friends of mine bumped into them—they said she was really dumpy and dresses like a frump. I thought she'd probably be some kind of glamour girl but evidently that's not the case. When Larry and I were married I weighed ninety-five pounds, all in the right places. I weigh one hundred and five now. Whenever I'd gain a couple of pounds he'd swat me across the rear and say, "Lose that weight!" I just don't understand it—a dumpy frump with a big mouth?

He's changed so much. I think he must be going through a midlife crisis or whatever you want to call it. He was always a very large man—a very physical person, proud of his looks and his build, his manhood. I think when men like that reach a certain age they realize they aren't getting any younger and they've got to prove to themselves that they are still manly. I think that had a lot to do with our situation. It was his way of expressing this and proving to himself that he is still a man. I think he wanted to make sure his sex life was still in operation and he had to do that with someone else.

The last time I saw him, about a year ago, I looked at him and I thought, He looks like an old man. He's gotten hefty around the middle and he looks haggard. I looked at him and I thought, My God, what happened to you?

The last time I talked to him was over the Christmas holidays when Greg was in an accident. He heard about the accident from Robby so he called the hospital in New York and found out that Greg was doing all right. He called to bawl me out because I hadn't told him. He said I should have called him—that maybe he could have helped. I said I had wired a thousand dollars to the hospital and he said he didn't mean money and I said, "Well, what the hell *can* you do?" That's the last time I talked with him.

Now I just wish I could find him so I can get on with the divorce. He and his partner split up and I don't know what that situation is. He's under a court order not to do anything with the business—not to sell it or change title. I've had three addresses for him, business addresses—so I don't know what's going on.

We have a legal separation but we're not divorced. In the state of California you file for dissolution of the marriage but you don't have to finish it—to get the divorce itself. Sometimes economically it's better not to. But you have a legal agreement about property and support. He was supposed to give me X number of dollars a month in alimony—they call it spousal support now—and child support until Tad is eighteen. The other two boys have gotten nothing from him. He said if they wanted to go to school they could pay for it. I was to get a new car every two years and he was to pay all my automobile expenses except the insurance. He was to keep medical insurance for Tad and me and take out a $50,000 policy on his life with me as the beneficiary.

I have the house, but that wasn't in the original agreement. And that's another strange thing that happened. A couple of years ago he called me up one day and said he was sending over some papers for me to sign. He wanted to take out a loan to do some remodeling on Gloria's house. The bank wouldn't make the loan because he was still married to me, and if something happened to him, then I would end up having an interest in her house. That was the funniest thing I ever heard of—me and Gloria with community property!

So he wanted me to sign off on her house—that means sign a paper stating I had no interest in it. I told him I didn't see any sense in signing away interest in something I had no interest in. He said I *better* sign—and I told him I'd talk to my attorney.

Before I had a chance to do that Larry called back and said he would give me full title to our house if I would do what he wanted. Well, my attorney checked into it and said it was a good deal. So we met with the escrow officer and I signed off on Gloria's house and Larry signed off on ours, so now our house belongs to me.

After we signed the papers we were walking out and Larry turned to me and said, "You are a real bitch!" I reminded him that it was his idea and I was just protecting my interests. He went barreling down the alley and that was the end of that.

But the strange thing was, I found out later, that the remodeling loan was for only three thousand dollars. He gets more than that each quarter from his trust fund so it was a very stupid move for him to make—and he's not a stupid man.

Until last September he was fulfilling all the terms of the agreement except for the life insurance policy. I could have put him in contempt for that but I didn't. I played the nice girl, which is dumb. In September he sent me a check for one hundred dollars and wrote me a note saying he wasn't going to be able to give me the amount we agreed upon because business was slow. I called my lawyer and he said, "He can't do that." He called Larry's lawyer, who immediately told Larry he had to pay the amount he had agreed on unless he went to court and had it reduced. He still didn't pay, so I tried to call him and that's when I found out he was no longer with his business.

Again I called my lawyer and he called Larry's lawyer, who told Larry I was worried about the medical insurance and the car. Well, Larry said, the accountants were going to come up with a price on his share of the business and that he would get his money the middle of January and that everything would be okay. Now it's the middle of March and we haven't been able to get any answers out of Larry *or* his attorney. So my attorney has filed for contempt and Larry is about five thousand dollars behind in what he owes me. My little business did pretty well last year but it's been slow since the holidays. I don't like having to go into my savings to meet expenses.

When I talked to him in September he wanted the divorce —wanted to go ahead with it. I said, "Fine, I do too. Let's sit down and talk about it." But then there was no communication. I think maybe he thinks he'll go to bed one night and he'll have a little piece of paper under his pillow the next morning that says it's all over. It just doesn't work that way.

I suppose I shouldn't have let it go on so long, but he had such a fit even when I filed for the separation. He said, "Why do you need that? I told you I'd take care of you." He just wanted to walk out and send me money and lead his own new life. He didn't think you had to go to court to do it.

Maybe he's afraid that if he has the divorce Gloria will insist they get married and maybe he doesn't want to do that. I'm not thinking about getting married tomorrow or the next day. It's just that I want this relationship finished. It's over —I don't care if I ever see him again. I never thought I'd come to that point but I have. It just takes time.

My life is entirely different now. There were a couple of men after I finally started going out, but nothing serious until last year when I started seeing Ray. Earlier there was a lawyer I'd known casually. He was separated and we went out a few times, but he was too much younger, and that just didn't work out. There was another man—a really nice man I enjoyed being with, but I knew he wanted a mother for his fourteen-year-old daughter and I didn't want any part of that. I don't want to raise anybody else's kids. I figure I raised mine—that part of my life has passed.

I didn't meet a lot of men—I'm not the sort to go out looking. I'm not about to go to a bar or a singles thing and meet somebody that way. I have no desire to do anything like that. But the fact that there were men who were interested was very important. For a while I felt I would never be accepted by anybody. It's a horrible feeling. But once you get out and find that there are people who enjoy talking with you, being with you, it does something for your ego and you begin to feel like a human being again.

I had known Ray for a long time, and we've been seeing

each other exclusively for almost a year now. Right from the beginning I felt so good with him—he's such a wonderful old shoe. I didn't want to go out with anyone else. He's divorced and has custody of the children but they're not little kids. One's away at school and the other will graduate from high school this spring. Ray's not looking to get married and I'm not looking to get married either, right now. We just enjoy each other and have a good time.

In a way, mutual friends got us together. Somebody said to him, "Why don't you call up Fran and take her out to dinner?" I had thought of calling him. You know, I thought of just calling and asking him to bring the kids and come to dinner—my kids know his kids—that kind of thing. But I just couldn't do it. I think I had a fear of being rejected. I didn't want him to say no he couldn't do that. After we started going together I told him, "You don't know how many times I started to call you up." He said, "Why didn't you do it?"

His wife left him and it's taken him a while to get over it. He's been able to talk to me about her, and it doesn't bother me, so it really started out as a friendship. We're very, very fond of each other. We enjoy the same things and the same friends. I don't know if anything will come of it. If anything more develops, that's fine—and if it doesn't, that's fine too. Either way, the relationship is a very important part of both our lives.

I wouldn't want to just live with him—or with anybody. I'm too Victorian for that. If I was going to live with someone I would want to be married to him. It took us a long time before we could even go away for a weekend together. I mean we were both brought up the same way and you just don't do those things—but we finally realized that we're not babies any more and that we might as well enjoy each other. That was a big stepping-stone.

It's an entirely different kind of world now, but I still have one foot in the old one. When Larry and I first separated I thought, My God in heaven—sex with another man? It really frightened me. And I've felt a little uneasy about the children. I haven't discussed it with them, haven't drawn any pictures—and they haven't said anything about what they think. About the weekends—there have been two of those —they just said, "Have a good time, Mom." And when I came home: "Mom, did you have a good time?" The other times Ray and I have been together the kids weren't around —so it isn't something that comes up often. They like him, they're interested. They want me to be happy.

I wouldn't say that I'm in love with Ray, but he is one beautiful person. He treats me like a woman—and like a lady. He puts me on a pedestal, which is something I've never had before. But right now his number one responsibility is the child who's still at home, and that's true for me too. I'd like for Tad to get rid of his surfboard and his skateboard and get his act together. I'd like to see Robby back in school. But you can't lead them by the hand. I'd like to feel that my business is well established. I'll probably be more concerned with what I'm going to do with my life as soon as these responsibilities are taken care of. Right now I just want to be able to support myself, to be available to my kids while they still need me—and to have fun.

I really don't have any desire to work for the rest of my years. I definitely would like to be married again. I enjoy being married—I like the security of it. I love taking care of a home, looking after someone—that's important to me. I don't want to be a big career woman. I'm a homebody, a wife in the traditional sense. But meanwhile—it's kinda fun being eighteen again.

Gabriel

Gabriel had been married to Julia for twenty-seven years when he became enthralled with a woman eleven years his senior. He is fifty-two, a musician and teacher, and the father of a son of twenty-four and a daughter of nineteen. This interview took place five years after his decision to leave Julia.

"We both just kind of retreated from that good, loving six-month period, knowing exactly what to expect, that we would go back to the old thing, those long, long periods of lack of contact and frustration."

I GUESS it was about five years ago when I read in the paper that an old friend, a guy I'd grown up with, was going to be guest conductor with the Symphony. At the time, I was teaching music to black kids in a high school—putting on shows, doing a lot of creative projects—and I considered my life to be reasonably happy. But something was nagging at me.

I'd never shown any real ambition, didn't seem to have eyes for the competitiveness that was needed—maybe for life in general, but specifically in music. Then, when I read about my friend, I started wondering where I'd been going, whether my looseness had been such a good approach— asked myself where I was at. And I got the idea of writing things down to help me sort it all out.

I began writing, and that process—the revelations that came from it! It was the first thing I'd ever done that gave me a feeling of genuine excitement and ambition. I think I'd kinda fallen into becoming a musician. My father was a cellist so I became one too. Nobody had pushed me into anything; there was simply a laissez-faire attitude. I had never really wanted anything for myself—not even my wife—so much that I'd be unable to fall asleep at night because of the excitement of thinking about it.

I fell into marriage as I've fallen into everything else—it just came my way. I've been lucky, have a pretty good personality, pretty good ability, I'm healthy, so things came my way and I took them and did the best I could under the circumstances. And if a job situation seemed to be working, well, fine, I'd stick with it. Even when it came to getting married, though I was very much taken with Julia, it was her mother who proposed the marriage. We were planning to go to Israel at the time and Julia said, "If we go, my mother wants us to get married." And I said, "Okay." The part I played was not good—standing back from it all, not particularly wanting to get married, being phlegmatic—and eventually it rankled in her.

I met Julia when she was sixteen and I was nineteen. She had just graduated from high school and I was in the navy—it was during the Second World War. I was a Zionist who wasn't all that hot about Marxism, and she was a Communist, very anti-Zionist. But slowly we both modified our opinions —I came round to thinking Russia was the greatest and she got imbued with the idea of going to a kibbutz, and in 1948, when she was eighteen and I was twenty-one, we got married and left for Israel.

As far as the Jewish scene was concerned, we were considered fanatics—loving fanatics. As for the gentile scene, they didn't know what the hell we were doing, and to the leftist political scene I guess we were considered nuts because why would we want to go to Israel when we thought Russia was the greatest something-or-other? So we were really minority, all the way down the line.

In Israel we were part of a compact, cohesive, very hard-working group of about one hundred and fifty people. We took over an abandoned Arab village in the mountains, about a mile away from the Lebanese border which at that time was peaceful, and we worked ten hours a day in 115-degree heat in the summer and in the snow during the winter. Exposure to the weather was terrible, but the terrain was gorgeous. And there was plenty of idealism.

Julia, who was a much more practical person than I, fitted in with the work routine, and somehow she managed to find a place for her music in the kibbutz. I was a little more—I guess if you said it in complimentary terms, I was of a more artistic nature—and so I didn't respond to the routine quite as well. In fact, I felt at odds with the group. I could never understand why it turned out that way because in general she is the more individualistic and I the more cooperative person. And I was the one who had been pining for the kibbutz scene.

We were there five years, and she got a couple of hours off every day to practice, which was unbelievable—in a working society where everybody is out in the fields, somebody being allowed to stay behind and play the violin! I felt jealous even though I didn't want to. I felt good for her, but a resentment started in me. When I'd first come to the kibbutz I hadn't been that involved with my music—the kibbutz became the big thing for me. But then as I started getting resentful, I had a resurgence of interest in music and I went to the city two or three days a week to play with the symphony orchestra there. When I'd get back to the kibbutz the guys would say, "Well, where were you fucking off?" I was working night and day to make a living and pay the kibbutz a little, traveling and practicing—a hard life—and I became at odds with the people because I felt they didn't understand me and I didn't understand them, and Julia had found this nice, homey place for herself.

Then our son Dov was born. Julia didn't like the idea of him growing up away from our kind of family unit—the kibbutz had a children's house—and I capitalized on that and said, "Hell, you're unhappy about that and I'm unhappy with the kibbutz, let's move to the city." I tried to get a job with an orchestra but it didn't work out. We'd been in Israel five years and the McCarthy era had canceled our passports and we were trying to regain our citizenship and oh God, all hell broke loose. Finally, after months and months, we got our passports.

When we came back we tried to forget about that whole scene—had a lot of guilt feelings about leaving the kibbutz, leaving Israel. But little by little, like children beginning all over again, we started a new life here. My aunt helped us buy a small house and I went back to school to get a teaching credential. Julia's mother had been with us in Israel, lived with us the whole time we were in the kibbutz and also after we came back. I was closer to her than I was to my own mother, who lived far from us. We were a threesome—Julia, her mother and I—plus Dov and a bit later our daughter Sonya.

Julia taught Hebrew at a temple in the afternoons, and after a day of classes or substitute teaching I'd often end up in the temple too and then we'd drive home together. We weren't paid too well but with both our salaries we were able to get along. Meanwhile she was practicing the violin and feeling very frustrated that she wasn't getting anywhere with it. She wanted to perform, yet was scared to death to perform, so she felt unhappy about that, boxed in. Julia was smarter than I, but she had no chance for academic development. I once took an anthropology course, broke my back to get a C in it, and then she took it and got an A. I said to myself, That gal is really smart, as far as being able to achieve in that way. She had more common sense than I did too. It was like that old joke—I could decide the main issues of peace in the world and she would take care of the smaller issues such as what we were going to do with the family.

I got my teaching credentials, taught for four years and then suddenly—I go through these four- or five-year cycles when a feeling comes over me that a change is needed—I told my principal I wanted something different and he said, "Okay, goodbye," and before I knew it I was out on the street. For a while I studied music in graduate school and again taught Hebrew and substituted. I enjoyed the subbing so much that I went back into teaching.

Julia and I were both so young when we met, and inexperienced sexually. I'd had a lot of what I would call frustrating petting sessions with dates and somehow, when I met Julia, I didn't want to get into that situation. So I held off for a long time, to the point where she thought I wasn't interested in her—I think about six months—and then I got very huffy that *she* wasn't producing sexually. It was stupid. I don't know what the hell was going on at that time, but I blamed her: Why aren't we having sex! She said okay and went to a doctor and got a diaphragm. I remember only that I was putting on rubbers and she was putting on her diaphragm and we were fucking a lot, but I don't remember any of the details any more. It was just kind of an activity.

We were both very affectionate with each other at the beginning, but shortly afterward, within a year, Julia became reluctant about kissing, holding hands, caressing, talking intimately, sharing—the whole scene. We discussed it then, and as I look back on it now I think it had something to do with the fact that she felt any show of affection on my part was a sort of demand for sex—I must admit she was right—and she was reluctant to start that whole process.

Then one day she came to me and said, "You know, Gabe, I'm very much afraid of getting pregnant and a girlfriend told me about oral sex." I said, "What's that anyway?" She told me and that became the bulk of our sexual activity during most of our marriage. We would go through long, dry periods where there would be a lack of contact, lack of talk, lack of kissing—she'd pull the old headache thing—and after maybe two weeks or two months or five months of anger and frustration it would just well over and then she'd get warm again. We'd have oral sex and then I'd go into her and that would be it.

We liked each other and wanted to get along, yet somehow we were blocked. I felt cheated sexually but didn't know how to produce desire in her, and she felt cheated that I didn't give her enough attention, make her feel more in demand. We lived a life of nonacceptance—those long, frustrating no-contact periods, and then the making up and a kind of grabbing at each other in a desperate way, not physically so much, but emotionally. And it seemed okay—I thought that was what married life was all about—except that underneath I knew there had to be something better.

We talked about it a lot—we're both talkers—but really *good* talk was rare. She might complain about something and I'd say, "Well, let's see what we can do about it," and maybe we'd forget about it or try to do something for a while and then it would drop until we'd get angry again. I don't remember any really constructive talking or any real listening. It was very hit-or-miss, but it was such a long marriage that even the hit-or-miss approach produced some sort of progress—things were getting better. We were moving by slight degrees to a higher, nicer plateau of getting along.

After we'd been married maybe fifteen years I got very uptight about the sexual situation and I said, "Have you ever thought of going into therapy?" So one way or another she went into therapy and she began playing the violin again, even began performing. Apparently what had happened was that she considered sex a demand performance like her violin playing. She didn't like to be told to play the violin and she didn't like to be told to play sex. Once she began performing on the violin she had what was from my point of view her first really good sexual experience. We had vaginal sex and she had an orgasm and I had an orgasm and—I thought we'd finally made it.

A few years later she went on the pill. Her pregnancy fears left her, she was more relaxed, more sexual, and much more loving. She was on the pill for six months and that was a beautiful time—life was so good. At last I really felt married, was really locked into it. Then one day she said to me, "Look, Gabe, I'm a little worried about the pill—feel like it's going to hurt me." And I agreed that I didn't want anything to happen to her. So we both just kind of retreated from that good, loving six-month period, knowing exactly what to expect, that we would go back to the old thing, those long, long periods of lack of contact and frustration.

It was right around then—Julia was either still on the pill or had just gone off it—when I read about my old friend being guest conductor with the Symphony, and out of the blue I started writing and it was a major turn in my life—a peak experience. Julia had gone back to school, was busy teaching violin and performing, and I was becoming deeply involved in writing. We were growing more separate. She'd be upstairs in the living room, practicing, and I'd be downstairs in what I called the catacombs, typing. I appreciated where she was at and she tried to appreciate where I was at, but we were not quite parallel. There was appreciation but not real support. She didn't want to accept my support for her playing—I don't know, maybe she thought it wasn't authentic. My writing was very personal, a kind of rebellious breaking out against a lot of things, and my friends, my children, everything in my life was included in it. A lot of people who read what I wrote reacted with "Hey! Is this me here? What are you talking about?" I felt beaten down by their response, misunderstood by Julia too.

I was taking a writing class, and one evening, after I'd read a few things there, this lady came up to me and we started talking. You know, when you're writing something very private—secret—you're like a little oyster working on a pearl. Most people see only the outer ugly shell and think that's all there is. Then somebody comes along and says, "I see a pearl." That's what got to me, that this woman had understood the message I was trying to get across, that I was *screaming* to other people. They couldn't get it, but she seemed to get it right away. And just from talking with her, I fell in love.

Then one day Julia asked me if anything was different and naively I told her no, I didn't think so. She said, "Well, you look different, you act different, you talk different. Has something happened in the writing class?" And I said, "Yeah, come to think of it, something has happened. I met a woman there." She said, "Well, how do you feel about her?" and I said, "I haven't thought about it. But I think I love her." And she said, "You better leave."

I called Margot, the woman, and I said, "I'm leaving my wife." She said, "What are you doing that for?" I told her about my conversation with Julia and she asked where I was going to go. I said, "I don't know, I thought I'd come over with you." She said, "I don't know about that." She'd been single for a long time. She was eleven years older than I, a very classy lady, a Vivien Leigh type. I said in an empty, braggart sort of way, "Well, if you won't take me I'll settle somewhere on my own." When I think about those words I realize how incapable I was then of carrying them out—coming from a marriage nest I thought it would be easy to set up on my own. But Margot said, "Okay, come on over."

We hadn't had an affair, but she'd built me up in so many ways—called me handsome, which was the first time I'd ever been told that. Commented on the way I talked. I thought I was a real bum, yet she made me feel like a prince. I blossomed, and when I went to her apartment and we got into bed it was like a revolution shook me. I became sensuous, loving, caressing, and I thought, God, that whole marriage was a waste! I couldn't have been more happy about leaving Julia. Even that nice period we'd had turned pale, and all the love that had been in me at the beginning of my marriage, all that demonstrative love, started coming out at the age of forty-eight. It was an explosion!

I was with Margot for a month and it was nirvana. There was just no problem. I got used to what you might call a super-dessert of sex-loving-understanding-talking-cooperation—God, it was unreal, like Shangri-la. Then we had one bad argument.

We had gone out of town to visit her daughter. Margot had middle-aged children, was a grandmother. While we were there we went to a party and spent most of the evening talking with a German lady. Margot was a gorgeous woman who knew how to take care of herself, and the lady was very taken with her, kept asking her what she should do about her hair, her cosmetics, her figure. With me she talked about the political and social scene in Germany. The three of us seemed to be having a wonderful time together, and when the lady said she wanted to come and visit us I said fine.

After we got back we went to see Margot's nephew and she started telling him about the trip. Instead of hearing it as it actually happened, I heard a whole distorted picture—how I was in love with that German lady and had even invited her to come and stay with me. I just looked at Margot, and I thought, What's going on here? Is she joking or something? By the time we got home she had made me into a guy who was trying to start an affair with a woman I didn't give a shit about, and suddenly she refused to talk to me. I couldn't understand it—after all that beauty, what had happened? Why such a misunderstanding? I simply couldn't take it, so I left a note and went to a motel.

A couple of days earlier Julia had written me a letter saying that she loved me and wanted me back. I'd answered saying, "Sorry, I'm in a different place." And there I found myself in a motel without either Julia or Margot. I called Margot and said, "Look, I'm over here if you need me," and she said, "I don't need your number, what do I need it for?" So I thought, Well, that's the end of that, and I called Julia at about three in the morning. We met in a restaurant and there was a very warm feeling between us. I kept trying to tell her, I said, "Julia, I know you're looking at me and I probably look the same to you, but I'm a different person in a different spot now." She said, "That's okay. I want you back." I said, "Fine, but I don't know what I can offer you because I don't know what happened to Margot. But, well, let's see how it goes."

I took her home, and like kids, we parked outside the house. We made love in the car and it was the first time we did it with caressing and sensuality and talking—new things for me that I felt I could pass on to Julia. She said, "Come inside the house," and I said, "No, I can't—I just don't feel like I can enter it. I'm different somehow." So I lived in the garage for two weeks. Julia would come out of that lovely house into the crowded garage and we were like lovebirds. For some reason I never set foot in the house. I guess my heart belonged to Margot and I wanted to reserve myself, not get involved again with Julia. And all the time in the back of my mind I was trying to figure out what had happened between Margot and me.

One day I called her and said, "Hi. Are you willing to talk to me?" She said, "Yes, why not?" So we met in the park and talked and she asked me if I'd had sex with Julia. I told her yes and she said, "That's it," and got up and started to walk away. I said, "Hey, don't do that, I still love you. Can't we manage this somehow?" And she said, "Well, you're living with her," and I said, "Oh, hell, I'll leave her in a moment!" And I did.

We looked for an apartment together but didn't find one and I went back to her place. Well, this isn't a very nice part of the story, but in an honest, mixed-up fashion I moved back and forth about nine, ten, thirteen times until Margot got so pissed off she didn't want to see me and Julia almost got to that point too. The way it finally ended up, I came back to Julia and did go into the house—I thought it was all over with Margot. And I had a kind of nervous breakdown. Julia took care of me through it and then I went into therapy after I practically—well, I won't say that I practically died, but it was horrible! My skin was burning for two or three months, night and day, just burning, and I didn't feel I could survive. For weeks I didn't even sit down, just paced the floor like a lion.

After four or five months of therapy I was talking with the doctor about how much I thought Margot hated me. We went over the ways she had phrased things and he said he wasn't sure I had come up with the right conclusion about her. For example, when I'd say, "Margot, do you still love me?" she wouldn't answer either yes or no; she'd say, "It's changed." Her answers were always couched in noncommittal terms and I didn't know how to read those messages. But the doctor did. He said, "You know, I think she's still involved with you. Have you ever thought of giving it another try?"

So I gave her a call, and by God, she said she was glad to hear from me and was more in love with me than ever! I practically flipped—thought this doctor must be a genius to have seen what appeared to me to be such an impossibility.

All during the time I'd been with Julia I'd been thinking that if I ever had the chance to be back with Margot I'd do whatever it took to make it work with her, and I'd start by reestablishing myself completely. I was scared shitless about that, but determined to do it. I moved in with a bachelor friend for about six months and then got an apartment of my own—a dumpy little place, but it was to prove to Margot that I wasn't going back to Julia and that I could stand on my own feet.

The real problem, the reason I hadn't been able to read Margot's messages, was that she was paranoid. That was what the whole jealousy bit was about—she'd believe anything that came into her mind and couldn't be talked out of it. But during the times she was okay, we'd get along fine. We got married, and after three days of a beautiful honeymoon she slipped into her sickness—I don't know whether or not to call it sickness because she's such a together woman in other ways, but still, there's a little screw loose. Then, after three weeks, she demanded that I leave. So for the year that we were married we were living in separate places and I was dating her. I finally had to stop seeing her because I was being destroyed—normally I weigh one hundred and sixty-five and I was down to one hundred and twenty. By the time we split there wasn't a thing in our lives that hadn't been warped and distorted. All the elements necessary for happiness were gone. We had nothing more to share.

When I first separated from Julia our daughter Sonya was fifteen. I was very close to her—she's a beautiful girl—and I certainly loved her more than I did my wife. I was a very strong father—not strong in the sense of being strict, but I gave a lot of my time and my energy and my thought to the kids. I guess Sonya had grown up seeing me be enthusiastic with her and not with Julia, and when she saw my enthusiasm for another woman it must have been very strange for her—must have seemed as if I'd abandoned her for Margot. At the time she was busy with her own love affair, but it came out later—the feeling that I had found somebody who was more important to me than she was. And by God, that was true. I didn't ever tell her so, but I couldn't deny it. Actually, now that I look back on it, it wasn't as serious as I thought. It was just that the whole love experience was so new to me—to have someone on my own level who I loved and who loved me. It threw me off kilter and I wasn't able to think too well.

Margot cursed the day I talked her into coming with me to Sonya's graduation from junior high. When we arrived Julia came up to me and said how dare I do a thing like that, bring that woman to Sonya's graduation! Until then it hadn't occurred to me I might be doing something wrong. You know, all I wanted was for the person I loved to share an event that was important to me.

Margot considered my love for Sonya incestuous. She never actually met my daughter—was afraid that Sonya would be antagonistic to her. She avoided my son too, and my friends, for fear she would be criticized as the cause of my leaving Julia. Margot tried to maintain a perfect image. Also, she wanted everything in my life under her control and she sensed she would have a hard job of winning Sonya over.

When I finally left Margot I spent about eight months in seclusion—didn't see Sonya, didn't see anybody—and when I was ready to be human again, Sonya and I made a connection. There was always a strong core of respect and love between us, and even though the ship had been in a very high storm, both of us survived quite well. We've been close again for about a year. I don't hear from her for long periods of time, but when we do see each other it's marvelous.

My son was traveling in Europe when I left Julia—he heard about it through letters. When he got back he didn't seem too excited about it all—took it not with a grain of salt but maybe one hundred grains and said something like, "Oh, Dad, this is another one of your escapades." I think Dov looks upon me a bit like fathers look upon their sons, sees me as being experimental, open, rebellious, a sort of unpredictable character, where his own tendency is to keep a more secure footing. Still, he's not all that predictable himself. He just changed his field from computer science to classical guitar. At the age of twenty-three he couldn't read a note of music, and then suddenly in grad school he's taking all these music courses. When we get together now we talk like two musicians.

As far as love is concerned, when Margot and I were finished I was worried that the machinery just wasn't going to be there any more. She'd imagined I was fucking with men and women and boys and girls and God knows what else, when really I was completely loyal to her. I thought, Jesus, without her I'll just go out of circulation. But I found this wasn't so, and having been a family man all my life the idea of getting married appealed to me. At first I tended to get involved with impossible women who would push me away —the Margot syndrome. Then I did fall in love with one woman—a bitch, but a very fascinating person—and the turmoil was enough to shake Margot's image out of my mind. I welcomed that. But after a while I found myself in the same situation of giving and being pushed away, so I broke that off.

I have a girlfriend now, a very loving, kind person. Margot was eleven years older than I and this girl is eleven years younger. Not that age is much of a factor. The only difficulty is that she's married. She has almost nothing to do with her husband—I've actually become her husband, the main man in her life. Nevertheless, she's still married and our relationship has been tumultuous. With her, instead of chasing after the impossible, I get the possible—after a lot of trouble.

During this last year I've actually been "sought after." There's a small group of women who think I'm a pretty good man and they want me in any way I'm willing to be with them. The only woman I'm intimately involved with is my girlfriend, but I have these other friendships and the women write me love letters, they tell me what a great guy I am, they want to talk to me, they call me up and ask for advice.

This is very new, very strange—instead of being on the begging end, other people are begging for me. It's too much, in fact, because I find myself pushing people away, using the same words that Margot used to push me away. It's too much to read your own script backwards.

I'm very involved now with myself and my relationships, looking for some kind of clarity to emerge. Reevaluating what happened with Margot—though I don't care that much about what happened with Julia. Trying to handle the new, beautiful tide of appreciation that's coming toward me. That's what my life seems to consist of, plus work, getting back to my music, a few other things. I feel like a retired president—all that experience and no place to use it.

With my writing I scratched the surface. Then there was the time with Margot, and finally the breaking away on my own. Those were the stages that brought me to where I am. A painful growth process that I wouldn't wish on anybody, but once you get through it, it's worth it. For me, knowing I'm going to have to step out, take that lonely step—it's frightening, it's confused, but I'm strong enough to do it. If I have to reach out for something and it's fearful, Margot doesn't have to be there, Julia doesn't have to be there, my mother doesn't have to be there—nobody has to be there except me. And that—the possession of autonomy—is comforting.

I don't say I'm a happy person, but there's nothing stopping me from being happy. I find myself going along as if everything that was real has already happened, that I'm like a ghost going through the rest—the ghost of my own past. I go to work but I'm not that involved. I have a girlfriend, the nicest relationship I've had in my life—I mean nice, not passionate—and yet I just don't feel she's the one for me. I'm an eight-piston car, working on two. The car is shiny and full of gas and everything's ready to go—there's just no race to enter it in.

Julia

Julia had been married to Gabriel twenty-seven years at the time of their separation five years ago. They have two children, a boy of twenty-four and a girl of nineteen. Julia, forty-nine, has been an accomplished violinist since childhood, but throughout most of her marriage was more wife and mother than musician. She now has a master's degree in music, teaches, performs and has remarried.

*"We were children when we got married
and we didn't grow up together—we just
grew old together. I guess that's the
story with a lot of couples."*

I THINK I may have the world's worst memory—I mean for
dates and facts and when this happened and when that happened. I can't think in those terms. There are feelings that
remain and a few incidents that stay in my mind, but so many
of the details are forgotten. Strange, I remember saying not
too long before Gabe left, "It seems like we're happier now
than we've ever been. We're getting along better than we
ever have."

Oh, we still argued—we argued plenty, we always had.
And we separated for brief periods a few times before the
real separation. I'd tell him to leave the house. I'd say,
"That's it—it's over. I don't want you around." And he'd go
off and get a motel room. He'd be gone for a day or so then
he'd call me and say, "We've got to get back together."
And a couple of times I left and stayed with friends overnight.

Some of the arguments had to do with the fact that he was
flirtatious and I would feel he was about to get involved with
other women, or he'd lose his temper about something, or
I'd feel trapped like there was no place to turn. It's very
difficult to pinpoint all this because during that time I was

busy. I had gone back to school and I was unaware of some of the things that were going on with Gabe.

We never had what you could call good communication. That was a continual problem. But I never thought that was so terrible—I thought that was the way marriage was sup-posed to be. So I wasn't really facing the fact that some things were wrong and that they were getting worse. I just didn't realize it at all.

It seemed that things had eased up when I started back to school. We didn't have a lot of the problems we had when I was home more. I think I saw him becoming more depressed in some ways, but I didn't realize it had anything to do with the marriage. I was kind of stupid.

I've gone over it a lot—over and over it. I've thought, Well, I was becoming more independent, I was getting stronger, stronger and happier with myself, and at the same time he was feeling less successful, having problems with his work. Maybe I became more threatening to him. It may have been something like a midlife crisis. He became very competitive and jealous of some of his friends who were more successful. And I think he felt that sexually he'd been cheated because we had married so young. I felt cheated that way too—I really did—all along in the marriage. He claims that for a long time he was just waiting for a relationship—a different relationship. He said it could have been anybody.

One day he called me from work and said he had met a woman and he couldn't control himself—he had to see her, had to be with her. I guess he was nervous about facing me. It seemed easier to do it on the phone. It was very odd, and of course I was completely tied in knots. I told him to come home and we'd discuss it.

So he came home and we had a big scene, really big. One minute I was angry and the next minute I was begging him to stay. It was "How can you do this? This is so ridiculous!" Then I told him I wouldn't be able to live like that and he'd have to leave. He moved out that day, and three weeks later he came back, saying the relationship with her was over. He said, "I walked out on Margot because we had an argument and I felt I couldn't live there because it was a strange home —a strange environment. Let's see how this works out. I don't want to go back to regular marriage—we're just going to try it."

Then he got a letter from her and he went back to her. It happened something like five times—the back and forth. I accepted it. He did it and I accepted it. We were both nuts —we were living in some crazy kind of world. He set the conditions; he was at that point totally in control and I was like a dishrag. I would have done absolutely anything then. I thought that was all I wanted—just to get him back. I wanted to have him come back mainly because of my ego, not because I wanted him. I think I knew that even then. But also, I thought we could make it. I mean the marriage was so old—such a long time—somehow I thought we could make a go of it. I was so irrational myself, so nervous and confused. I never thought a month ahead or a week ahead. I just acted spontaneously.

Each time he'd leave it was a different story, but it would end up that he had to see her and settle something. He'd say he still loved her and I'd say, "Okay, goodbye." Then he'd call up about a week later and say he was in a panic. He'd say, "I've been smoking all night and I'm in a panic . . . I'm afraid I'm going to lose you . . . can I talk to you?" Then he'd come home and he'd say, "I'm trying to find a way to leave her." One time he came back and said, "I'm taking back my house." It wasn't to be with me. He just moved in—he was going to live here because it was his house. He was completely confused. And I guess little by little he began to find things about her he didn't like.

This woman was 10 or 11 years older than Gabe. You know, that's a little odd, to put it mildly. He told me a lot about her and if I'd ask him a question he'd really give it to me. I'd ask one little question and he'd start in. He even told me what she was like in bed—word for word descriptions. He'd tell me, "I take you for granted . . . I love her" . . . on and on. He had started to write and he became very flowery at that time. He'd write everything down—all his words, all her words, all my words. I was in agony—absolute agony.

One time he went back to her because she wrote him a letter saying she was dating someone else. Another time he said he just wanted to see her as a friend. And one time her daughter was very ill and Gabe had to go comfort Margot and they got involved all over again. He'd even say, "Why don't you go out? I'm going to see Margot now—why don't you go out?" Crazy!

When he would start to talk about wanting to stay with her, I'd say, "Go! I don't want you here." He'd go but he'd leave his clothes. He'd call and I'd say, "I want you to pick up your things and get out." He'd say okay, then he'd call again and say he was in a panic. A couple of times he really lost control, literally lost control of himself, and was screaming and talking such wildness. I mean he was really *ill*—had to have a psychiatrist. When I wanted to see a psychiatrist he said, "But *I* came to take care of you . . . I can't stand to see you suffer . . . that's why I'm here . . . I'd rather live there but I'm living here because I can't stand to see you suffer."

This went on for almost a year. One time he was home for about three months, then it would be several weeks, then he'd go to her for a week, then back here. I took all this partly because I wanted him back, because I was scared, and because I thought I had to give it a chance. His sister was here at the time and I was very close to her. She'd say, "It's going to blow over, it's crazy, you can see it's going to end."

Finally I felt like I'd lost my entire ego, all my pride. I hope I never get to that point again. I knew I couldn't live like that. It was causing me so much pain to have him around the house—having to worry about, Is he going to stay this time. Is he going back to her? It was much easier just not seeing him. I realized I was getting along very well when he was gone. Then he'd call and play on my guilt or my pity or something and he would threaten all kinds of things—he didn't say suicide, but I kept thinking he was going to do something.

I talked to my friends constantly during that time. It was as if I was always on the phone, mostly when he'd come home. Every time there was some kind of anxiety—and there was plenty of it—the way I would work it out was just to call someone. It was as if I could not be by myself. I had to have some communication, some feedback like "You're okay, Julia" because I felt like nothing. So I'd call friends and they would give me advice. "Let him go. What do you need him for?" Or "Let him play it out. Just forget about it, go on about your business." I couldn't follow the advice but it made me feel like I was getting some attention. That's what I wanted.

But I knew at one point that I just didn't want to have this any more. The fifth time he left I served him the divorce papers and that was it.

We knew each other four years before we were married. We were very young when we met. I was sixteen, he was nineteen. It was one-sided from the beginning. I felt I was more in love than he was, that I was more attracted and he was doubtful. I wanted him right away, I was sure immediately, he was my ideal man. He had a lot of other girlfriends and I was very jealous. I felt he was always holding back. He'd come to dates late, talk to other girls, flirt with other girls. I was never secure with him. For twenty-five years there was always that kind of thing going on. I don't mean that he was having affairs, but that he was flirtatious. Gabe was very charming. He'd seduce people, envelop them almost—then drop them—insult them if he didn't like their ideas, and never see them again.

I think we got married because he couldn't get out of it, something like that. I met him through a Zionist organization and we got turned on by the idea of going to Israel. We went there as immigrants and had planned to live there for the rest of our lives. There was no adventure after the first day, it was just plain grueling work, but it was fun, I enjoyed the whole life style. But the feeling of adventure, the romantic part of it was gone very quickly. He became very disenchanted—he was just not that kind of person. He was very individualistic, spontaneous. Emotionally he couldn't take the discipline of a kibbutz—couldn't stand any kind of control. So after five years we left, mainly because of him. I didn't want to leave but we did. I think then I began to feel that we were living according to his wishes, that everything we did was because of him—his needs. I know that's silly but that's the way I felt.

We got along very well for long periods of time. We agreed on a lot of things, thought the same way about many things, liked music together—we're both musicians—but we just had different expectations, neurotic expectations, I guess, and those would cause problems.

When the kids were born was probably the calmest period. Gabe was a very loving father, very good with the kids. During that time he went back to school and got his teaching credentials. He was working most of the time then, but as he got older he would quit more jobs. He'd take summers off— we couldn't afford it but he just decided he wasn't going to work in the summer. He was always a very irresponsible person, very difficult. You couldn't count on him to hold a job, to fix something, to be at a certain place when you needed him. This was true almost throughout the marriage. He was very emotional, very uncontrolled. If some idea would come into his head, if something seemed unfair to him, he was ready to write a letter to the editor and expose this or that without any thought of who was going to be hurt, who would be affected. He was erratic—once he came home with his head shaved because he'd gotten in with some ·group that shaved their heads. I couldn't believe it! I'm a controlled person. I think that was a basic conflict, a kind of difference in our personalities that started to grate.

I still feel kind of guilty that a lot of this was my doing. He would often say, "I want you to go along with me, I don't want you to be critical, I want to be accepted for the way I am." I was critical, but I wasn't open enough, so it was all covered up in a kind of pseudo-hostility. I was angry about the things he would do but instead of expressing it in simple terms like "I'm angry and I'm not going to live like this," I'd nag, I'd repeat myself, I'd go around with a long face.

I really see that my own problems were very much a part of this whole thing. I had problems with being up front about my feelings—lots of problems—especially with expressing anger. It was very hard for me to really confront him in a positive way. It's still a problem for me—generally, I mean —but with him it was especially difficult and it was crucial. He'd say, "I'm not critical of you—why are you critical of me?" And I'd say, "Well, you're just like a child. You dump your shit there and what am I supposed to do? Just accept it?" So he felt I was constantly pulling him down and I felt he was constantly doing things which drove me up a tree, where I couldn't get out, where there was no way to maneuver.

But I always cared for him—oh, not always—but I knew there was a basic feeling of caring which sustained me. I'd get very mad but I always cared about him. I still care about him in many ways.

Throughout the marriage I think we were sexually compatible except when there was anger, and there was a lot of that. There were times when we didn't have sex for a month at a time—one time for three months he didn't even talk to me. I don't remember what started it but he literally didn't talk to me for three months. I tried to talk to him—I was always the first one to try to make up. In all of our arguments I would come to him except during one period when I was in therapy and I got to the point where I could get mad and yell and throw things. And he'd like that—somehow he liked it. So he would respond by coming to me when I'd get really mad—when I was definite and strong. But generally I was the first one to make up. And then we'd have fine sex, until the next argument.

Gabe could have sex even when he was mad. I couldn't. He would want to make up sexually. You know, he wouldn't say a word for hours, then suddenly, "Let's make love." Here we'd just had a big argument and he's already touching me, and I couldn't do it. That was a big thing to him that I would reject him in that way. He would sometimes talk about sex —he'd say he needed it more often. So I'd say, "Okay, all right, you want to have sex, I can have sex—but I can't pretend I'm aroused when I'm not." (I found out later that a lot of women do pretend.) But he didn't want to do that, and I can understand not wanting to have sex with someone who's not in the mood—I wouldn't either—so in that way I guess I got to him. But maybe that's the way women are . . . much more . . . well, sex has to be a culmination of something and it has to be nice and in a special atmosphere—you can't just jump in bed and do it.

Finally it got to the point where I felt totally ineffectual where he was concerned. I became very unhappy. Obviously he didn't feel very gratified by that. He was unhappy, too. The only way I could feel any satisfaction was by getting out —going to school, doing my work—so we ended up in our own little worlds. He had started writing, so he was doing his thing and I was doing my thing. But I didn't realize there was anything wrong with that. I thought that was what happened. You see, we were children when we got married and we didn't grow up together—we just grew old together. I guess that's the story with a lot of couples.

After I served him with the papers there was no more of that crazy business. All the anxiety was just about over and I started feeling good—really great—about myself. I got more pupils, was teaching more, and I was busy at school. At that time I was about to finish my bachelor's and I began to think of ways to go out and meet people—even fantasized meeting some man and all that. I didn't really do much dating but I did think about it—how to do it, where to meet people—and I felt strong and proud of myself. I think I felt free for the first time, more like a person on my own. It was very good for me and I started thinking, "Actually, he did me such a favor." When I began to really analyze the problems we had had, the breakup was a blessing in disguise.

That first year I wasn't really anxious to get involved with anyone. I didn't do any of those singles things. I'd go to concerts, to friends' houses for dinner, to parties. I had two dates—one was a blind date, the other I knew casually—and they were both just terrible. I didn't enjoy them at all. So I was mainly involved with school and working.

The really important ways in which I changed had to do with some of the fears I had. I was almost phobic about a lot of things—flying, performing—also I was something of a hypochondriac. A lot of that went away during the separation and after. I just gathered my strength together. It wasn't conscious—it just happened. For instance, I used to be afraid of speedboats. My daughter used to water-ski and the whole idea of going that fast on the boat—I thought, Ohhhh, it's going to tip over. But during that bad period we went on the boat and I got in there and sat down at the wheel and it was just like I was tempting fate—to hell with it, who gives a damn! And I flew to New York a couple of times and wasn't the least bit nervous. And I used to be so fearful about performing as a soloist, but a lot of that diminished during the separation. While we were going through all that it just seemed that nothing else was very important. Performing didn't seem that much of a life-and-death thing—I wasn't afraid of anything. Some of those fears have come back. Funny—I lost them during the time I was depressed, and they've come back since I've been feeling better.

Gabe was difficult during the divorce. When he first left me he said, "You can have everything." He felt guilty, I guess. Then later he wanted me to sell the house and give him half the money. He was earning very little at the time. I had a feeling it would be very hard to get any money out of him—I didn't want to sell the house. So I got the house and gave up all child support and alimony. We had an antique collection—some valuable pieces. We divided those. But there wasn't a penny in the bank. I had to work, and as it was I borrowed quite a bit of money from my family. I worked hard, but it was worth it. I'm pleased about that.

He did some things that were nasty and any conversation we had about the divorce was negative. And he did some things with the kids, so for a long time I was just so mad at him I couldn't talk to him, look at him, anything. But things worked out after the divorce, and when I saw him about a year later he was friendly and I was friendly and it was almost like he was just an acquaintance. I guess it took about two years in all to get to that point.

I can't remember how we told the children—exactly how that went. Dov was in Europe. I remember Sonya was upset, quite upset. At first she didn't want to meet this other lady; she considered her an intruder. Gabe kept pushing that on her. He once told Sonya he would give up everything for

Margot, including his family. That caused a lot of anger, but he's like that, he'll say anything that comes into his mind.

Sonya doesn't seem to be angry at anybody now, but I think there are some effects from it—some hurt, the way it was done. We wrote to Dov. He wrote back and said, "Don't you think you can patch it up?" Then he came home so he was here for part of it. Every time Gabe would come back, the kids would think, This is good, this time he'll stay. But after a while they began to take the whole thing in stride.

When Gabe finally left—left for good—he lost contact with the kids for quite some time. He was so involved with himself and with this woman—with his own problems—he just didn't call the kids or see them. And of course I was no great model of a parent at that time either. I often was verbally critical of him in front of them. I'd say, "God, how could he do this? He's so selfish" or "so nutty" or "so mixed up." I've felt bad about that.

After the divorce was final, he married Margot. They were together for three weeks, then he moved out and they got an annulment or something. Then *that* started going back and forth.

So for a time he was just like a phantom as far as the kids were concerned. But for that matter they didn't call him much either. They were involved with school and their own lives. Now they see him more—not on a regular basis but maybe once a week or every two weeks, and they talk to him on the phone. He's much better now, much more human.

I met Mel a little less than a year after I filed for divorce. We started going out and I knew that was what I wanted. He's very different—very different from Gabe. On the one hand I was excited about the difference, but I also had to adjust to it. He's very responsible, very stable, but the relationship is more demanding in some ways—there's much more interaction so there's that kind of emotional responsibility.

I didn't have any definite ideas about getting married. I think I wanted to meet somebody but I didn't think about marriage right away. I wanted to leave it open—not feel too committed. I was enjoying a certain independence. So I didn't necessarily see marriage for myself, and to begin with I was very doubtful I would find someone I could love again. I went out with those two men, and I couldn't stand them. One of my friends said, "Go out, go out with everybody—do it." I said, "I can't. It's not worth it." I know women who've been single for years. They can't seem to have a relationship with someone they really care for. It seems to me the single women I know are much nicer than the men they go out with. So I didn't think I'd ever find anyone—I was very pessimistic about that.

But Mel and I got along very well right away. It was so easy—it happened so easily, a nice, warm, comfortable good feeling—and caring. When we decided to live together, it just sort of happened. Sometimes I'd stay over at his house, and once in a while he'd spend the night here, so we figured we might as well try it. . . . One day he asked if it was all right if he moved in. I told the kids and I was a little concerned. Dov said, "Gee, I hope I'm going to like that." He felt like he was being edged away or something like that. I told him how I felt, and that I didn't intend to do anything that would limit him in any way—that we would all have our own lives, our own privacy. Dov never complained after that. Sonya didn't say anything negative about it.

Mel and I were always open about what was going on with us—there was nothing secretive. I never really talked to the kids about that. I never said, "I'm your mother but I still have sexual feelings." Nothing like that. We just took it for granted they knew what we were doing. I have never made them feel that sex was a bad thing. I think they have a healthy attitude about it.

So Mel and I lived together and then we decided we wanted to be married. It seemed right.

The thing I worry about is that I overreact sometimes when he tells the kids to do something, gives them an order or a direction—or if he gets a little angry because one of them parks too close to the front door or leaves a mess someplace. I tighten up. That's the maternal thing, the need to protect my kids. But that's my problem. Mel is much more open—when he's mad, he's mad. He has said, "Julia, anger isn't the worst thing." But I still have this terrible problem with it. It interferes with my whole life.

My life with Mel is obviously very different from what I had with Gabe. There are many more satisfying things, and there are some strange feelings too. Sometimes I tend to romanticize the first marriage. I forget the real problems and remember some of the nice things that happened. But all in all my life is much more calm, much more relaxed, much less anxiety. I can count on the next day—the next hour. When Mel says he's going to be home at such and such a time I know he'll be home.

He loves music and he's very supportive of me. Thank God, because music has been a big, big part of my life since I was seven years old. It's something of my own. I was a child prodigy and I suppose all kinds of problems resulted from that. In many ways it's been wonderful and in many ways very anxiety-provoking. There were a lot of expectations I thought I didn't fulfill—things I didn't do, people I disappointed who had hopes for me, fantasies of being a great concert violinist. I didn't do it; I did the opposite. I didn't purposefully defeat myself. I always played, but I didn't really pursue it. I was scared, too fearful to pursue it more strongly. Instead I got married and lived in Israel. Someone who really wanted to make a career of music wouldn't have done that. I just didn't try to make anything big out of it. But it's been nice for me—I've played in a small milieu and it's been very gratifying.

I think what I learned from my first marriage has been very helpful in this one, but no matter what, it's still hard to change yourself. I know where I have to change. I know I can't go along and hold back angry feelings the way I did with Gabe. They are potential dangers. I think I'm much more able to say I want this . . . I think this . . . I'm angry about that. I do it, but it's still hard for me. Sometimes it takes me two or three days. I think about it, I rehearse it— I'm afraid of the reaction. I'm changing, but it's very painful.

I've been in therapy off and on, many years ago for a couple of years; then during the separation I went for a while, and it all helped. Mainly it gave me an ego boost and a little strength. But changing is so hard. What I have to fight in myself is to keep that feeling of strength and independence that I felt after the separation and not to fall into a kind of pattern I've always fallen into. "I'm not worthy to want this . . . or to feel this . . . or to say this. . . . If I do this or say this my husband's going to leave me. . . ."

One of the reasons I hesitated about getting married again . . . this may sound like a small thing but it isn't. I didn't want to have to ask somebody if it was okay for me to buy a dress. This is really my problem, but when there's a joint financial situation and one person is earning a lot more than the other, it's just not easy to spend a hundred dollars without the other person approving of it. I feel a little squeamish about it, like it's his money. I have an income but it's not very much. I'd like to be able to say, "Look, I want this because I want it." So on some points we have differences—but we're working on it.

The question was "What happened?" It's so easy to say Gabe needed someone and Margot just happened at the right time. Friends have said to me, "Well, he was depressed and he needed a change in his life. You were becoming too independent." I can't really make any judgment about it any longer—mostly because it just doesn't matter. For a long time I tried to figure it out so I wouldn't feel so lost—rejected—but I realize now it doesn't make any difference. Midlife crisis? Women's lib? Mother figure . . . father figure . . . craziness . . . What's the difference now?

Things are 100 percent better. I know that. I'm much happier than I was. Whether I can be totally happy is up to me because I think I tend to be more comfortable with pain. If I'm happy one day I'm going to be punished the next. Can't stand it if it's too good. It sounds screwy but it's true. I don't know if it's the Jewish suffering complex, or maybe all religions do that to people. You know . . . sin . . . you shouldn't be too happy . . . true happiness is not for this world. But I'm trying.

Stan

Stan left his wife after twenty years of marriage because of her alcoholism. He is fifty-five, an actors'
agent, with two sons, now eighteen and twenty-three,
both of whom have had drug problems. Stan and his
wife had separated seven years prior to the interview.

*"I'd worked very hard and I wanted to
enjoy it—I wanted to enjoy me. I wanted
to be able to come home and laugh and
have a good time, but every time I did, it
would end up being spoiled."*

MY WIFE was an alcoholic. She wasn't during the early years,
but it grew and became a problem for her and obviously for
me too. I don't know exactly when Jackie began to be unable
to control her drinking, but it certainly became evident during the last four or five years of the marriage. It was finally
the cause of my leaving—I just couldn't handle it any more.

I would get home from work and she would be tight—
sleepy drunk. Toward the end she was falling-down drunk.
So she would go to bed and I would sit alone and watch
television, which didn't seem to me much of a marriage.
Actually it was from *that* that I began not to come home,
because it just seemed silly to come home to watch television, and we had nothing going for us by that time—I only
stayed because of the kids. So after work I'd either meet with
a client or go out and have a few drinks, have dinner, do
whatever guys do when they don't want to go home—get
drunk, get laid, go to a movie. Or sit around with a bunch of
other guys, laugh and play cards—that's what I did. I didn't
have a girlfriend *per se*. I did have some friends who were
girls and whom I would occasionally visit and with whom I
had sexual relationships, but they were not romantic and not

a threat to my marriage—really didn't relate to my marriage —they were just separate.

More often than not I would be home by eight or eight-thirty, sometimes midnight or later. In the last years, even if I got home for dinner, Jackie was already drunk, trying to conceal it and not doing very well. We talked about it a lot. She was in analysis for a long time but it didn't seem to help her. I assume—I know—that the drinking problem was symptomatic of a set of other problems, some of which had to do with her parents, and others were my responsibility.

She wanted some things from me which I could not give. I could be her husband and her friend and her brother and her father at various times, and I could be her mother, but I couldn't be all of those all of the time. And that was the demand. I'm sure that as I talk there will be areas where I will expose certain other inadequacies of my own. I don't think I could recite them, but I'm sure they will come out.

I may have left out "lover" from that group of things I was supposed to be because that really was never very good. The physical relationship was never particularly satisfying for either of us. I don't mean that it was bad, it *got* bad. It wasn't bad at the beginning or for most of the marriage, but it wasn't one of those terrific "Oh boy, I can't wait to go home and jump on her" things. During the last few years of the marriage we occasionally had sex, but it was more dutiful than anything else, on both our parts.

I wish that Jackie had been more experienced sexually, more responsive. She wasn't frigid, she was a loving lady, but physically she couldn't cope with sex well. She just didn't, or I didn't. She would never have an orgasm. I don't think she had an orgasm during intercourse the entire time we were married. I don't know how important that is to other women, but it was important to her—a big problem for her —and I think it created enormous amounts of resentment. Whether it was my responsibility or hers was never determined, but I had this image of myself as responsible, and now I have the feeling that somewhere in there I should have done something—could have done something—that I didn't do. I have no idea what. I'm not looking for—you know, a *mea culpa* thing. I just feel that I should have done more than I did. I guess what I regret is that I wasn't better or smarter or whatever, but I really did do my best and it just wasn't enough for either of us.

Jackie was twenty-three and I was twenty-eight when we got married. Her parents didn't want her to marry me because I was Jewish. They were Congregationalist, supposedly a very liberal group of Protestants, but her father was liberal about *nothing*. He was the first man I ever heard say, "Some of my best friends are Jews," and he said it straight! We had a number of major problems with her father—not her mother so much.

We were supposed to get married and come to California. I quit my job and on my last day at work when I went in to say goodby to everybody I got a call from her saying the marriage was off. So I went up to Connecticut where her parents lived and found her in bed, having a nervous breakdown. After much conversation back and forth I said that I was leaving for California and she could call me over the weekend and we could still get married. She did, and we did get married as scheduled, and her parents came to the wedding.

Jackie was beautiful and a terrific woman, she really was, and I did love her. So when she left home and gave up her relationship with her parents—because that's what it seemed to be at that point—and *did* marry me, I was so grateful that for a year anything she did was okay. I mean we didn't have a quarrel about anything because whatever she said, I agreed. Later I regretted that, but that's the way it was. After the first year we began to have the normal give-and-take, but I discovered by that time I had fallen into a pattern of giving and not demanding back and I never did really break that habit—I was always the one who gave in.

Jackie had three miscarriages and then she was in bed for seven months of her pregnancy with our first son. I used to get up very early—I would walk our dog and feed him, then I would make Jackie's breakfast and make her lunch and place it close by where she could reach it. If she needed a bath I would give her a bed bath and then leave the house by eight-ten in order to get to work by nine. I'd work all day —didn't get home till about six-thirty at the earliest—and I'd walk the dog and feed him again and then I would make dinner. That was what I did and it was terrific—I mean, I wasn't that unhappy. I was exhausted, finally, but I wasn't unhappy about it. I didn't mind looking after her. You know, she was going to have the baby, she was going to have *my* baby, and she had lost three and I wanted a child badly and she wanted it badly, so that was fine.

But after the baby was born I was still father to her as well as to the child, and during the first two years of Rick's life— with the exception of maybe a dozen times—I was the one who got up with him every morning. I changed his diapers, I gave him breakfast, I played with him and put him back to bed, and then I went to my job, while she slept on. I didn't even object to that most of the time.

Actually, it really was a problem when the baby was six months old—I guess we'd been married about four years. I woke up late and I said, "Jackie, I don't have time, you've got to get up and take care of Rick." She wouldn't do it—she refused! I ended up not going to work—and I moved out. It was the first time we separated. After that I recognized that I had fallen into the pattern. I moved out because I just had had it—I was not satisfied. It was not that I wasn't happy getting up with the baby; I was unhappy about its being a one-way street. Relationships have to be two-way streets, and this one wasn't. I just didn't think it was fair.

I was gone less than a day—we ended up going to see friends, tried to get it straightened out, and I moved back that night. It just seemed silly to stay in a hotel. I tried to talk with her about it—that's when she first went into therapy. It didn't solve any problems—no, it really didn't solve anything.

We had probably been married about a year and a half when I had the first affair. She was a woman who was a friend. We spent some time together by chance and—it happened. As a matter of fact, I wasn't even the aggressor. I think we went to bed together two or three times, that was all. But we stayed friends—nothing interfered with that. Almost all of the ladies with whom I had affairs were married and were often, along with their husbands, personal friends of Jackie and me. I was never very good at having an affair with someone I didn't care about. I don't seem to do anything well with someone I don't care about—can't do business with them, can't represent them, and I can't have sex with them. I don't feel that the earlier affairs were anything more than opportunity. They were nice and they were warm and it was pleasant and it was good for my ego, and I assume it was good for the ego of the lady. It happened and it was done, and that was fine. I have been very lucky with ladies.

I did have a serious affair, a romance, when we'd been married about seven years. She was not a friend of Jackie's. She was an actress and I was taking care of her career—had done good things for her career—so we were thrown together quite often and I did fall in love with her. I mean, I was going to leave Jackie. This actress was married, but her marriage was not a good one and it was about to end. But then Jackie got pregnant with our second son and I couldn't leave. It did not work, leaving Jackie at that time—it just seemed self-indulgent. So I broke off the affair.

I broke it off because I was not capable of sustaining that kind of relationship without being with her—it just didn't make any sense. I couldn't afford to keep her on the side—pay the rent and do all that stuff—and I'm not sure that I would have done it even if I had been able to because it would have been sleazy. I liked her too well, and it seemed to me she was much better than that and I felt I was too. Also, if I had done that I would not have liked myself for letting my wife down. I cared about Jackie, have always cared about her—she just didn't make me happy. And I've always liked her. She did some things I didn't like but I don't dislike her—never did. It was not my intent ever to hurt her, or anybody else.

So things just dragged along. We were married and we had the kids and we had the house, a rented house. My career was certainly not startlingly successful. It never was, and I've never been any major hit at anything I've done. And we had the same kind of problems—she was too passive, she relied on me to do everything. She did *nothing!* I even ended up cooking more often than she did. I mean the whole structure of our lives was disproportionate.

Later on we bought a house. I worked my ass off all week and then on the weekends she would give me a list of things that had to be done. Many of them were things she could do, she just never did them—they were all left for me. And I really resented it, grew progressively more resentful. If I didn't go out and do the gardening on Saturday or Sunday morning, if I played tennis on Saturday and then watched a football game on Sunday, I paid for it. As soon as the game was over I had to suddenly be up and about and doing, not of my own volition, but because I'd be nagged. None of it was that important—a lot of it was stuff she could have done, but she chose not to. It was *my* responsibility. I was responsible for the whole fucking world! That was just unacceptable.

We argued about it and I'm not good at arguing. I'm good at fighting but arguing depletes me of energy. Oh, I talked about the way I was feeling, but after you say it three times, why say it again? It's done nothing, it doesn't mean anything, it's not being listened to even if it's being heard. I'm not a grievance collector, but my wife was, so when I would say something she would say, "Well, seven years ago when . . ." and she would give me a date and a time and a place and a conversation that I never remembered. From my point of view arguing was fruitless. It may have satisfied her needs, but it didn't satisfy mine. It made me angry and I began to live with resentment and I wanted to leave but couldn't afford to. At least I *said* I couldn't afford to leave—financially, and also because of my sons. You know that whole conventional "We'll stay together for the kids' sake"—unsatisfactory, and dumb, I think.

When we were married about ten years—I can date it because my mother was in the hospital dying—I left again. That was a complicated time because I was very close to my mother. She was a very strong lady and she took a long time dying, and we knew when she went into the hospital that she was never going to come out alive. It was traumatic, extremely painful for all of us. And I was having problems with my wife and I moved out. I was running my mother's business—it was a financial shambles, and I was trying to put it together at the same time that I was trying to run my own business and spend time at the hospital, which was far away. Jackie was very unhappy and she kept asking me to come back, and after three weeks I did because of the boys and—I really couldn't deal with everything at once. My mother finally died and I went East and buried her. I took over her business and made a deal with another agency, and having accomplished that—worked it out so that her debts would be paid—I suddenly found that I was incapable of making any kind of decision about anything.

I was an actors' agent at the time, and a client would come in and ask, "Should I do this role?" My mouth would open and either a yes or a no would come out but there was nothing behind it—I didn't know what I was going to say or why. And though I'd gone back to the marriage, I was not happy with it. I also had a sister who was a major problem to me—she was the most selfish person that I have ever known in my life, and I was trying to cope with that.

I realized that I was not doing much of a job and that I was totally immobilized, so I went to a psychiatrist one day a week for about three months. I would meet with him and then would get through a week, and I would come back and tell him all that had happened and all that I was dealing with, and between us we would get me together and I would hold up for one more week. And then I would come in again and have the same conversation I'd had before. I was coping, but I hadn't gotten one iota better, so I knew that I needed more than that, and I ended up going into analysis four days a week. It was very Freudian—I think he said seven words the whole two and a half years. I was looking for a father figure and when I met him I told my wife that he was about six feet five and about six years older than I. After two and a half years in analysis he was about my height, or a little shorter, and about six years younger than I. But when I needed him to be Daddy, I made him Daddy. He was not my father, I discovered.

Later I was in a therapy group with the psychiatrist that Jackie was seeing at the time. It was the best experience I've ever had in my life—she is a superb lady, best I've ever known. Then I was facilitator for her in another group and we had some conversation about forming a group of married couples and I would be her facilitator and her mate for that group. This did *not* work out. We ended up having an affair and I did not handle it well. And that relationship ended.

When Jackie and I were married I thought we would have interests in common, but we didn't. We didn't even like the same television shows. She didn't read and she didn't like to play card games or board games, and we really didn't do anything together except have the kids. Two or three nights a week I had to go to the theater and mostly she wouldn't go with me—she was beginning to drink. If she did go with me and I had to visit backstage, she would wait, wouldn't come with me, so I was always under pressure of "Jesus, I can't spend too much time here, gotta go." So everything was ugly and unsatisfactory and debilitating, really!

At first, however, we had fun together. I like to be around people and I like to entertain. I love being a host, and I'm good at it, and in the early years of our marriage we gave a lot of parties—we had a lot of fun. But by the time we moved to our own house in the suburbs, Jackie wasn't entertaining much at all. We were out there and that was the only way we could see people, and it was deadly, because she didn't like to entertain. We had a pool and all the suburban conveniences—but if we entertained twice in a summer, that was a lot of people, that was a big deal—and it got less and less until we would go months without seeing anybody from our earlier life. We had our new group of people who were all suburban big drinkers and boring as hell, and all you could do was get drunk. That's what we did—I did—a lot. I like to drink—matter of fact, I'm beginning to be aware that I may be having a problem with alcohol.

It's very strange to try to talk about the overall marriage because it almost comes in sections, depending on where I was at a particular time and where Jackie was at a particular time, and those are hard to recall. As I said, I'm not a grievance collector—not a recollection collector. Memories are stimulated and come back from something that triggers them, but it's very hard to relate things in chronological order.

In fact, I skipped a whole period which was really a major portion of my life. I had cancer of the throat and Jackie was the one who recognized there was something wrong with my voice. This was about six years before our marriage broke up. She was very supportive and terrific and that was a good period of time for the marriage—I was aware of how much she cared for me.

They removed one vocal cord—that's why my voice is so deep. I just have the one vocal cord, didn't have to have a box. And I smoked for ten years afterward to prove it wouldn't happen again—and it didn't.

It was really funny—when Jackie and I went to see the doctor to find out the results of my tests, he told me I had cancer and I didn't hear him say it—I thought he said I was okay! So the next day I was walking around the house, feeling happy, singing, and Jackie said, "What are you so happy about? The doctor just told you you have cancer." And I said, "Nah, he didn't say that, you heard wrong. He said everything was all right." And I really believed that—didn't have the slightest memory of him telling me it was cancer.

I don't have many physical ailments. I don't allow them. I get aches and pains—everybody does, I guess, when you get into your fifties. They're boring as hell—boring to talk about and boring to experience—and the result is I don't give into them. I'm busy physically—play racquet ball, play tennis, do sit-ups. I'm fat but I'm still in good shape, and I don't give in to colds too often. I know that if I get one I'm going to have it for two weeks so I take all the pills that hide the symptoms and get through it, you know? I don't stay home when I'm sick.

Anyway, I guess we'd been married about sixteen or seventeen years when Jackie became an alcoholic—when the symptoms became clear. We both became aware of it and tried to do something about it. She joined AA and I went to the meetings with her. She was never dry more than a month. At one point, during the last year of the marriage, she went away and stayed at a halfway house for six weeks, and I went and visited her twice a week. I was with the kids every night —I was both parents. She came home just before her birth- day and she got drunk on her birthday and I knew I was in trouble. After that she was falling-down drunk. One night she fell and hit her mouth on something and the next morn- ing accused me of having hit her. Well, the boys had been there and seen that she had fallen, so it was okay finally. But it was ugly! And the screaming and yelling and fighting and —I was filled with hate by that time. She threw things—she threw plates—accused me of not caring about her, which by that time I guess was partially true, but not to the extent that she imagined.

The first time I was impotent, it was with Jackie—a couple of years before I moved out. Later on it happened with some regularity—as a matter of fact, it became the exception rather than the rule when I could have intercourse with her. I was impotent with her because I just couldn't do it any more, just didn't want to do it any more. I grew to accept that as a way of life with my wife—that part of our relationship just didn't exist.

I was impotent a second time about six months after the first. I was having an affair with a client, a young actress, who was romantically involved with me, not I with her. She was sweet, she was darling, she was very attractive, and our affair lasted several months. But one night I was impotent with her and it was very distressing—it was mind-boggling and *scary.*

These things happened around the time I was thinking seriously that I had to leave. I've heard it said that people give up in their marriages and that's why they move out. I don't believe that's true. I think that the reason people move out now more than they did is that they *refuse* to quit. I believe it's almost always positive—done in the hope of something better. It's much easier to say, "Well, fuck it, I'm an old person and my life is over and I'm miserable, but our *kids* will be happy if I stay"—which is bullshit! I finally decided—I was in my late forties—I made up my mind that even though the kids were going to suffer they would just have to suffer and hopefully I would be able to get them into therapy so that they wouldn't be scarred forever. But even if they were, it was okay because I insisted—I *demanded*—I wanted to be happy in my own life. I just couldn't live that way any more, was not willing to live the rest of my life in misery. It wasn't worth it. I deserved better. I'd worked very hard and I wanted to enjoy it—I wanted to enjoy *me*. I wanted to be able to come home and laugh and have a good time, but every time I did, it would end up being spoiled.

During the last few months I'd stay away for short periods, alone at a hotel about ten minutes from the house so that I could be there to do whatever was necessary. Then one Friday night she was just roaring stinking drunk and I said *Fuck it* and I took the kids and we split. I didn't take them far because it was too complicated—we went to a nearby hotel. She found us the next day and begged and pleaded, and we went home on Sunday. But I knew that I couldn't live this way. That kind of pressure was too much for me and I felt that if I stayed I would eventually begin to do what she had accused me of—I would hit her—because I was getting that angry. And I realized that I could do nothing. I couldn't help her. Finally one night she got drunk again and the next day I went and got an apartment and I said, "I'm leaving Saturday. I'm moving to the apartment and that's the way it's going to be, I'm not coming back." And I did just that.

She was not drunk when I told her. She said that she was going to kill herself, then she said she wouldn't drink any more. I said, "Don't tell me that when you know it's not true. You know it and I know it." She said she loved me and that I no longer loved her. I cared about her, you know, but it was over—I couldn't care about her in the same way at all. And I was doing her no good and doing myself no good and the kids weren't being helped by my being there. It just seemed futile for me to stay. It was very difficult when I left.

I furnished the apartment, sort of, and it was okay. You know, she never came to that apartment for the five months that I lived there. My youngest son used to spend every weekend with me, *every* weekend, and I would see the older one, although by that time he was into drugs. He was chewing mescaline, dropping acid, smoking a lot of grass, and he was dealing, along with some of his friends. And I gather the younger one was smoking grass occasionally too. They were then eleven and sixteen.

After five months of my living in the apartment, she called me one day—she couldn't cope with the boys. So we switched—I moved back into the house and she moved into the apartment, and that made it much easier for both of us because I was there with the boys and they responded very quickly. Within three months the older son had quit drugs and the younger one got himself straightened out too.

The switch was good for Jackie, too, because she didn't have any responsibility and she didn't have to come to the house except when she wanted to and for big occasions. On her birthday or the kids' birthdays or Christmas or Easter I would have her either by herself or with a date and I would make dinner. So it worked out very well, and finally I was her friend.

But she wanted to move back, and she'd come to the house and try to seduce me. I was very tough and I wouldn't allow any of that to work because I didn't see any reason for it—it just seemed purposeless, tantalizing rather than productive. And besides, I wasn't turned on. The real reason, I guess, was that I would always remember her drunk and it was a nonromantic memory. I'm sure I make her sound very unattractive, and toward the end she was, to me, but when she was sober, when she was together, she was bright and charming and wonderful—and always pretty. Beautiful—a beautiful woman.

I never filed for divorce because it seemed to me she didn't want it and neither did I. I felt it would be an extra slap in the face to her and I didn't see any reason to do that —I knew we weren't going to get back together so I didn't feel any pressure. It also made my life simpler because then I couldn't run around getting engaged to other ladies.

Jackie made many suicide attempts. She was a Valium lady —she would take a bunch of Valium, drink a lot of booze, then call for help and have her stomach pumped. Afterward, the emergency room would always phone me to pick her up.

Finally she tried to kill herself four times in one week. The last time she was having dinner with the husband of one of her best childhood friends and apparently he made a pass at her. She got terribly drunk and swallowed some pills. He took her to the emergency room and called me. He had to leave, so I went over there and they wouldn't release her unless I agreed to stay with her. I got her home about 2 A.M., got her to bed and stayed until five. She had gotten rid of everything and seemed calm, so I left and went home. Then I stopped by to see her later in the morning and spoke to her that afternoon, and both times she seemed okay. The next day a friend of ours went to see her and found her dead. She'd had some kind of cerebral hemorrhage. Technically it wasn't a suicide, but in my opinion whatever she had done to herself through the week accumulated and finally caught up with her. We did not have an autopsy. I've regretted it since because I wish I knew precisely—but it just seemed so obvious what had happened that I didn't.

When they found her I was with another woman. I was in bed—and I had that whole image, which was ugly. It was Saturday afternoon and they couldn't reach me because nobody knew where I was, so they called my older son. He didn't go and see her but he called the funeral home. We had neighbors who were very close—I was a surrogate father for the family—and they took care of things. When I got home they told me what had happened and I had to tell Danny, my younger son, and—that was hard.

I didn't feel responsible. As I said, Jackie had been continually threatening to commit suicide and I didn't know how to deal with it. I talked about it with Jackie's psychiatrist—the one I'd worked with in the group—and she explained to me that it was Jackie's body and if she chose to destroy it there was nothing I could do about it. There was no guilt, you know? Which is fine to say—but I didn't believe all of that. And then when it happened, I did feel a good deal of guilt—which was helped a lot by my father-in-law, who was convinced that if he had known that she was in trouble he would have been able to help her. We had become fairly friendly over the years—they had finally accepted me as the son-in-law, always with an enormous amount of reserve. But he would never admit that she was an alcoholic—didn't want to know about that. She did try to talk to him a couple of times and nothing came of it. And when she died he explained to both my sons that it was *my* fault—which I thought was terrific of him!

The kids hadn't been seeing her regularly. When she could get her stuff together she would come over and see them. Christmas was a problem, and birthdays, because those were big occasions in our home. But other than that, they had grown accustomed to not seeing her, not being with her, and they knew she was having problems. I didn't hide that from them, because it just seemed wrong, in case something happened. But Danny was very, very upset. He was thirteen and it was hard for him. Rick was fairly grown up, quite mature, so that's been okay.

I have a great relationship with my sons. They're wonderful and I'm good with them. That's the thing I have probably done best in my life—I've been a really good, successful father. When Jackie took my apartment and I moved back to the house, the boys were both in trouble. Danny didn't acknowledge that there was anything happening and Rick wouldn't talk—he was very uncommunicative, into drugs which were distorting the mind, so he was off on his own trips. When I moved back it became a clubhouse—all the kids came there and one of Rick's friends lived with us for about six months. We cleaned the house together and we gardened together and everybody took a turn cooking— doing something—so that we were all equally responsible for what was happening. All of Rick's friends would come to our house and it was quite open. They would smoke grass occasionally and it was okay.

Rick went off acid on his own—did it himself. I guess what *I* did was I treated him as a man, as an equal, and gave him some responsibility without laying too much on him. It worked. It was October when I moved back and by Christmas he was finished with the acid and the mescaline, by January he stopped dealing, and he stopped smoking grass by March or April. I didn't even know he was doing it all. I knew vaguely that he was into some drugs, but I didn't have any idea how much. It wasn't till afterwards that he told me what he had been doing, and that he had stopped. I really can't take any of the credit for that—it's just that our relationship was the kind that allowed him to quit without feeling pressure.

My sons have been an absolute joy and *they* provided *me* with stability at a time when I could very easily have gone bananas, like a lot of guys I know have done. During the five months I was in the apartment I was really bed-hopping, and I think I would have fucked a snake, as the saying goes, and it didn't matter. I was not involved in anything except winning, and winning meant getting to as many women as I could—jumping on the bones. When I moved back into the house I realized . . . I don't know that I realized anything . . . but just being around the boys put an end to that. I didn't do it any more. I don't mean that I didn't have affairs but there was a different quality—it was a relationship first and then it was or it wasn't sexual.

Toward the end of my marriage, just before I moved out, I wasn't having any affairs. I was so disturbed by my whole life I didn't see anybody, didn't care to see anybody. But when I moved out I had fantasies about all those young girls I was going to get. I made up a list of women that I wanted to date and called a few of them every night. I always called at five o'clock because that way if they didn't want to go out with me and they said "I'm busy" I could rationalize that they really were busy. After two weeks of this, one of these ladies finally took pity and she said, "I'm busy, what about Wednesday?" And I had a date with her and it was terrific and I became freer. You know, rejection is not my strong suit —I'm not too good at that. I think my ego is delicately balanced. Anyhow, I went out with a lot of those ladies on my list.

And I used to go to my office wearing jeans and all that shit. I did that for a couple of years but I stopped—don't do that now. But I didn't put all the jewelry on and dye my hair and boogaloo. I did not pretend that I was younger than I am —I am who I am. But I've always liked to be around young people. Most of the friends I spend time with now are in their mid-thirties to early forties. I see people my own age, play tennis with guys my own age, but when I go for laughs I like to be with younger people because I don't find most people my own age very entertaining. I've heard all the conversation that they have, just as they've heard all mine, and they have nothing new to say. I'd rather be with people who are younger and have fresher ideas. I thought it was terrific when my sons' friends would congregate at our house and I'd be able to sit there with a bunch of teenage kids. My being older didn't seem to bother them, so I would hear what they had to say and what they were feeling and it was really interesting and wonderful. I learned a great deal.

I don't find women my age as attractive as I would like to. Logically, I think that I should be with them, but it doesn't work—just doesn't work at all. I am very aware of sensuous things in people—touching makes me really happy, I love to be touching someone. I don't know—it just doesn't work the same way with older women. Touching them doesn't seem to be as satisfying.

The majority of women with whom I've had lasting relationships—I mean three to six months—well, they were in their late twenties, they're now thirty-one or thirty-two. Those are the ladies whom I find most interesting, and they're also the most difficult, because if they have been married they want to get married again, and if they haven't been married they want to be. And that is not really uppermost in my mind.

I don't think I want to get married—don't think I'm prepared to work that hard any more. I'm not sure I'd be good at it. I think I used it all up—the patience and all the willingness to understand and accept. I don't want to do that any more. When my sons move out I'm sure I'll try to get some terrific lady to move in with me, but I have no idea if that will succeed because I find when I go away with women for weekends, by Sunday noon I think, God, what am I doing here? Leave me alone! And these are nice ladies, you know, nobody that I dislike. It's just that I wanna do what I wanna do. I don't want to be understanding. I don't want to accommodate. I want to be selfish, and I can't do that when I'm with someone—it just isn't fair. The ladies I've spent the most time with have been soft and very giving, but also very dependent. I don't *think* I like that, but my experience is that I do like it—feel more comfortable with it. It puts me in a position where I am giving and I'm more comfortable that way—at least until Sunday noon.

I've been in love once since I left Jackie. She fell in love with me—and she fell out of love with me—very painful. We were together for six months—that was four years ago, she's now thirty-three—and I proposed marriage to her and I think that frightened her. Then I had a bad period emotionally. I was down, and I think that turned her off. So we didn't see each other. She started going with another guy and I would see her and take her to lunch occasionally. Finally I realized I was punishing myself. That seemed purposeless, and I'd just talk to her every once in a while, find out how she was. She was living with this guy, and then about a year ago she moved out and we went out a few times—had no sexual relationship—and I realized that that was not good for me, so I don't see her any more, haven't seen her in about three months, since about the time I met this new lady who I'm seeing most often. She just turned thirty, is in show business —a bright lady, and she's been around a little, so she's not young in that sense—really a wonderful woman.

Impotence has been more of a problem in the last year than ever before. I find that it happens quite often, and I think it may well be that I'm jaded—just getting laid doesn't really do anything for me now. I'm not sure what it is but I know that I have some sexual dysfunction—not all the time, but often enough so that it's always a problem whenever I'm in a situation where I am going to get it on with somebody. I worry about it and feel a terrific sense of relief when it doesn't happen. But I've grown to expect that it could happen any time and—it's dreadful.

I wouldn't call myself a happy person—no. I'm not rich, I'm not a star, I do not have an emotional connection—I'm not in love—so I'm not happy. It would take some combination of two of the three. I have a reputation as being successful, but I look at the bankbook and I know that I'm not. I think if I had a lot of money, enough money so I wouldn't have to worry about money, ever—$250,000 at the moment would seem like a lot of money, and I'm sure that if I had it I'd say, "Yeah, but if I had $500,000" . . . and so on. So I recognize that that's a snare and a delusion. Nonetheless, it is quite evident to my accountants and to me that I am not wealthy enough to stop working for more than twenty seconds.

But if I were to have an emotional connection now and want to get married—if I were in love and the lady were in love with me and we were really going great—I would worry about the financial aspects of marriage too. Sure, I make enough to have a woman live in my house—I have my two sons living with me, and if I'm supporting them I could support her. That isn't what I'm talking about. I would like to live with some grace and some ease. I don't mean that I'm worried about paying the rent or about groceries, but the kind of easy life that I would like to have is not within my grasp at the moment, and to take on the responsibility of a wife at this point I would want a more stable financial situation than I presently have. And I'm sure that if I were desperately in love and if she were desperately in love with me, all I've just said would go right by the boards and I would say, "Let's go, let's do it!" I know that.

I'm not happy and not unhappy—I'm in a holding pattern, vaguely discontented. I see things just a little out of my grasp. I'm talking about money and satisfaction. I know that something's going to happen and when it does, it's going to be terrific.

I also don't know what I'm going to be when I grow up, I really don't. I sound like an absolute idiot to myself, but I don't know that I'll be doing the same thing for the rest of my life. I have always wanted to be a producer and a director. I was a producer for a few short moments, and I would expect that some day, if I get the chance, I would do it again. And even as I say "the rest of my life" I don't know what that means either, because I'm not sure that I'm going to die. So far nobody has told me anything terrifically attractive about dying and I really don't see any need to do it. I know that logically there's no sense to that—I understand it—but it is true that is what I think much of the time.

You know, I love what I experience. When I went away to college I was seventeen and I moved into a fraternity house. I was there two and a half years and *every* night I was the last one to go to bed. And when I went into the army I was always the last one in my group to go to bed and I never understood why. But I do now. I've always thought that sleeping was a terrible waste of time, and if you stayed up, *maybe* you would have that one great experience—that one super moment that would be perfect. I've probably had it and don't remember it. I still don't like going to bed. I'm not afraid of dying in my sleep. I don't need an enormous amount of sleep and if I stay up maybe I'll see the best movie that was ever shown on television or I'll hear the best joke that was ever told or have the best sexual experience that has been known to man—or something that I can't even describe will happen and will be the best. I've been doing that all my life, so I am not unhappy at all. I'm just waiting for something terrific.

What I would *really* like—I would like to be desperately in love with somebody who loved me back. But I think that I'm too cynical at bottom to allow that to happen—or jaded, or cautious—whatever the right word is. But—I may find out that I'm wrong.

Ellen

Ellen was married twenty-three years at the time of her separation. There are four living children—girls, twenty and seventeen; boys, nineteen and fourteen— and a history of numerous pregnancies that ended in miscarriage, and infant and childhood deaths. Ellen is forty-six, has a bachelor's degree in literature and is highly active in religious and community affairs. She had been separated six months at the time of this interview.

"My marriage, as a sacrament, will last forever—until death—even though he's not here. I don't care what the state has to say—I am married forever."

ABOUT SIX MONTHS BEFORE Stefan announced he just *had* to leave, I sensed a withdrawal and bad moods coming more and more often. He's always been a moody person, but during this time four weeks couldn't go by without a seventy-two-hour withdrawal—silence, not pulling out of the mood —and the mystery which bothered me was I wouldn't know for sure what had brought it on.

On the surface—well, if the children were making noise or came in a little late, he would lose his temper over things that hadn't seemed to bother him in the past. I thought, well, I myself find the teenagers enjoyable and rather a challenge but he might find this phase difficult. Then I began to think, No, it's probably me, because he began picking at little things. He'd say something like, "Things are just not right around here. I feel uncomfortable." I tried to keep things quiet and running more smoothly but I don't know—it was just an unhappiness.

And finally one day, almost like a bolt from the blue, I just sensed it. I didn't say anything because I had been so used to dealing with reality and this was something intuitive that I hadn't experienced before—it was just a plain knowing— knowing that what he really wanted was out.

It happened on a Sunday morning. I have to go back a little—for about three or four years now the children have helped with the housekeeping. Every other month I have a cleaning service but the in-between vacuuming and dusting and so on the kids have done. I was into my own activities and figured these children benefit from their nice surroundings. They can cooperate—they can help. The chores were written down—a checklist was put on the refrigerator—and they would eventually get done because I had made up my mind I wasn't going to do them. And Stefan didn't like it when I'd remind them, in a voice that meant business, to do those duties.

One day he said *he* would take over. He took the children into the living room for a heart-to-heart and then said to me, "Ellen, you are not going to have to worry about *that* again." I thought, Yippee and good luck! But from then on they did absolutely nothing. And that was a disappointment for him. They hadn't kept up the bargain, and he was too proud to remind them. So he would do the work himself. They'd run up and say, "Dad, let me help—I forgot—I was busy." And he'd say, "No," angrily, being the martyr.

The third time he took the vacuum himself, I said, "Stefan, this is not working—I'm willing to take this job on again. You shouldn't, on a Sunday morning, be doing the vacuuming—this is ridiculous." He said, "It's fine, don't worry about it." Then a few breaths later, "I've got to get out—I've got to have my own space."

Of course it wasn't the vacuuming, or even the disappointment. But he had failed in what he had attempted to do. His children had disappointed him and I had to remind him he had failed. Why not? I didn't say, "I told you so," but I guess my words conveyed the message. At this point in my life my energies were going into studies, into groups I was enjoying —I didn't have time for the bullshit protection game I used to play with him. I didn't care—I really didn't. It must have showed.

Then after the business about needing space he said, "I've been unhappy for six months." And I said, "What about me? Try twenty-three years on for size."

That really set him back. I shouldn't have said it—it just came right out. But I was so angered, not about the needing space, but about the "six months." The space—well, who doesn't need space now and then?

Then sometime later he said he was going to look for an apartment. I remember saying, "Okay, Stefan, if you have to go, okay—but remember this. I don't *want* you to go. We have this family—I see no sense in it—it's an embarrassment I'm willing to endure." He said, "Why should you have to endure?" And I answered, "Because I always have."

It's true. I had programmed myself to endure because marriage is forever. Some things are that simple to me. And it's nice that some things are that simple—that you just don't debate. Like there *is* a God—it's that simple. There's no proof. It's like honor thy father and thy mother. Your body will tell you if you quarrel with a parent—it'll eat you up. You don't need Moses to tell you that. There are certain basics that are for me beyond discussion. It's that simple.

I said, "I am willing to endure *now* . . . God knows . . . a month . . . two . . . three . . . but will I be later?" And now it's six months since he left and absolutely not—I would not be willing to endure. He might say, "Okay, Ellen, I'll never be moody again." He could put it in writing, but how do you write away moods and blackness and silence? I think maybe it's a chemical thing. I think he can wake up in the morning and it's just there. I don't know . . . I don't know. . . .

I said to him, "You know, it amazes me—you tried to break my spirit and it never happened." He said, "I didn't try that." And I said, "Oh, yes you did, but it didn't happen." I just had to say that because a thousand thoughts were going through my mind—the trials, sorrows, unhappiness that have

gone into these twenty-three years together. It's quite amazing—I don't know how I did endure it. It must be some
power to block certain things out.

So I thought, why fight it? It's just as well. Let's find out
what this would be like—a little peace and quiet. And I think
I was disgusted with his dramatics.

He moved out two weeks later on a Sunday. I had made
up my mind—decided life was going on according to my
routines. Sunday afternoons I visit the sick. As he was getting
together the furniture he needed for his apartment, he kept
looking at me sideways, and I said, "Well, it's almost one—
it's time for me to go visiting. I'll see the apartment sometime." Out I went and talked to the sick people I see on
Sunday afternoon.

That evening I saw his apartment—he had it all arranged.
Matt, our youngest, was helping him. It was very nice—Stefan's very good at that. He brought me back home and later
I called my oldest friend, told her, cried a little bit. She
couldn't believe it. That *he* had left. Over the years she'd
say, "Ellen, what are you doing? You don't have to take that."
She'd bring up things, such as how once, in the midst of the
babies, I packed a bag in the middle of the night with no
place to go. That was a foolish thing which is unlike me. I
never did a thing like that again.

At first, those first few weeks, I was afraid of embarrassment—I really was. I wanted to talk with my friends one by
one. I had the idea I might be put to the test—that it would
pass through my friends' minds—Why did he leave her?
What did she do? What's wrong with her? But not one had a
question about what had I done wrong. The usual reaction
was, What's Stefan doing this time? But it is a bit of a failure
—no matter how well you think you've done. After he moved
out, we did see a counselor, a wonderful woman. We each
went to one session and one dual session. In the dual session, she said, "Well, Ellen, do you worry about loneliness?"

I said, "There is nothing as lonely as being under the same roof with a person who really isn't there."

There was the illness earlier—and I've wondered if that had anything to do with the changes in him. He had a coronary in September of '76. During the recuperation I wasn't aware of anything different about him. But after he got back to normal activities—to his practice, to his archeology trips —he began to change.

We were at a meeting in Seattle when Stefan had the heart attack. Thank God I was there—I wouldn't have liked to get a long-distance phone call that my husband was in intensive care. He never lost consciousness, never turned blue, but if he was not a doctor he probably wouldn't be alive now. He was in the emergency room and they couldn't find whatever medication they needed to stop the arrhythmia. He spotted an emergency cart in the corner and told them to look there. If the cart hadn't been there, he'd be gone.

When it happened, I couldn't believe he actually had a coronary—I thought perhaps indigestion from the big meal. And when the doctor said it actually was a coronary I still couldn't quite believe it. I stayed at the hospital that night, and in the morning Stefan said, "Ellen, you better get back and stay with the children." I said, "I'm staying here until you're out of intensive care—that's three days. I'll talk to the kids." He kept insisting that I go and I thought, Well, he's upset. . . .

He cried the second morning and said his life was no longer in his hands—he was no longer in charge. It wasn't fear—it was sadness. And I remember saying, "Knowing you, that's only while you're recuperating. You'll be back at it as usual if not more so." Which turned out to be the truth.

The day after he moved out of intensive care and was doing well, I came home and stayed three or four days with the children. Then I went back to Seattle. My plan was to stay a couple of days, but the doctor said if I stayed three I could take him home.

The day we were to fly home, Stefan said he thought he should go to a motel for a couple of days to think things over. And I said, "I'm going to sue the hospital. The hell with your heart—they gave you too much oxygen and your brain is gone."

It didn't register on me. The look on his face—I know now, but then I was just thinking, He's trying to pretend he can be in a motel. This is stupid when we have to have a wheelchair coming and going. But he insisted on walking. The wheelchair was at the bottom of the stairs at the Portland airport—but he walked.

So, these were indications. I think he would have gone to a motel for a couple of days in Seattle. Those three days in intensive care must be an experience only a person who's gone through it would understand. I filed it away—I had too many things to do—I didn't dwell on them, but the words, his wanting to "think things over" stayed in my mind.

While he was recuperating, I apparently was in the habit of looking at him, watching him breathe. He said, "Will you stop *staring* at me? I'm breathing just fine." I wasn't aware I was doing it but I was. I'd even wake up in the middle of the night to see if he was breathing.

That passed like everything passes, with time—you get accustomed—you can't live forever on a tight tether and survive. And basically I'm a survivor. But all these thoughts went through my head. The thing is, he was not about to be a semi-invalid.

I became very angry with him when he planned a trip to a remote place soon after his recuperation. It was a four-day dig in a place where he'd be over an hour's drive from a hospital. I think I said, "You're going that far away—you might as well put a bullet in your head." He said, "It is my life and the quality has always been good and that's not going to change—the quantity is not all that important."

It was difficult—very difficult—while he was gone, but by the time the second and third and fourth trips rolled around

I was fairly relaxed about it. It's a bit of a gamble perhaps, the way he lives, but he's in good shape and I suppose he could go on forever. He did the stress test with flying colors. Still, once a person's had a heart attack, I would think it would make him sit back and worry a bit. He's given no evidence of that. From the moment he was up and about, there was more activity—more concern about this *quality* of life, more intensity—and more moodiness.

And sex—there were changes there too. In a marriage where there are ten pregnancies in ten years, I suppose sex cannot help but be an issue.

Until Theresa was born, sex was, in a sense, fine. Ah, but after the advent of that first child one does get reticent. Theresa wasn't the first—our first was premature—born within nine months of our marriage. He died in seven days. And after that there were the miscarriages. And someplace in my mind I thought, Well, these miscarriages aren't so bad and sex is good and maybe I won't have children. I wanted children eventually but . . . So, there were almost four years of marriage by the time Theresa came along. And as is the case with many women who miscarry, once they have a successful birth, they have many afterward.

We have four living children. One boy, Paul, died when he was seven. There were problems with all the pregnancies, all the births—but no—I would never have considered birth control any more than I would have considered divorce.

There were times during Paul's illness when I would feel bogged down. There were times when I prayed I would die. I was standing in the shower just a couple of weeks before Matt was born, and I was praying to God, saying, "Well, this baby will probably have something wrong, too." I'm standing belly to the sky and I'm saying, "God, let this be a healthy baby and let it be the end—or let me die. I can't go on like this. . . ."

I was tired of life at thirty-two. I didn't want a career or romance or "space"—I just wanted out from under. I didn't talk to Stefan about how I felt because there was no sense in it. He couldn't have handled it and what the hell could he do about it? I'd have opted for belated celibacy if you please, for a breather in between these pregnancies. Take me to a nunnery—I would have gone gladly! Sometimes I would kid Stefan. I'd say, "For God's sake, you got through medical school and you can't count to twenty-eight?" Really! I would have to laugh sometimes to keep from crying.

Over the years I learned I couldn't discuss my unhappiness with him. He could never bear to see me cry. I cried with friends. He, of course, was and is my friend, but I learned early on that I would have to save my tears for people who could share them with me. If I had talked about the times when I felt pressured with the mothering duties, I would have probably ended up in tears and he probably would have left the room—not out of indifference—some people would say out of guilt—but no, it wasn't that in my view. It was a loving thing—and it would have been too much of a burden. I guess I protected him, and maybe I made a mistake by doing it. Maybe I was wrong—well, there's no way to be wrong in human relationships—but maybe there are a lot of things about him I don't understand.

My mother was the one I talked to. Thank God for my mother. If I ever have a crack-up, it'll be when I lose my mother. She's been a brick—over here, helping every day through those rough years.

I would look forward to the kids getting on the school bus one by one. I never shed that kindergarten tear when they were off into the world away from Momma. As the kids themselves said, never would I get the Mother of the Year award. And yet I have that prize—because they're good children. I am not one to cling to them that much. I want them to get out there and say, "That's my mom, didn't she do a hell of a job? . . ."

But . . . I was talking about sex. When Matt was born I had

a ruptured uterus and they took everything. I knew at thirty-two I could no longer become pregnant. Sex hadn't really died—I could enjoy it. I had experienced orgasms even during the period of all the pregnancies, though not constantly, not every time. I'm sure that through all the ages there have been many women who never experienced an orgasm. Probably there wasn't even a word for it in centuries gone by. Women were not expected to enjoy—it was kind of naughty.

But I must say I was intimidated after the heart attack because it occurred approximately a half hour after a most pleasant intercourse. So when before he went back to work he said, "We shall make love . . . get in the mood . . ." and all that, I was frightened and said, "Oh, you know we can do without . . . God forbid . . . you're recuperating . . . I feel like I could be a threat . . . really." And I did not enjoy that particular intercourse, let me tell you, but then again, you get over this nonsense of worry, so we got back on a normal pattern.

Our pattern was never intense, once, twice a week—I can't put numbers on it—maybe sometimes less. It didn't seem to matter one way or the other. We were probably pretty well in tune in the sexual department. But then there were times, especially with moods and stresses, when he would want to have sex and it just wouldn't happen—no erection. He'd say, "You're not patient." I'd glance at the clock and think, Well, I've been working at this for an hour. . . . I mean, really, it was rather bizarre. And this goes back even before the heart attack—his not having an erection on occasion and finally his leaving to go out and sleep in the family room. He would never admit that he was embarrassed—it was just that I was not patient enough. But if pleasure also entails a great deal of work, it can cancel the pleasure.

I like the nice warm holding/comforting situations—not quite orgasm or whatever, but very pleasant sensations—who says we need more? I mean *always?* Just because you

begin something does not mean you have to go to what the
world says is the ultimate goal.

I would always say yes, this was very good, and he would
claim he could tell if I had an orgasm. I don't know if a man
can know that about a woman—for sure. But after the coronary, he got to the point of demanding that each time we had
intercourse, I must have an orgasm. Well now, didn't that
defeat it right there? He said that way it was more pleasur-
able for both of us. So we're putting a little guilt trip on that,
right? He'd get quite incensed sometimes. I'd say, "Well,
I'm comfortable . . . this is fine . . . I don't have to go any further and I don't care to." I suppose that was something of a
rejection. Again? But I was being more myself.

But I gave up. Later, when he'd say, "Did you experience
this pleasure?" I'd say yes, and he was satisfied—so he
didn't really know. That's playing a game and whatever, but
in order not to get a sermon about not having an orgasm, I'd
fake it. I was looking for the easy way out.

I wouldn't say there was any change in frequency after the
coronary—it was in intensity. I suppose everything in a marriage, sex included, does color the situation that ends in separation. I doubt strongly that sex would be at the top of the
list—if there is a list—but it's in there. I dislike the idea that
not having an orgasm every now and then is bad. It's the
warmth—the closeness. With so many a bride, the big disappointment is we no longer hug—kiss—the so called fore-
play goes downhill after that initial intense passion, but one
misses it. The holding hands, the touching . . .

We've not had sex since he moved out—nothing like that.
Our relationship is amiable for the most part. Oh, sometimes
if he's in a mood, I will get a little angry. He will kind of
mumble when he's in a mood and I have to ask him to repeat
what he said. And sometimes he'll walk in and I'll say,
"Would you like some coffee?" "No." Indication—bad
mood. In years gone by, too, if he was angry with me he

would not have his dinner—and I didn't care. I said, "Well, you know how much I care about food—if the kids want a peanut butter sandwich instead of what I cook, so be it. I'm not your Jewish mother. I don't equate noodle soup with love. If you don't want to eat, don't eat."

Another thing that's irritating now—his just dropping in. He knows I go to five o'clock mass on Saturdays, yet a couple of times he's walked in around twenty to five and I didn't have time to talk to him. I've been tempted to say, "Stefan, I have a schedule. I am running a family here. It would be courteous if you would call ahead of time and say when you're coming." He hasn't done that. In his mind I'm still always here—but I'm not always here. My life has become quite busy. I haven't brought it up to him because I want everything friendly.

So, when he does come here in a mood, I feel a little twinge and a little unhappy about it. He usually won't stay long, won't have his cup of coffee. And when he leaves, the mood and my feeling of worry about it leave with him. This couldn't happen when he was living here. I felt kind of responsible. And perhaps I was, with something I'd say. He is very sensitive to the way I put things, and I did get careless as time went on because I just didn't want to be bothered thinking ahead. I used to do it, but I just got tired of it. The caring was still there, but the putting myself out fell by the wayside, and I was aware of it happening.

But all and all, our relationship is better. Our talks have been mostly good. And he's more concerned—he asks questions about what I'm doing. He actually remembers that I visit people on Sunday. He came over one Sunday recently and said, "Now isn't it about one o'clock that you go out?" Whereas for the last seven years that I've been doing this, I would start out at one and he'd say, "Where are you going?" Things like that.

With his schedule, we hadn't seen an awful lot of each

other anyway, and now things are more pleasant. And the ridiculous guilt and sense of responsibility I felt about his moods I don't have any more. It's almost like another child has left the nest and I don't have to worry, and yet the love is there and the wanting to be in touch. It was always a friendship—you know you can have trying times with friends, too.

Since the separation, we have both said, "I love you," and that will always be there. The existence of love is like the existence of God—either it's there for you or it isn't. We once had a neighbor who was always reading books about love— Erich Fromm and Rollo May—and always asking, What is it? What *is* it? If you can't see it, forget looking for it. It's either there or it isn't. You can't define it. For instance, you can say, I love my baby, and let it sit in filth and not feed it. But isn't it beautiful? I love it! Well, you're kidding yourself—then love's a four-letter word. With me it has to be an extension of self—an empathy. Each person I love in a different way, so how can I lump them together? Love for Stefan . . . love for my mother . . . love for my children . . . for my friends—and it's an ongoing process. It's a faucet and once it's turned on, I've never been able to turn it off.

I'm remembering a talk I heard about the "fire of love." In Hebrew, Adam was called Clay until he was introduced to Eve, and then he became a man. There is the fire of the early time of marriage. Eventually the flame goes down—joins with the clay and we get a solid object of art. It no longer needs the flame—it's solid.

I've heard the term "mourning the loss of a marriage." I think that's it. I haven't really lost the person—I've lost the *state* of marriage. There are certain things I don't do—places I won't go without a male escort. I don't see myself alone on a vacation, for example. Thank God, in a way, we didn't have much of a social life these last few years, so I haven't lost much in that department. Oh, we did some things together, had some shared interests. He always did the cooking when we had guests—the Julia Child thing—and I was in charge of the cocktail hour. It would be my night to socialize, and besides he did an excellent job—and he liked the applause. The ladies would say, "Are you noticing that, Harry? Catch that, Fred. Do you rent him out, Ellen?" And bless him, he always cleaned up the kitchen, too.

And I would go on some of the short collecting trips with him. We'd go to concerts, but I didn't basically enjoy them. We would go to the ballet, which he didn't enjoy—then we did some things separately too; and we never had to be side by side at an occasion. Even as "youngsters" in our marriage, and all through it, if we went to a party we would split at the door to find new people. I didn't want to sit there and listen to a story that I knew. There are married people who absolutely must be side by side at a party, boring each other and everyone else, I'm sure. There was never that kind of social dependence on one another.

So, it's not a loss of *him*, because I have more of him now than I did last year. It's a way of life I've lost. My marriage, as a sacrament, will last forever—until death—even though he's not here. I don't care what the state has to say—I am married forever. I wear the ring. I will always wear my wedding ring. . . .

To my knowledge, there never has been and there is not now another woman. If it happened, I doubt that I'd be devastated. I know there'd be another hurt—and maybe it's already happened, I don't know. I would hope it wouldn't be such a possessive relationship that he would lose contact with me and the children. They need him and I'm still needing advice. Also, I like to see him and know how he's doing. If he got into a passionate affair where he dropped the rest of the world, I'd find that difficult and I'd worry. Yes, I would worry. Yet, I know if there would be another woman involved, it couldn't be on a casual basis—not a one-night stand—and that is threatening, because I don't want to be locked out of his life.

I don't think he's worried about his manhood—he has a good self-image. In other words, I don't think he has to prove anything like some men I've heard and read about—you know, Am I still a man? Can I still attract women? I think he's in a position to know that he's still attractive to women. Many women, I'm sure, reveal that they find him attractive. He is.

I worry about practical matters. When I saw the lawyer, when he told me the facts of life—that I would be responsible, when the property was split, for paying whatever premiums on whatever policies would be mine, and all of a sudden I thought, This had better be done well, because I have no other source of income. With my religious scruples, I will not remarry. So I worried about money and that depressed me. And I told that to Stefan—that the lawyer had really shocked me into the twentieth century. He said, "Why should you worry? You've never had to." But the lawyer had already said that even though this is a friendly separation, he had noticed that when things get down to money matters they can become unfriendly. So he jarred me into considering money more than I ever had in my life. There is money —but I do want to feel I can manage.

And I worry about *forms*. This year we'll have joint income tax, but from there on in I'll be taking care of that. And paperwork—I've had my own checking account for eighteen years, and now I'm handling more—the house payments and insurance—but paperwork tends to be something of a problem. But again, it's not on me all at once—it's gradual. I'll learn.

And there's being alone. Of course, three of the children are still at home, but sometimes when I'm wandering around here by myself I'll have a bad time. I haven't ever ceased to function. There's not been a depression, if that means not being able to rise from the bed or not wanting to. But sometimes . . .

I've never lived alone. I find it difficult to picture myself alone, but then in my study groups there are women who've been widowed or separated for years. They read, they're active in the community—vital, interesting women. My closest friend has been alone—she's raising her son alone. Another dear friend has been a widow for ten years, and another for three. So the people closest to me, people I love and admire, are women on their own. Whenever I feel a little sorry for myself, I sit back and think, I am really blessed. I have good friends. Right now I am still with my children. The mothering duties I have are very good—being there, talking with them, being aware of what's going on. The contact I have with Stefan, when he isn't in a mood, is pleasant, so therefore why should I brood about the future? But I have thought about it. I've thought when Matt leaves the nest I'll be by myself—but then I feel encouraged when I think about my friends who've done well on their own for years.

I do like male companionship—the male point of view. I'd like to have a male friend. But again, with my scruples . . . so, if it isn't possible, I had better cancel that need. If something is good for me I will do it; if it's bad for me I won't— I'll drive it out of my mind. I can do that. When Paul was sixteen months old, we learned he was going to die—he lived to be seven. But there were times when he seemed so healthy. I'd look at him and think, my God, he looks marvelous—then I'd say to myself, But never forget, Ellen, he's going to die. It was my kind of healthy reminder to not con myself into thinking that a miracle had happened.

I have to do this—talk to myself—and to other people. When I found out about Paul's illness I was telling everybody that the doctor says this, and this is what the prognosis is, and this is the way it's going to be. When Stefan had the coronary, I called people I hardly knew to explain about it. It was a way of saying to myself, This has happened . . . this is a heart attack. I had to keep saying it. Whatever tragedy is going on in my life, I must verbalize it to another individual.

The kids would say, "Your telephone calls are all the same
—why do you keep saying it?" I told them, "Because I've
got to believe it." And I think it's a good thing—in my case
anyway.

I don't like to project too far into the future right now. It's
one day at a time. I'm relatively content where I am. I didn't
get my master's degree and I'm not going to write any term
papers at this point, but if I ever would go out for a career it
would be in adult education. You don't really have to have
the degree if you're in the right place at the right time. That's
what I'm working in now as a volunteer, leading study
groups. I have no plans, but if it came to a career I would talk
to people I know and say, "Can you get me into such and
such on a paying basis?" It's possible. My work is well
thought of—I received an award last spring. I led a group in
comparative religions beginning in September of '77 and I
intensified the work during that painful period in January
when we separated. By March and April I was giving even
more of myself to it, simply because there was more of myself to give. There was dramatic growth, I would say. I really
felt good about it. I didn't use the work as a distraction—it
was something already begun, an enjoyed obligation.

I have tremendous faith. My faith has pulled me through
the loss of two sons—it will see me through this. I firmly
believe there is a mosaic or providence in our lives. I don't
mean we don't have free will—but that God in certain ways
directs us, pulls us through things. And one of the tenets of
the faith is that we are never expected to have a burden that
with God's help we can't handle. So that's been the core of
my being—my faith.

I'm not saying that faith and good health or whatever are
everything. We all suffer through a separation, and it is, I
presume, entirely different if you are the one who leaves or

the one who is left—but I cannot consider myself betrayed. I think Stefan has a very sincere need—and he probably had it in Seattle when he wanted to go to the motel and think things out. Probably he was saying, I need to think out my whole and entire life. It was nothing but hard work for him, coming here after the war, learning English, working through school, through medical school—marriage, work, raising kids. I can see that. I am not betrayed—this is something that perhaps has saved his life—to be by himself.

There's an old lady I visit. She said, "Oh, I'm shocked. I've heard about you and Stefan." And then she said, "You know what, Ellen? I'm sure he loves you—he probably was doing you a favor." And maybe he did. I didn't want him to leave—but coming back to this mosaic of life, maybe the Almighty had a hand in it too. Maybe He felt I'd done enough time in a certain way, and He wanted me to be freer to serve and to learn and to enjoy the community. It isn't all Stefan and myself.

But it's been good—pain and all, it's been good. And it happened. It's a part of my life, and time is a great healer. At first it was difficult—there still are moments—but it gets easier as time goes by.

EPILOGUE—FIVE MONTHS LATER

I knew something like this would happen, but the reality of it is very painful. It was my mother-in-law who let it out, wondering where she would be for Christmas—at my place or at Ruth's.

I called Stefan's office. I said, "I'd like you to come over this evening if possible to discuss Christmas plans, and who the hell is Ruth?" This was about ten-thirty in the morning. He said he'd be over at noon. And I found out about Ruth and that he had introduced her to his mother and had had the children over for two dinners with her. I said, "Why didn't you tell me?" He said he hadn't wanted to hurt me and he'd told the kids not to say anything unless I asked.

Hurt? God, there isn't any pain quite like this. There were a couple of days when I was weak, hanging around in my bathrobe, crying. I had anticipated it . . . a Ruth in his life . . . but I had no idea how it would feel. He said he met her in April. He left in January—and in only three months? Was it only his body that needed something? There are seven sacraments—marriage is one of them. It's the basic family unit . . . the commitment . . . for our whole lives. *We* are a temple . . . God dwells in us . . . our bodies are sacred . . . our sex belongs to one another. He has defiled the temple. His vessel is no longer held in honor. That is in my *roots*.

The painful thing, too—I feel that in a sense doors are now closed. This relationship with Ruth might be a permanent one, I don't know—but it makes me feel lonelier because now I see a closed door and I'm trying to prepare myself for the loneliness. The kids are growing and about out of the nest. Instead of the travel and good times without the care of children and concern—I'm alone and will be. It's scary. Before Ruth I felt it, but not as deeply.

She's the most jolting thing that's happened. And something has happened! I'm hoping there's not much soul or intellect there to go along with it. I want her to fall flat on her face—and him also. Oh, yes, I devoutly hope that this Ruth —this Ruth thing fails. I don't want any success—*her* to bring something that I couldn't.

I want him to appreciate my worth—the value of me over the years, the investment in the marriage, of what we together have accomplished. I want to know that I'm one of a kind and there is no replacement possible. I don't know *what* I want—I know I want something.

I've heard that the other woman is the most devastating part of the whole thing and I have to believe it. I've experienced it now. His death of a heart attack at forty-five would not have been as devastating.

Stefan

For twenty-two years, Stefan took it for granted that he and Ellen had an ideal marriage. Then he suffered a coronary, the first in a series of events that led to a drastic shift in his viewpoint, and less than a year and a half later he moved out of the house. This interview took place a year after Stefan left Ellen. He is a forty-seven-year-old physician, the father of four children.

"I believe Ellen left me as much as I left her. She left me a long time ago, except that we continued to live together."

I'M AWARE that when I discuss my marriage it always turns out to be a very one-sided story. There are three sides to it —my side, Ellen's side, and the truth, which is probably somewhere in between. Our reality isn't objective, it's what we feel. Ellen's version of the story is undoubtedly quite different and, to her, just as real as mine is to me. One of the unfortunate things about all this is that we cannot reconcile the two—to each of us, the way the other sees the situation appears as a distortion. And yet—we are trying to be friends.

Up until the last two years I thought our marriage was happy, sort of an ideal thing, what a marriage should be like. I thought the fact that we had divergent interests—did not do things together and spent much of our time apart—was a good thing. I used to say, "At least we're not smothering each other like so many other people do." Then I realized that something was radically wrong. I felt an increasing amount of tension, anxiety, and just general dissatisfaction in our relationship. In connection with this, there are two incidents that stand out in my mind—I had a coronary in September of 1976 and was off work for about three months, and then the following March we went to a seminar on creative marriage.

The coronary happened while we were in Seattle at a medical meeting. It was a very relaxed gathering, one of those tax-deductible vacation trips. Ellen and I had gone to a few sessions, then out to dinner and back to the hotel. In the middle of the night I started to have a chest pain that wouldn't go away, and even though I hadn't had anything like that before, I knew what it was. I got up and was sitting in a chair when Ellen awoke and asked what was the matter. I said, "I think I'm having a heart attack." She asked me why and what, and I said, "I'm in a lot of pain and I think you better go to the desk and call an ambulance." Somehow or other she procrastinated an awfully long time and she tried to talk me out of it, saying, "I think you're imagining it," and that sort of thing. And she said, "Maybe if you put some hot towels on your chest it will go away."

By this time about an hour had gone by and I said, "I want you to go to the manager and call an ambulance because I think it's being unfair not just to me but to the kids. I can die, and the first hour or two is the important time when things can happen." She finally said she would and she very slowly got herself dressed. I said, "Don't bother getting dressed! Just put on your robe and go down the hall and get the manager." She said, "Oh, no, I couldn't. I have to get dressed first." And she very deliberately and slowly put on her clothes until she was completely dressed and then went out and talked to the manager and the ambulance was called.

It was a little bit upsetting to me at the time—I'm not sure —I really don't know quite what to make of it. I think it was probably fear on her part—fear that this thing was actually occurring. She's told me many times since then that she wished I had died, that she feels it would have been better for all of us. She would have gotten the insurance money and the family would have been secure and she wouldn't have had to suffer so much during our last year together when I was always in those ugly moods. And she wouldn't have had to put up with all the crap of my leaving. Ellen talks like that when she's had something to drink and doesn't know what she's saying.

They took me to the emergency room of the hospital and for a few minutes there was a little problem keeping me alive. They had me hooked up to a monitoring machine, and of course I knew what this was all about. My blood pressure went down to zero and my heart went into a very abnormal rhythm and I realized that my chances were very slim because I could see the monitor going down. I found that all the popular clichés about dying—fright or regrets or your whole life flashing in front of you—that doesn't happen. I wasn't at all frightened and I found it very interesting: So this is what dying is like. I watched it all like an amused bystander. It didn't seem very bad at all. Then they got things under control and I spent a few days in the intensive care unit.

I recall one day when I was extremely depressed—depressed because somehow I sensed that Ellen was really disappointed that I was still alive. I don't remember how this came about or what she said. I was really down in the dumps and it may have been a physical reaction. After a coronary many people become depressed temporarily, so I may have misinterpreted the whole thing.

Then when I'd been in the hospital about a week I wrote her a long letter which was pretty much of a love letter. Even though she flew back and forth from Portland to Seattle two or three times and came to pick me up, I didn't give it to her then, I waited a few months and gave it to her for Christmas. I said, "This is something I wrote for you and I would like you to read." She put it aside and said, "I'll read it later," which hurt, because I thought it was something very special. I guess she read it the next day, and she said, "Thank you for your letter." And that was the only reaction I got! I don't remember exactly what the letter said, except that it was an attempt on my part to get us going. I think I sensed that things were wrong—knew it was the last-cry-for-help type of thing.

When I got out of the hospital I told Ellen it would be better if I went to a motel rather than come home. I guess I expected that things at home were not going to adjust themselves to my being there, that I was going to be a big nuisance to have around, someone who had to be watched over and waited on—a big aggravation. Throughout the years Ellen has said she cannot tolerate illness because her father had been quite ill and she was aggravated by people who needed care. The fact of the matter was, I didn't really need or expect any care. I was capable by the time I got home of taking care of myself, and I did. I rested a lot—didn't do much, didn't drive for a week. And I remember that three weeks after I had my coronary I scrubbed the kitchen floor.

I don't think I had a coronary because I smoked too much and drank too much coffee and that sort of thing. I'm doing the same things now—smoking and drinking a lot of coffee, and I detest exercise, so I don't get any, except when I go backpacking on the spur of the moment. The coronary didn't precipitate any feeling of "Gee, I've only a short time left and I missed something in life and I have to run out and get it"—none of that! I'm not the least concerned about the length of my life or my impending death—whether it's tomorrow or twenty years from now—or having another heart attack. My own interpretation is that episodes in our lives, like a major illness or a catastrophe, are pretty well programmed. I think they are reactions that we have on a very subconscious level to permit us an out from the stress we're under. In retrospect, I think that's what happened to me. I was under a great deal of stress at the office and I was under a great deal of stress at home. I didn't really know any way out of this. I could only continue in the same way, working harder and putting in more hours. A coronary is a way of getting three months' rest that nobody can blame you for. I *have* changed my life style in terms of walking away from stress a lot more than I used to, and I just don't get myself into positions where I'm being aggravated. In other words, at present I have nothing going on around me that I'm aware of to make me need to use a coronary as a way out—I can find much less dramatic ways of handling my problems.

I've read that midlife crisis is frequently precipitated by a major illness. Personally, I have come to the conclusion that it's the other way round—that it's a crisis which precipitates the illness, or that the illness just happens to be one step in the progress of the crisis, maybe accelerating it. In my case the illness was nature's strong warning signal saying, Do something, because if you go through this a second time you'll have had it! And it also gave me a three-month pause to look at the situation.

Actually, I don't think there's anything to this "midlife" concept. A crisis can happen at any age, twenty-five or thirty-five or what have you. The reason that changes occur at midlife is because the *opportunity* is so much better. There's a lot of guilt in leaving a family and you don't easily get up and walk out when you have young children. You worry a great deal about what it will do to the kids, and ten years ago I would probably have said, "No, I can't do this."

I'd always imagined that if I weren't there, my office would fall to pieces and my livelihood would go down the drain, but I discovered that, after having been away from my practice for three months, I'd only lost five or six patients. I realized that I'm a very good doctor and very much loved by a lot of people. There were baskets of get-well cards, comments that people had cried when they heard about my heart attack. It did something for my ego—made me aware that there was a difference between what I was at home and what I was to the outside world—brought out the reality that I am a worthwhile person, not just the guy who brings home the bread.

One thing about Ellen, when a crisis arises she becomes very different—not the dependent person who normally can't handle things, but someone who is extremely capable. After my coronary she got everything straightened out in my óffice just like a pro. But over the years we've played this game of her being incompetent and me being the competent one. For example, she has *never* packed a suitcase because I "knew how to do it right"; she was unable to do anything around the house because I "was so good at it"; she couldn't do any Christmas shopping because I "did it so well." I would practically have to beg before she would run an errand for me that had to do with the household. Then I'd have to look up the address of the place in the phone book and call to make the appointment and draw a map for her on how to get there. I accepted that role, and that was my fault—I played along willingly. I think there was a great deal of ego involved—I was the guy who knew how to do everything. Yet a lot of it also made me very angry. Not only did I have to go to the office to work, but I had to do all those other little things.

And whenever anything went wrong it was I who took responsibility for it—not overtly, but somehow by implication, I was the one made to feel guilty. My relationship with Ellen was based on guilt, and I can see now where this was a continuation of the relationship I had with my mother. I was raised on guilt—it was what my mother used to control me. I'm not putting any blame on Ellen here, because when you're dealing with guilt it takes two—one person to assign the guilt and the other to accept it—and I played along with this game. It wasn't intentional, but Ellen was able, by everything she did and everything she "endured"—I have to laugh because this is a word she uses so often—to make me feel as if I were to blame for whatever happened that was bad.

I think this really began causing a serious problem when our son Paul died. He had muscular dystrophy and was sick from the time he was a year and a half old. Then he went through a period of six years being very sick and Ellen was deeply involved in his treatment—she spent the better part of her time taking care of him. The way Ellen presents it, she took care of Paul and I had nothing to do with it; she is the one who suffered with him, I didn't; she is the one who carried the burden while I was out in the world having a good time. It doesn't matter how often I've tried to tell her that I suffered just as much, that she really wasn't the only one to carry the burden, that there were many nights when I was up with him. I couldn't be there with him all day because I had to earn a living to support his illness, to support the whole family. But none of this has registered, and somehow, what came through was that his illness was my fault, his death was my fault. And I played along, accepted all the blame, and very wrongly so.

After Paul died we never talked about this. His death was never resolved between the two of us. The guilt, which I think is a normal reaction for any parent to feel when a child dies, was always placed on me and I accepted it. I don't any more. To Ellen, having children was the price she paid for our relationship. A phrase she used repeatedly was that she "paid her dues" in the marriage by being pregnant—a situation forced on her by me because I had an interest in something resembling a normal sex life.

Ellen and I were very strict Catholics during the first ten to fifteen years of our marriage. Birth control was not practiced in our house, and any time she became pregnant she considered it my fault. I think this was a cultural thing. In her family the men were just sort of cut off—birth control was practiced by total abstinence. Her parents had separate bedrooms after she was born. I wasn't willing to go quite that far.

At the time we got married Ellen wanted a big family, although now she says she didn't. For the first few years we didn't use any contraception, but later we used the rhythm method—which, of course, doesn't work. As the years went by, she was counseled by the priest that it would be permissible for her to use the pill. At the time I had rather strong religious views against this—didn't feel that using the pill was any different from the other artificial methods of birth control. So I said, "No, we're not going to use the pill."

I don't believe contraception was an issue at all for the first nine or ten years. As a matter of fact, I never thought about it until just before Matt was conceived—he's almost fourteen now. At that time Ellen and I were in disagreement—I didn't feel we should use contraception and she felt we should. The only thing we were using was the rhythm method. Then she became pregnant with Matt, which was rather an emotional upset for her and also for me because we were concerned that he might be ill too. But Matt was healthy and has been nothing but a joy to us, so I can't say I feel guilty for having fathered him. I'm very proud of him and so is Ellen. After he was born, Ellen had a hysterectomy so, as there was no further pregnancy possible, that problem was solved.

Ellen was pregnant about fourteen times. She had a lot of miscarriages because we have the gene for muscular dystrophy. Statistically there is a good possibility that every male child that is born to us will have this disease. We lost our first child to it when he was only a week old. He was premature by two months and died of a bowel obstruction. Our oldest son, Luke, was born with a kidney tumor. It was presented as a bowel obstruction—it didn't turn out to be but we thought we were in for the same thing all over again. He was operated on immediately. The kidney was removed and he's been fine ever since. To Ellen's way of thinking, she is the one who suffered and endured all of this while I had no reaction at all!

Then there was the second incident I mentioned that had to do with the dissatisfaction I began to feel in my relationship with Ellen. A few months after I was back at work from my heart attack we went to a weekend seminar on creative marriage sponsored by the University. The seminar was designed for people who were happily married but felt they were still missing some aspects which would make the marriage more successful. Ellen and I did a fair amount of this sort of thing—attending classes and seminars—and this course was being taught by a marriage counselor we'd known and liked for several years.

Well, when it was over, we both felt it had been a very boring weekend. We were the oldest couple there—the others were in their twenties—and to us the marital problems they were discussing seemed to be completely inconsequential, kind of ridiculous. They talked about things like which of the two of them would water the lawn and who would be responsible for doing this, that or the other thing in the house. I felt that we didn't fit into the group because we didn't have those kinds of problems—the discussions didn't apply to us. Then, a couple of weeks later, I suddenly realized that even though we had laughed about the problems of those people, at least they had enough of a common direction so that maintenance of the yard and housekeeping were important things to argue about. With Ellen and me, our lives were so completely divergent that we didn't have even those *minor* problems—we had nothing holding us together, really. We were leading separate lives under the same roof without a common goal, a common direction, a real sense of cooperating, of helping each other.

During the seminar, as a technique for making the marriage more rewarding, each husband and wife were advised to make three lists. First we would write down our non-negotiable demands—those we considered essential and which we expected from the relationship. Next we would write down the things we wanted but were willing to compromise about. And finally, a list of items we didn't consider important enough to quibble over. I suggested to Ellen one night that we go ahead and do this just to see what would happen. After twenty minutes she handed me her list, and everything on it was non-negotiable—not a single negotiable or unimportant item—and I realized that we had *nothing* to talk about. There was nothing that permitted any adjusting or giving in to each other, and it was a shock to me that we were so apart—far, far apart. I told her I didn't think she ought to present only non-negotiable demands. One thing on her list that sticks in my mind was that we should have people over for dinner once a week. As far as she was concerned, this was non-negotiable. To me, this was the type of thing that we should have been able to discuss. I don't think we talked much about this afterward. I don't think we talked much about anything.

During the next few months things seemed to always be bad. We were constantly arguing, in a continuous state of tension that you could cut with a knife. We argued mostly about little things, like the responsibilities—who was going to do what in the house. And money suddenly became a matter to argue about, which hadn't happened much before. But after my heart attack the situation was a little tight financially for a while because I really lost my shirt while I was off work, so it became necessary to do without a few things. For example, before my heart attack we'd always had a janitor service come in and clean the house. The house wasn't spotless by any means, but, with a bunch of kids, it was acceptable. Also, we'd maintained a gardener who was supposed to keep the yard in shape, but I didn't think he was efficient. The reason he was around year after year is that Ellen makes friends with all these people, so pretty soon the gardener could not be instructed to do a better job or be discharged, because he was a friend who belonged in the house. And the cleaning man, who was a friend too, spent more time drinking coffee than he did cleaning.

Anyway, after things started looking up again financially, I said I did not think we should get back into having people come in to clean. I felt that with six of us living in the house it should be quite possible to keep the place clean ourselves and that this should not be a big problem. Well, this is where we began to have arguments. Ellen said that under no circumstances would she clean or vacuum or do anything like that. If I and the kids wanted to do this it would be all right, but she was above this kind of work and she was not going to participate.

I tried with the kids—we set up schedules to clean the house. Of course they realized that "If Mama doesn't do it, I don't have to do it either"—so it got to the point where I was doing all the housecleaning, which made me feel very put upon and hurt. I'd work all week and then Saturday I had to start vacuuming the house. It was that sort of thing which brought us into constant contention, and undoubtedly I was not easy to live with—I bitched and complained about it a great deal.

For many years we'd had a strange family life according to other people's standards. We never had meals together except on holidays, never had breakfast together because Ellen never got up for it. I fixed my own breakfast and the kids fixed theirs, and we were all on our own—there was no structure. At that time this seemed to suit everybody fine. Then, suddenly, it began to bother me—or maybe I woke up to what was going on. I'm not blaming it on anyone, but Ellen and I argued constantly. There was an awful lot of tension in the house and I would find myself staying late at the office, reading, because I was more comfortable there than at home. I was depressed, started to withdraw more and more, and I was very unhappy.

Some of my anger had to do with my idiosyncrasies, which I thought should be respected. For instance, I am a poor sleeper and usually cannot go back to sleep after I've been awakened during the night. So I felt that getting eight hours of sleep should be of prime importance in my house—everybody ought to realize that my going to work in the morning supported the whole show—and I'd get furious at being awakened at midnight or 1 A.M. by people slamming doors or television sets playing. I have to get up at six but Ellen doesn't get up till nine or nine-thirty. As far as I'm concerned, I think she led a very luxurious and spoiled life with few responsibilities—nothing to do except what she wanted to do.

She complained about having to endure my—I forget the term she used, either temper tantrums or moods—and there's justification for that. I have a terrible time expressing angry feelings to people at the time I get angry. I've always been like that. The way I was raised, children were never permitted to express anger of any sort, so maybe that's where it originated. I have this problem with the people who work for me, with all my relationships. When I get angry I hold it in, and then some minor thing that has nothing to do with the real cause of the anger will trigger a sudden explosion that might be called a temper tantrum. Or else I go into one of my withdrawn moods where I don't talk for a day or two. I play that game very well. It's a poor way—I'm getting better.

Besides the tension between Ellen and me, there was also tension that involved the kids. Ellen and my oldest daughter, Theresa, have been in a constant state of warfare since Theresa was about fourteen years old, but Theresa and I have always gotten along extremely well. I think maybe the kids started taking advantage of the whole bit—started playing us against each other, but I don't think that was a big factor. All I know is that during this period I became more unhappy and depressed.

My angry feelings also had to do with the day-by-day frustrations that get pent up, the little snide comments that hurt, the little sarcasms, the put-downs. I don't blame Ellen for this as much as I blame the bottle. There's a great deal of difference between what she says and does when she's sober and when she's been drinking. When drinking, she can say things that are absolutely cutting. She doesn't remember them afterwards, or if she does, she remembers them in a completely different context.

Ellen's increasing dependence upon alcohol has become a serious problem in the last few years. I'm not saying that in a condemning way by any means because I used to have the same problem myself. I never drank until I was in medical school, and at fraternity parties I would get horrendously drunk—never knew when to stop. Later, in the Air Force, drinking was the custom, and it took less than a year for me to become alcoholic to the point of actually sneaking drinks. When I started my medical practice I drank very heavily but only on a restricted basis—never while working or on call. We lived in a neighborhood with a lot of boozing and parties and there was a joke: "As long as I don't drink more than my doctor I'll be all right." It got to be a way of life for both of us. Ellen was quite accustomed to drinking at a social level at that time but she didn't drink to excess. I would drink at night, not have any hangovers, and it went on like this for years with no problems.

Then I started having the physical symptoms of alcoholism —the morning vomiting and the morning drinking—and I wasn't functioning as well as I should have. One Sunday morning I got up hung over and in terrible shape, so I had a couple of belts before going to church. It was in the middle of mass that I realized I was half drunk, and that I couldn't go on living like that. So I called my partner and explained the situation—he hadn't known about my problem—and he made all the arrangements for me to go to a private hospital for a few days to dry out. Afterwards I didn't drink for about six weeks—and then I fell right back into it again for another year. I would measure out a pint as my daily ration, which wasn't much, except that it was more than my body could tolerate, and I had the shakes and severe hangovers every single day. Not only that—I was getting myself into ridiculous social situations and using frantic activity in an attempt to conceal my drinking. Things had gone entirely too far so I admitted myself to a state hospital and spent a month there. It was rather a horrible experience—we were locked up and dried out cold turkey.

Ellen was fantastic during that period—I'll always be grateful. She couldn't have been more supportive or helpful or nonjudgmental. She visited me every day and never once made remarks, nor did she ever let me feel that she was not behind me, really trying to help me, and that the only thing in her mind was to get it over with and get me well. At that time we had been married thirteen years—it was a year before our son Paul died. Certainly in those days she and I were still really together, still had a lot going for us.

I haven't touched a drop since, but I think it was about that time that Ellen started drinking more heavily. It's a common thing—when one partner stops drinking the other starts. She very seldom lost control and it wasn't a problem until the last four or five years, when she sometimes went through a fifth a day and had periods when she couldn't remember what she said the night before. We have talked about her drinking and I've asked her to do something about it, but I don't think she acknowledges it as a problem.

Ellen has two distinct personalities, and she changes suddenly from one to the other when she drinks. Sober, she's an intelligent, charming, delightful person to be with. That's the way she is on Sunday morning, but not by Sunday night. When she's drinking she's an aggressive, sarcastic, angry individual who has a way of putting people down, of not listening and of interrupting, of making caustic remarks which she thinks are funny but really are not funny at all. She prides herself on her sense of humor, but it isn't humor—it's a way of hurting people. The kids are aware of all of this too.

I also used to get very disturbed by Ellen's preoccupation with the television set. Life revolved around the fact that Dick Cavett came on at a certain time in the afternoon and then "Upstairs, Downstairs" came on at eight and had to be watched to the exclusion of all other activities—another "non-negotiable." By the time I came home in the evening it was nearly time to turn on the boob tube. I wouldn't watch it, so I would sit in a different room. It seems like Ellen and I spent our entire lives sitting in different rooms. And sex had become infrequent—my own needs were in constant competition with the movies shown on Channel 9. The moment she got an inkling that I was interested in having sex she just would *not* come to bed—because she was so engrossed in watching Channel 9. She used to say that as far as sex was concerned, she could take it or leave it—it was of no importance to her.

When we got married we'd been dating each other exclusively for three years and we were both pure, totally inexperienced in sex. For the first ten years or so our sex life was satisfactory for me, but I don't think it was ever satisfying for Ellen. I don't think she ever got much out of it. She told me she considered this normal, and we didn't think of it as a problem. I felt occasionally frustrated, but in general it was satisfactory—to a great extent because I didn't know any better. I was a very ignorant person then—didn't know what sex *could* be like. I think that during the last ten years of the marriage sex was something that Ellen endured—did not enjoy at all in terms of orgasms or in any other way—or she enjoyed it maybe once or twice a year. Sex became unsatisfactory for me too because of her lack of interest.

An incident stands out in my mind from the last few months that we lived together as husband and wife. Once, after intercourse, she said something like "I tried my best not to have an orgasm but I did anyway and it really bugs me because I didn't want you to have the pleasure of knowing you could satisfy me." This is what our sex life was like—it had become a battleground, and I think that had something to do with my deciding to leave. A woman has ways, if she wants to use them, of castrating a man psychologically. This is what happened to us and I became less and less interested in sex—less and less able to perform. It was done by little remarks here and there, little comments, nothing that was stated directly—there was none of the openness between us necessary for a discussion of it. The problem of impotence —it's obviously a very psychological thing. When you're in a bad situation, when there is absolutely no encouragement or response, your self-esteem suffers a great deal. I've found that potency does come back under different circumstances and—it's no longer a problem.

From my present perspective, I don't think our poor, inadequate sex life was the reason for our splitting up. It was one of the factors, but if everything else had been all right, if we'd had a common goal, a common direction, a common interest, the lack of sex is something I would have endured. But we spoke only of superficial matters. I couldn't have a discussion with her because she constantly interrupted and made me feel that I was a dummy. That's the way it's been over the years. What I've said has been broken in on, comments have been made that were totally irrelevant to what was being said—I'd be halfway through a sentence and it would be completed for me—or somehow, by insinuation, I'd be made to feel that what I'd said was not worth listening to.

I don't think Ellen ever listens to anybody—I think the words just sort of go by her. The only way I've been able to talk to her recently is to literally sit her down and tell her, "I want you to sit here and I'm going to talk for the next twenty minutes and I don't want to be interrupted and I want you to pay attention and find out what it is I've got to say to you!"

It was what happened at the end of the June vacation that precipitated my decision to do something about our situation. For the past fifteen years we'd taken the kids to a family resort on the Coast for two weeks each summer, and it was a holiday we all looked forward to. But in 1977, the summer after my coronary, we were not as flush as usual, and I said we could only manage one week and that I would not go at all because I couldn't afford the loss of income from my practice. Also, by this time the vacation had become a little bit boring to me.

So I drove them down on a Saturday, stayed overnight and returned home. They were going to come back the following weekend, but my oldest daughter had to be back a day early for her summer job and she brought with her all the dirty laundry that had accumulated from the family. I thought it would be a nice thing to do, so I went ahead and did eight loads of washing, got it dry and put away, and then proceeded to clean the whole house and get it ready for the family's arrival. On Saturday Ellen walked in after a week's absence and greeted me with "Hi, well, we had a wonderful time. Everybody there sends you regards and I have to go and watch Dick Cavett now." And that was it—she went out to the family room and turned on the TV. She didn't give the least bit of recognition to the fact that she had been absent from me for a week or indicate in any way that she had missed me. And there was also no recognition that I had gotten the house in order and done the laundry. I was really hurt about that.

It just suddenly struck home that our lives were so completely apart—that there was no community there at all. It was just a matter of living under the same roof. A few days later I sat down with Ellen and told her I was really very, very unhappy, had been unhappy for several months, and that I absolutely did not want to go on like that. I felt that either we should get some counseling and see if we could get things back on the right road, or else we ought to separate. Her response to this was something like "You must be kidding! I've been unhappy for the last ten or fifteen years and you mean you didn't know?" I really *didn't* know that she had been, as she said, putting up with me and all my crap. To me this was completely new—she had never told me, had never expressed in any way that she was unhappy.

I think this was the first time that we really talked in a long, long while and it became apparent to me that our basic orientations toward life are completely different. To me, life is basically good, with occasional episodes that are bad, and I do anything I can to get over these bad episodes. But for Ellen life is basically bad, something that one suffers and endures, with occasional high points—but happiness is not to be expected as a part of daily life. I realized that we were completely different, had different outlooks on everything.

Ellen was unwilling to have any kind of counseling—she considers all that worthless—so I said in that case I wanted to leave. I started making some preparations, looked around for an apartment—and then she asked me if I wouldn't please stay for the kids' sake and for financial reasons. I agreed to this on the condition that we would separate our lives and just share the same house. We would move into different rooms—I would get one room in the house to sleep in and another to sit in. I would insist on coming and going as I pleased and she could do the same.

This went on in a halfhearted way for three or four months and didn't really solve anything because it was an impossible situation. You *can't* really lead separate lives in the same house—it doesn't work. You can't come and go as you please, you still meet in the halls, you still talk. The tension is still there and the little unpleasantries are still exchanged. But we went on like this until after Christmas.

There was another factor which probably was significant in pushing me toward the decision to move out. A girl who had worked for me years ago and whom I'd always liked a great deal had come back to Portland to be with her parents for the holidays. She had just got a divorce. We saw a lot of each other—she came to the house a couple of times to say hello to Ellen—and we did our Christmas shopping together. In our family Christmas shopping has always been my responsibility and it's been a big chore. Last year I had forty-two people to buy presents for. Anyway, this girl and I went out together five or six times to shop in the evening and usually we had dinner too. There was nothing romantic about it, we were just good friends. For the first time I really had fun Christmas shopping. It was a discovery to find that I could have a good time just being with someone, and it opened my eyes to the understanding that there might be something else out there—that life had some enjoyments that I had not yet taken part in.

After Christmas I thought, I'm going to get this thing out in the open—but what precipitated my moving out was the housecleaning, which had become a focus for our differences. The kids and I had planned to clean the house together on Saturday. Saturday morning arrived and none of the kids could be seen or found, so I ended up cleaning a six-bedroom house from top to bottom by myself—including waxing the kitchen floor. I don't think I said much all day or all evening to Ellen—I was too mad. But I told myself, "I'm not going to put up with this any more," and the next morning I announced that I was going to leave. I felt the only alternative was to split up, and I agreed with Ellen that it was right for her to stay in the house and continue to take care of the kids, so I moved out.

She told me when I left, "I want you to understand one thing very clearly—once you walk through these doors you are never coming back. I'm not going to put up with any of this yo-yo in-and-out business." Some of our friends had done just that, moving in for six months and out for six months. She claims now that she never said this, but I know she did—I have no doubt about it—and I have been living my life on the assumption that this is a permanent arrangement.

After telling Ellen I was leaving I called all four of my kids together and what I told them, basically, was that I had been very unhappy for several months, that I was not going to continue to be unhappy, and I was going to move out. Matt —he was only thirteen—was kind of shook up at first because he didn't realize—he thought I was sort of disappearing from his life. I think it took him several days to comprehend that I would still be around and that he would still see me. The comments of the older kids were "We've been wondering why you didn't do this five years ago!"

My relationship with the kids has become much better. We don't spend as much time together but we spend better time together. They feel free to come over to my house whenever they want to and they stop by the office. We see each other all the time. There were a few problems at first, but very minor ones. I mentioned that Matt was upset until he realized he wasn't losing me. Then Luke, our oldest boy, who knows how to handle things pretty well, started playing Ellen and me against each other. The moment we saw what was happening we stopped playing that game with him, and he's not done it since. He's really grown up lately—sort of become the man of the house. It's done him good—it's done everybody good. Ellen says that Matt is very maladjusted because of the separation but I don't think that's true— haven't seen any evidence of it. He seems to be perfectly well-adjusted and perfectly happy. It's very easy to blame everything bad that happens on my leaving, but I don't think it's so—don't see that it's hurt the kids one bit.

At first, after moving out, I felt terribly lonely. Suddenly there comes this great big vacuum and you think, My God, what's going to happen now? And you start going through this panic—Did I do the right thing or the wrong thing? I'd moved into a dinky apartment and there were those four walls staring at me. Also, I experienced some social ostracism—there were neighbors who would look the other way when they saw me or call me by my last name, which they hadn't done in fifteen years. You get a feeling that you're a dirty dog and it takes a while to get over that.

Ellen went through a period of great euphoria after we split up. She thought, Gee, this is great! I finally got him out of the house. At least, that's what she expressed to me. She told me how much happier she was, how she wasn't aggravated by me any more—didn't have to put up with me any more.

I had suggested that we get some counseling, see if we could get things back together, and she absolutely refused. Then one day a friend of ours for many years called, and when I told him we'd separated he said he wanted to have lunch and talk with me. He thought we were just a couple of silly kids having a spat and sort of considered himself my big brother who was going to get it all settled. He said, "If I convince Ellen to get some counseling, will you agree to go too?" I said sure.

So the next morning—it was a Sunday—he called me and said triumphantly, "I just talked to Ellen on the phone and she's willing to go to a marriage counselor." I said, "Fine. And thank you very much." Ten minutes later Ellen called and said, "We're going to a marriage counselor." I asked her what brought about the change of mind and she said, "I haven't had a change of mind, but Leo insists we go, so we'll go a few times just to satisfy him and make him happy." I said, "You know, it's ridiculous for us to spend the money and waste our time going to a marriage counselor to keep *Leo* happy. If you don't think it's going to do anything . . ."

She said, "Of course it's not going to do anything. It's not going to change my mind in any way, but we certainly don't want to offend Leo. He'd be insulted if we didn't go." Maybe I'm much too sensitive about these things, but for Leo she was willing to go—for me she was not!

Okay, we went to a marriage counselor. I went first, then she went, and then we both went together. At the end of my session the counselor—who I think is a fabulous person— asked me if I would be willing to try getting back together again. I said, "I certainly am." She asked if there was still a feeling of love within me and I told her I thought there was —in both of us. Afterward I thought about this a great deal, and two weeks later, when Ellen and I had our session together, I said that I'd changed my mind—I was willing to have counseling but I doubted the success of it. It seemed to me that Ellen and I were on such different tracks in life that it would not be a matter of changing just a few things—it would require a complete change in our personalities.

Then the counselor said, "I just wanted to be sure how you felt about it because Ellen feels that way too, and after talking with both of you I don't think there is anything I or anybody else can do for you except a superficial patching up." She said that we shouldn't end communications, shouldn't stop talking to each other—that the doors should be left open.

Well, for me this was final. I had left, and Ellen had expressed satisfaction that I was gone, and an expert thought there wasn't much that could be done about it. In a way I felt relieved and in a way very sad.

I did not proceed immediately to a lawyer because at first we thought we could probably handle things informally. Then an old friend, a lawyer who does not take divorce cases, begged us to get things settled. He felt we were living dangerously by not having a legal separation. Under the circumstances, Ellen would be totally unprotected in case something happened to me or if I just wanted to waltz off to Africa.

So we got separate lawyers—expensive lawyers—to handle the matter for us. They wanted to hire all kinds of appraisers—I guess lawyers frequently try to make enemies out of you—but I certainly didn't want to get into any hassles over a property settlement and we decided to settle it very simply ourselves. We spent a few hours working out the property settlement, and it's fine, although it's not the way the lawyers wanted it. From a practical standpoint it's not a fifty-fifty division. Ellen wound up with 70 percent of the property and I wound up with 30 percent, and I have no objection at all to this, no bad feeling. At the time she felt that this was a fair settlement; I don't think she feels that way any more. Now she feels she got the short end of the stick.

She's getting the better part of my income right now—sixteen hundred a month—plus I'm giving one hundred fifty a month to Luke, who is going to college, and he gives a hundred of that back to Ellen for room and board for staying in the house. So she's getting seventeen hundred a month and has no obligations beyond the house payments. We have our interlocutory, and getting the final divorce decree is only a formality, but I haven't done it for financial reasons—it's less expensive to keep Ellen on my health-insurance policy than it would be for her to get her own.

After I moved out, she rehired a janitor service. I feel a little angry about that. Also, another boy has been living at the house for three months—a friend of the kids' who doesn't get along with his father. He has plenty of money and Ellen's been charging him a hundred dollars a month for room and board. He's a nice boy, I like him, but I'm sure he's eating up twice that much, so it's not a fair arrangement in the first place. Then last night she told me he's going into the Navy, and she gave him fifty dollars as a goodbye present. Now this is kind of hard for me to take, because I'm always hearing how she doesn't have a cent of her own. Also, last night I watched her give Matt and Chris twenty dollars to go buy themselves dinner. Well, to my mind that's a lot of money for two kids to buy dinner.

I don't think I'm a tightwad but I equate money with work. I know how many hours it takes me to earn such-and-such amount of money, so whenever I see either Ellen or the kids throwing money away it bothers me. It's like throwing away my labor. For example, a couple of years ago I bought my oldest daughter a water bed for three hundred dollars and now the liner has a hole in it. I told her to get it patched or get a new liner for thirty or forty dollars but she said, "Well, it's an old water bed and I don't want it any more so I'm going to get a new one with my tax refund." On the other hand, when her car broke down she was on the phone immediately for me to give her four hundred dollars. I get upset about this sort of thing because money represents a certain amount of work I've put in, but her attitude is, It's only money. And when I mention this to Ellen she says, "Well, it *is* only money." This is the kind of conflict we used to get into and are still getting into. I don't usually say anything at the time, but the anger sticks—and finally explodes.

Ellen expects to be supported for the rest of her life, and we're at loggerheads about this. I think it would be very bad for her—she ought to stand on her own two feet some day. And it's not fair to me. Even though I put such a burden on her for all those years, it's not fair that I should have to devote the largest share of my work to supporting her. I'm willing to do this for a while, but not forever. It would limit my future to a great extent—I wouldn't ever be able to cut down on my practice. I've made it clear many times to her and in front of her lawyer that in a year, when Chris turns eighteen, I'll go back to court and ask for a reduction in support payments. The judge will probably not grant it at that time. He'll probably say I have to continue support at a certain level, but meanwhile Ellen must get some training to prepare herself for a job, and that reduction in payments will be reconsidered in a year or two.

Ellen has a bachelor's degree, and although she's taken I don't know how many university courses over the past many years, they've all been audited—she's refused to take any of them for credit, so she has nothing to show for it. But she has a great deal of practical experience that could be made into a paying proposition. For instance, she recently organized a visitation program for elderly people in convalescent homes all over the county. I'm sure somebody would be glad to hire her, even on a part-time basis, to do this sort of thing. But Ellen won't hear of it. Unfortunately she has very strong feelings against earning money. She'll do something as long as it doesn't pay, but when the potential for earning income arises, she drops the project. To her, earning money has a negative connotation—any paying job is way beneath her.

Ellen is convinced that she has a special gift from God and a special mission from God—that she's in the same category as the mystics and prophets. As I see it, she believes her mission is to help others and enlighten them as to what life is all about—to bring knowledge of the happiness and joy of the life hereafter. That's why she refused to work, says that she will always refuse to work for money, and that if a judge were to reduce her support payments to the point where she would be forced to take a job, she would make herself sick and go on welfare.

I enjoy religious studies too, but this does not necessarily become a part of me as it does with Ellen. To my mind, her religious involvement almost borders on the fanatic, and this has become a problem for the kids as well as for me. She has a relationship with her God that is far, far deeper than I have ever had, and it may well be that a hundred years from now she will be known as one of the great mystics. But—it's been pretty hard to live with. When problems came up it's frequently been, "That's the way it is because I, Ellen, say so," or, "God said so," and therefore there is no further discussion. Very non-negotiable.

My own religious convictions have pretty much gone down the drain in the last ten years. I haven't been to church in a long, long while, and I don't believe in it any more. Several years ago I began reading Eastern philosophy, and this had a great deal of influence on my ideas in terms of what I wanted out of life, and it probably separated my thinking from Ellen's quite a bit. There was a gradual progression —Alan Watts, Suzuki and Ram Das. I was suddenly questioning much of what the church was teaching—and rejecting it. Over the last couple of years I've been reading the works of Krishnamurti, and I think they've been a major influence on my thinking and on the way I'm living now.

I met Ruth shortly after I moved out. She came to my office —she had been my patient about six years earlier, and when she returned I didn't remember her. I debated with myself whether I should mix business with pleasure, realized I had a unique opportunity to meet people in my office, and decided to ask her out. On our first date we went out to dinner and then I took her home, and it wasn't till the next day that I realized I'd spent five hours with her in the restaurant, completely oblivious to the passing of time, thoroughly relaxed and at ease. That's the way she is—not what you'd call the world's greatest conversationalist, talking about big issues and that sort of thing—but somehow making everyone with whom she comes into contact a little bit happier.

Ruth is six years younger than I, a widow. I think that by not having a lot of preconceived notions about what I was looking for in a woman—like blonde, blue-eyed, five foot six —I made the opportunity much greater for myself to meet a person with whom I get along so fabulously. Although Ruth isn't shy, she'd be very easily overlooked in a crowd. She's a nondemanding sort of person—makes no demands on others, no demands on life, and our time together just—goes along so well. There have been no startling high points and absolutely no low points in the six months we've been together. It's so different for me—something I've really not experienced before. I look forward to coming home in the evening, just quietly reading and having her sit across the room from me. It's just—pleasant—doing things together, the normal, everyday things. If I say, "Let's go shopping," she says, "Okay, let's go!" and we have a good time shopping together for groceries. I had no idea what fun it can be to spend time with someone in the kitchen, or how enjoyable it is to clean house together on a Saturday morning. It isn't a question of "I do this for you" or "I'm putting out for you" or "I'm suffering and sacrificing for you" because I know she's enjoying it just as much as I am. I have the feeling of being appreciated as a person, not being taken for granted, and I appreciate her as a person too. There's something so good about understanding one another, about sharing our lives. I'm starting a part-time business and Ruth is going to manage it for me.

At present I'm living in a state of great euphoria. Everybody keeps telling me it's going to stop, but it's been going on for six months—since I've been with Ruth—so maybe it will continue. I'm leading such a happy life that I don't have any goals except to go on in the same way, and that's a great state to be in. I honestly never thought it was possible to feel like this.

Suddenly I'm aware of what life is all about and I can see, in looking back, that I missed an awful lot, didn't know what a good relationship could be, didn't know what it was like to be relaxed with somebody instead of being in competition with them—what it was like not be put down day after day, to be made to feel bad, responsible, guilty. I'm just learning what it's like to have someone who looks after me—it's a fantastic feeling to come home to a dinner that obviously has been prepared with affection. And, quite aside from everything else, until I met Ruth I didn't know what sex was all about.

The day I left Ellen I only had a year and a half of unhappiness to look back on. Now I can see that the unhappiness had been building up for many years—the year and a half was only its conclusion. I'm not writing those years off as nothing but unhappiness, not by any means. As I perceived them then, they were very happy—and when they stopped being happy I changed to something I thought would work better. That's the way I feel about it now.

I can't commit myself and say this relationship with Ruth is going to last until I'm eighty-five years old—I've learned that statements like that don't work. But as long as it lasts I'll be a very happy person, and it's awfully nice to know that she'll be a very happy person too. I don't see any reason for getting married again—I don't need that piece of paper. But I may get pressured into it. From a practical point of view, what I've got right now is the same thing without the legalities. And I wonder about Ruth and myself—perhaps the fact that we're not married makes us try just a little harder. Maybe if we did get married there'd be the idea, okay, now we're married and we don't have to put out any more. That has me a bit concerned. But there are pressures from "society"—people who do not feel that this is proper behavior for a doctor in their community, and some of my friends invite us to dinner with that raised-eyebrow attitude. I don't know that this really bothers me, but it is a pressure. My mother wants a daughter-in-law and she's putting lots of pressure on me to marry, but that's a minor thing. Then there's some pressure on Ruth's part—I think she feels a bit insecure about our current status. She knows I don't do much planning for the future and I think she would feel better if she knew where she stood.

Ellen is now interpreting the words of the marriage counselor—"You should leave the door open"—as meaning we should really try to get back together, and I'm saying no, because nothing has changed. If anything *has* changed, it's that I feel more dissatisfied with the life I led before and a greater satisfaction with the life I have now. Ellen is also trying to make me feel responsible for depriving her of sex and companionship for the rest of her life because her strong religious convictions prevent her from ever getting involved with another man. I really don't think this is my doing. I feel that if Ellen doesn't want to remarry or have a relationship with another man, that is her free choice and I am not to blame. She's making a choice about which is more important to her, her religious convictions or her other needs, and that's something she has to work out for herself—I can't accept the blame for that.

And she's giving me a lot of flak about the breaking of the vows—frequently drops remarks like "*Some* of us keep our vows." Well, I don't think twenty-three-year-old kids can make a vow that binds them for the rest of their lives and have it be a sensible one. The vow we took implied that if you stay the same and if I stay the same, then we'll live happily ever after. But we don't stay the same—we change.

Ellen has a way of getting to me like nobody else can. For instance, we went out to dinner last night. This came about because a couple of weeks ago she called me and she was unhappy and crying, saying she felt I had deserted her and was no longer interested in her. I've really tried to keep a friendship going between us and there are strong feelings for her on my part. One does not live with a person for all those years and suddenly cut it off. I wish nothing but the best for her and I do love her. I can't live with her any more, but I do love her very much. Anyway, during the phone call she complained that I had not asked her out to lunch or dinner or invited her over, and I said to her, "Look, it isn't my fault if we haven't gone out to lunch—you have a telephone just as handy as I do and if you and I are going to continue to be friends we cannot function on a basis of guilt, I won't accept it any more. You can pick up the phone just as easily as I can and suggest we go out to lunch."

So she called earlier this week, and last night I took her to dinner. I picked what I consider one of the best restaurants in the area—one that I knew she hadn't been to. We walked in and she said, "Oh, this is just like Olde Sicily," which happens to be the lowest-grade pizza parlor in town. Then we talked about some books I had given her to read that I thought would interest her, would help her understand me a little better. Each of these books took me a couple of weeks to get through, but she had sent them back with one of the kids after four days. She said she'd read them but that they were extremely shallow and had nowhere near the depth of the sort of thing she was accustomed to read. Which was her way of saying, "Your brain isn't really very much."

From my standpoint the evening was a complete disaster and I didn't sleep most of the night because I was that upset —about the things she'd said to me and how she said them and how she was able to push the same old buttons again, which make me feel just as guilty, just as responsible as before. She put me down just as she has done for years and years. When the evening was over she said she'd had a very good time and she hoped we'd do it again very soon. I don't think she even realized what she had done to me.

Last night I told myself that I should really call her and tell her, but then I thought it would only hurt her more and I don't want to hurt her. She still has that going for her—she can make me feel like I'm hurting her. Then I feel responsible and guilty again. The vicious cycle is still going around. And this business of who walks out on whom—pinning guilt on one party—I don't think that's right, don't think it's ever the fault of one person. I believe Ellen left me as much as I left her. She left me a long time ago, except that we continued to live together. I'm talking now about the difference between the physical leaving and the actual leaving. I think Ellen left me right after Paul died—maybe even before. She left in the sense that I stopped being the important part of her life, and our life together stopped being the center of the family activity.

You know, when you talk about crises—I think Paul's illness and his death, even though we expected it and knew it was coming—I think that was a terrible crisis. And I think that's when the walking out took place. I'm not saying she walked out on me or I walked out on her. I think that's when we really split, went off in different directions.

There was a lot of hostility and poor communication between us during the time Paul was alive, and I think Ellen blames me to this day for a lot of the burden she carried through his illness. There was nothing I could do about it, it wasn't my fault, I didn't make him that way—but she blamed me for it. We were put in the unfortunate position for a long time where I was taking care of Paul medically, and you know, there were some things that didn't go right and there was blame associated with that. It was the sort of thing many families do when a patient dies—they blame the doctor. It wasn't a spoken thing. Ellen never came out and said, "You messed him up," but I think there was a lot of that kind of feeling. And I didn't do all the right things—I don't know of anybody who *could* have done all the right things for him all the time. There were a lot of times when a decision had to be made about what was important for Paul, and I made the decisions because somebody had to. Many of those decisions were wrong ones, but I did the best that I knew how at the time.

The main thing is that we did not go through Paul's illness

together. It was not the two of us suffering along with Paul
—we each kept our sorrow very private, very personal—it
was never shared. And there was a great deal of competitiveness in a negative sort of way—you know, the "I hurt more
than you hurt" type of thing—no comforting of each other,
and when Paul died there was no sharing of that—each of us
to our own grief. I think to this day Ellen doesn't believe that
I grieved for him, and if there's anything you can pin it on,
that's where we went wrong. Somehow or other that never
got resolved, and after Paul's death we took off in different
directions in our lives and never got back together again.

I mentioned before that one thing Ellen brings up quite
often is the breaking of vows. Well, I admit that I have broken the vows by not staying around till death do us part. But
she, or both of us, broke some of the vows a long time ago—
about honoring each other and cherishing each other. You
know, when those went down the drain, the rest of the vows
weren't really that important any more.

Roger

Roger and his girlfriend wrote to each other daily while he was fighting in the Korean War, and upon his return they were married. For twenty-one of his twenty-two years of marriage, Roger engaged in clandestine affairs. He is forty-nine, a businessman who returned to school at the age of forty to get a degree in law. His son is twenty-two, his daughter twenty. This interview took place two years after his separation.

> *"I felt badly for my treatment of Lila be-*
> *cause she deserved better. I was always*
> *seeking elsewhere, wasn't able to give*
> *her what she should have had. I feel*
> *sorry for her for having to live with me*
> *for twenty-two years."*

LILA AND I had an affair—we slept together over a period of perhaps a year. You know, in those days affairs weren't quite so common, but still, it wasn't any big thing. Then I went to the Korean War. I was in the infantry, in the front lines, and I was sure I was going to get killed. She was my latest girl-friend and kind of my tie to life—my link with home and the future—so I wrote every day and I expected a letter from her every day. By the time I came home she had convinced her-self that this was going to be "it." Of course, as soon as I got home I realized I didn't need her. I was free, out of the Army, and I wanted to play around a little bit. But she wanted to get married and I felt guilty about the whole thing —and I married her.

Really, I didn't want to be married—never wanted to be married. I'd never had the freedom that comes with bache-lorhood. When I was in school I didn't have the time or the wherewithal to do a lot of dating and screwing around—I was a serious student. And I went from school to the service to marriage—when I came home from Korea I was married before I was even discharged.

At the time I didn't think Lila was pretty enough for me.

She's a great lady, I mean I really feel that way about her, she's a fabulous person, but she wasn't pretty enough for me. And she was too old. When we got married I was twenty-four and she was twenty-eight.

The idea of leaving her came to me very early, during the first couple of months. But we were married in December and by February she was pregnant. The week before she found out she was pregnant we had a fight and I went to the movies by myself. I remember walking down to the theater and hoping that she would have gone home to her mother when I got back. I was thinking, Oh, good, it's all over! But when I returned there she was, begging and saying everything was all right and let's make up. We had twins. One died at birth and the other died within a month. So again, there was more guilt on my part and I thought, How can I leave her now? Soon after that she was pregnant again—we had a boy and then a year and a half later, a girl.

It was never a particularly happy marriage in that I've always had my eyes elsewhere. I was always looking at other women, was always interested in them and hoping to make contacts, playing around, although I didn't have an affair until we'd been married about a year. It was very easy to meet women. I was in a sales organization going from office to office and I was quite attractive in those days—women would hustle me as much as I would hustle them. The relationships would last several months, a year maybe. I'd be involved with three or four different women at a time, seeing them each once every two weeks, something like that. They all knew I was married, was still committed at home, and that I'd be seeing them on a short-term basis. Sometimes they'd meet men who were potential husbands and then they'd stop seeing me, or I would meet other women and lose interest, call them less and less frequently. I suppose in a sense I was using them, but I don't think so—I was sharing.

Occasionally friendships have developed with women

after the sexual part is over. For instance, I began an affair years ago with a woman who was having serious sexual problems with her husband. She finally divorced him after twenty years of marriage, but during the first ten years we had our affair—the only affair she had—and it helped her, made her feel like a woman. Since then we've maintained a very good, warm friendship. I met another woman eighteen years ago and we still keep in touch. In fact, she invited me to a party at her house last New Year's Eve to meet a beautiful single lady.

I admit I have made passes at women who should have been out of bounds, friends of friends or friends of my wife's —her single friends, mostly, but some married ones, some great ones! Some of the outstanding women in my life were Lila's girlfriends.

I don't know that anything could have salvaged the marriage. I remember there was a period of jealousy between me and the children—not jealousy, but anger at my wife because I would come home from work—I was a salesman and struggling, working my butt off, doing a very hard, competitive job—I would come home bursting with enthusiasm to tell her about the dragons I had slain and she would say, "I can't talk to you now, I've got to prepare dinner . . . got to take care of the baby." You know, this, that and the other thing. So I would be squelched, and feel hurt and frustrated at not being able to talk to her about the things that had made me happy during the day. I thought it was my fault until I told the story to a friend—you know, a social friend, the wife of a friend of mine—and she was so shocked she told Lila, "My God, that's terrible. Your husband comes first, you've got to listen to him." So then I thought maybe it wasn't me, maybe I was right—maybe I had the right to talk and be listened to.

Lila always made me feel that I was wrong. She's a very critical lady, always thinks she knows what's right—as if I weren't smart enough to know right from wrong but she was. My approach was a little more philosophical, a little more conjectural. If I did anything Lila didn't like she'd put me down for it and I'd feel very badly. All through the marriage we probably put each other down a lot in different ways.

Sex was not as good as it could have been although *when* we had sex it was good. But there were many times when months would go by and we didn't touch each other—we didn't talk and we didn't touch each other in bed. Well, I was getting it elsewhere so it didn't matter. It became a good excuse for me to go out and play around. I'd go out at least once, maybe two or three evenings a week. I'd use a business meeting or a card game as an excuse, and as time went on I was home less and less often.

It's hard to remember now what caused those long silences between us. I guess any little disagreement that came up would shut us off. Her anger would last a long time. I'd be angry for a night and the next morning I'd wake up feeling fine. I'd come home from work and she'd still be angry so I'd say the hell with it. It was easier not to have to talk, and I was having a somewhat adequate sex life outside, so . . .

Lila wasn't too interested in sex, wasn't loving enough to me. Very often she would pick bedtime to say something that would turn me off, and then I just didn't want to do it. I felt she'd said it deliberately. So we wouldn't talk to each other and she'd go to bed and I'd stay up late and watch television. I have a big sexual desire, that's the way I am—I want to get laid every day. Sometimes I even want a different girl every day, but one way or the other, I want it every day.

Once I sort of fell in love—I felt very special toward a woman. I was introduced to her at a social event, saw her only for a fleeting moment, and later looked her up in the phone book. She was beautiful, a delightful woman, and we were extremely compatible sexually. She had just separated from her husband and I saw her for about a year. Then I left my wife for two weeks. Those turned out to be two really miserable weeks. It's an interesting thing, the thrill just wasn't there any more when I was free—something had happened. Physically I couldn't perform like I did when I was living at home and our meetings had to be clandestine. It just didn't work out well, and—I was still interested in other women. If I saw her two nights in a row I'd say I was busy the next night and make a date with someone else. I just wasn't that committed—still wanted to play around. So in two weeks I found out it wasn't love.

I missed the kids—they were only about eleven and twelve then—and I felt guilty, so I ended up going home. My wife was glad to have me back and I didn't see the other lady any more until Lila and I separated two years ago. I saw her then for a while but she was very possessive—I shouldn't say possessive—I mean I'm sure again it was my fault. When I was with her I was making passes at other girls, checking out the action just like I did with my wife—same old pattern. It had always upset Lila when I did this, but after I left her and came back and she realized I was actually *seeing* other women, then, of course, she would get *very* perturbed, to say the least.

I really don't think I've ever been in love, but I am in love with the idea of love. You know, I imagine some beautiful woman—not beautiful in the conventional sense, but someone who turns me on, who's sexually exciting, stimulating intellectually, with interests similar to mine. I keep hoping I'll meet a woman like that who doesn't smoke and she'll turn me on so much that . . . it might be interesting to fall in love. I don't know, maybe being in love is if your sexual drive is directed toward only one person instead of toward the world in general?

I've been accused by some women of not being affectionate enough. I give them sex, myself and my time, my body, but probably not yummy affection. There was one girl—I didn't like the fact that she smoked but she was cute and I had a nice little friendship going with her. She complained she couldn't get enough feeling out of me, that I didn't tell her how I felt, and that aside from loving her in bed I wasn't affectionate. She said she didn't want to be *only* a lover. Well, it was pleasant, and she was great physically, but I really didn't like her that much—wasn't interested in getting into her head or her getting into mine. She sensed she wasn't going to get anywhere so she stopped seeing me. I've been told often enough by women that I don't communicate on a feeling level, so I believe it. I believe what they tell me—I don't know what they want, but I know they're not getting it from me.

I haven't been able to communicate much on the feeling level with anybody, including my wife. Well . . . I shouldn't say . . . I do talk with some of my girlfriends, and there were girlfriends I could talk to when I was married. Also, I saw different therapists over a period of years. It was my wife who urged me into it—felt that the problems I was having with her were rooted in the fact that my mother wasn't loving enough. She thought that was why I didn't communicate with her, but the real reason was that if I'd spoken honestly I'd have had to say, "Look, I don't love you, I'm not interested in being married, and I want to go out and play around." She misinterpreted my lack of communication as a problem from childhood, but really, I couldn't tell her the way I felt—it would have hurt her too much. And probably broken up the marriage.

When I went to a therapist I felt all he was going to say was that I should get out of the marriage, which I already knew I should do and I didn't need anyone to tell me. Actually, the therapists never told me anything—they listened, and they collected money. Sometimes I'd get a catharsis—I was able to tell my story and cry a little and that made me feel better—just to express the sadness, the sorrow I felt at never having experienced the joys of bachelorhood and promiscuity, the dating game, the thrill of having various encounters.

Part of the sadness was not having the great loving relationships that I might have had if I'd been a different type of person. I felt badly for my treatment of Lila because she deserved better. I was always seeking elsewhere, wasn't able to give her what she should have had. I feel sorry for her for having to live with me for twenty-two years, and sadness for my boy, who is a doper, who isn't a happy person, never was. I feel responsible, although I don't feel I caused his problem. Lila thought that my philandering had led to my son's alienation, his escapism. I don't agree. There are some things that happen no matter what you do. I've seen men who were not philanderers and who ostensibly had a better family life, and yet their children are still messed up, worse than mine in some cases.

When our children were little they were both beautiful and I loved them—I thought. The reason I say "thought" is that I was always being accused by my wife of not having given enough, not playing with them enough. I don't remember that I was holding back, but I have this feeling that maybe she was right. They were both breast-fed so they got a lot of affection from her, and I thought I also was warm— tried to give as much as I could, remember hugging them as much as I thought was appropriate every chance I got, and I enjoyed it—I liked them. We took them with us everywhere. From the time they were born we carried them around with us, to the beach, even on vacation in Europe.

Once my son was refusing to move his bowels, was holding back, and we took him to see a lady who I feel had a profound influence on his life in a negative way. Up to that time we'd always made a big fuss over him. Every time he'd draw a spot on a piece of paper we'd say, "Oh, how beautiful, how lovely!" And this lady said we shouldn't do that, we should wait until he did something really good and then tell him. So we didn't continue to pump him up. She told us not to make a fuss over the little things and to wait for the big ones—but if the big things don't happen, then the kid doesn't get praised. Unfortunately, at that time I wasn't strong enough, wasn't sure of myself in knowing what was right or wrong in raising kids, so when a professional who had a degree told me what was right I figured I'd better listen. But you know, sometimes those professionals don't know their ass from a hole in the ground.

I tried to give my son whatever I had in terms of values. I couldn't teach him to play baseball or football because I wasn't an athlete, but I did show him how to use tools, work with his hands to make things and fix things. And at least twice a week I would pick him up and take him across town to his music lesson and home again. Later, when he was a teenager, Lila felt I wasn't spending enough time with him and she suggested we get tickets to the college football games. So we started going, went to three or four games, and we were both bored out of our minds—we both hated football. He didn't care and I didn't care so what the hell good did it do? It was an attempt on her part to believe that if we were together it had to be healthy. But it was already too late —my son was sixteen and had already been on dope a year, year and a half.

I thought I treated both my son and my daughter about the same, but she turned out to be a hard worker, an achiever. She's a lucky, happy girl and an optimist—thinks that good things are going to happen to her, and she makes them happen.

Lila always says she can't remember anything about her own youth, but I remember everything about mine. My father was a working man and we were poor. My parents often fought about the normal things—money, him looking at other women. He was always flirting—I'm probably follow-

ing that pattern in my own life. I have a sister three years
older, but I was the favorite—for my dad, at any rate. My
sister and I were never close. She's been living in Europe
for the last twenty years and we don't write or see each other
too often. Both my parents were extremely handsome people, and very youthful. My mother didn't start aging until her
fifties, and in her forties she and my sister were taken for
sisters, with my mother the better looking of the two.

I'm not really close to my mother. I liked my father much
better. She's a very self-centered woman, and vain. At sev-
enty-two, she just had a face-lift and she looks terrific. And
she's tremendously energetic—I get my energy from her. At
her age she works four hours a day and spends the rest of the
time helping women who can't drive to get to their doctors
and their banks. Last year she was offered a full-time job at
ten thousand dollars a year, teaching deaf children—she
learned how to do that at age sixty-five when she worked as
a teacher's aide. But she decided she'd rather have her free
time. Pretty independent for a lady who lives on social security plus a little bank interest. So she works part time for
fifty a week instead.

I have my problems with her—she's always calling me to
complain that I don't phone her often enough, and when she
does that, she's a good hard pain in the butt. I mean, she's
my mother and if she really needs me I'm going to be there.
When she was sick recently I visited her in the hospital
every day for several months, but now she's back on her own
and she's very capable of taking care of herself. I have a lot
of respect for her—the fact that she's working and driving
her car and is self-supporting. I just don't want to hear her
complain about being neglected because I don't call her
twice a week.

Anyway, when I was a kid we did a lot of things, had a lot
of adventures with my folks. I remember the summers we
spent on a farm—in those days you could stay at a farm for

practically nothing. And I remember how my father would take me out—maybe because he was having a fight with my mother—on Sunday trips to visit museums. I don't know how much he ran around, or even *if* he ran around, but there were fights and several supposed suicide attempts on the part of my mother. She would run into the kitchen and turn on the gas while my father was there. If she'd really wanted to kill herself she could have done it when no one was home. But now she remembers all of the happiness and none of the sadness. She was sixty-three when he died, and even though she was a great-looking woman she never went out on a date. She said the guys she met were little old men compared to what my father had been.

He went to the doctor on account of a sore back and they X-rayed him and found a spot on his lungs. The doctor said it looked bad. They took him in for a biopsy and the biopsy looked even worse. When the pathology report came back the doctor sat down with my father and said, "You've got a tumor, we can't do anything about it." My father said, "What does that mean?" and the doctor said, "That means you're going to die."

I felt badly for him because he was such a big, strapping guy, had such a zest for life. Like me. I felt bad—I felt terrible. It's not the kind of thing you can talk about, that you can describe. I mean, your father's going to *die*. I guess there was the feeling of being glad it was him and not me—and the guilt of not giving your father enough love and so forth. But there's nothing you can do about it.

So the doctor sent him to a chest specialist just to get another opinion. They told him that some people do recover, but in his case there was no chance for any miraculous remission. Still, when my father heard that some people recover he figured he was going to get better. The doctor who did the tests said to me, "He's going to die and because he's so enormously healthy, so strong, he'll die in two years, not six months. He'll fight it all the way—his heart is as strong as can be, his chest is strong, and the cancer will kill him slowly."

The last year and a half he had to use two canes to walk until they operated on him for a mass of material that had gone around his spine from the lungs. After several operations he was able to get up out of bed and move around with the help of a walker. But lung cancer is agonizing—they could never give him enough morphine to deaden the pain. The cancer had metastasized—spread throughout his body. If you're a woman or a weak person, it can get to the heart and kill you. But if you're a strong man who weighs over two hundred pounds, it's got an awful lot of material to eat up before it gets to your heart. Your body is there in pain while your heart keeps beating away, still strong—so you live with the pain and you fight it. He never allowed in his mind that he was going to die. At times he said he wanted to kill himself, but when the doctor finally told him he could have as much morphine as he wanted he would wait until the pain got so bad he couldn't stand it before he took another shot. Doctors don't give enough pain-killers. When a person is going to die, why make them suffer? They should have kept him sedated completely. It was awful—terrible—he weighed two hundred pounds when he went to the hospital, and when they buried him I don't think he weighed seventy-five. A man six feet tall, husky, barrel-chested, big hands, big feet, and when he died he was just a withered up little shell—nothing left.

My father smoked all his life and died before his time at sixty-seven—his family lives to be eighty, ninety. I am physically and psychologically turned off by smoke. If I'm in a closed area with someone who's smoking, it's hard for me to breathe, and the terrible dependence of it annoys me. I realize it's not easy to stop smoking, but—it smells. I've got girls coming into my apartment with their hair smelling of

smoke, mouth smelling of smoke, clothes smelling of smoke.
I just don't like it.

I used to smoke when I was in Korea. I smoked a lot then
because they gave us free cigarettes all the time. Combat
troops got the benefits of the largess of the tobacco compa-
nies—cigars, cigarettes, roll your own, chewing tobacco—
everything. It was cold, and sometimes just holding a cigarette would keep your hand warm. I quit because one day I
was getting shot at and I was running for my life and I was
coughing. And the cough tasted of tobacco. It was so obvious
that smoking was taking the wind away from my lungs, re-
ducing my ability to run and to survive. So I quit.

Smoking used to be a big factor in my choice of women.
Lately I find I'm meeting some women who are so interesting that I put up with their smoking. But if a woman is dull
and smokes in the bargain I won't put up with her at all. And
I don't want to have anything to do with a woman who drinks
a lot—a bottle of wine or more than two cocktails in an evening is more than I can handle. It bothers me that they're
dependent on a drug, alcohol-dependent. I know so many
good, capable people who drink too much and I see their
lives and their productivity being affected. It really bothers
me—I'm very narrow-minded about this. My father, who
could not hold his liquor, drank a little too much at times—
often, I guess. A beer at lunch was enough to put him to
sleep and a beer at dinner finished the rest of the evening.
Even the little bit he drank was too much.

The time around my father's death was a period of evalua-
tion for me. In fact, that's what really triggered my going to
law school. Most of our friends were professional people—I
remember once having about thirty people over to our house
for a party, and I was the only man there who didn't have an
advanced degree. And the idea of becoming a lawyer had
been in the back of my mind for years—I liked the identity
it gave me. I discussed this with a dear old friend and she

said, "Now that your dad's died, I'm sure you're thinking about your life and what's going to happen. You've always wanted to go to law school—why don't you go?" Just those simple words. I immediately went down to get an application, and I was accepted.

I figured that going to school would be a way to use my excess energy—I've got more energy than anybody I've ever known. Also, just before I was forty I had some serious back trouble, was laid up at home for two weeks. So my chronic bad back was another factor to consider—in case I couldn't work any more at my business, the back trouble wouldn't prevent me from practicing law. My work involves bending and lifting things that weigh as much as a hundred pounds. The more I bend and lift the better business gets, and the better business gets the more I bend and lift. I'm aware there's a psychological element with my back—on vacations it never hurts me. When we went to Europe with the children we were dragging luggage from place to place every day and I didn't sleep on boards or special pillows or any of that and my back never bothered me. And it hasn't given me any serious trouble in the two years I've been separated.

Then, too, there was the idea of getting old—would I rather be an old salesman or an old lawyer? I was thinking about my father, who hadn't accomplished too much, hadn't had the gratification of an education, which he would have enjoyed. He was a fairly bright man, he could have gone to college. But he had to work through high school to help support the family. And I just thought, Gee, here I am, forty, yes, what the hell! If I can do it, why not go to law school?

I also thought it'd give me a chance to get out of the house, maybe meet some women to play around with. That didn't work out too well because I was too busy. I had a few affairs but most of the girls were a little too young, a little too bright to get involved with an older married man. Although age was never the particular problem. Girls in their mid-twenties have said to me, "If you weren't married there's no question I would go out with you."

I was in law school from the age of forty-one to almost forty-five. It was exciting—great fun. I was working all day and going to school at night, so Lila and I had a sort of weekend social life when we would see people or go out together. But often we didn't go out—a lot of my time was devoted to study when I wasn't working or in school, and in a sense we were each living our own lives. At forty-five I graduated, studied for the bar and passed. By that time I had my own business, which paid my way, so I stayed with it. I have people working for me and can take off time to do my law work, but I'm only accepting cases I want to handle, and only one or two at a time.

Actually, I'm not as interested in practicing law as I thought I would be. I was fascinated by law school, loved it, but practicing law is not so gratifying. I've found that many lawyers are sons of bitches. They price themselves too high —a hundred dollars an hour—and then they begin to have the illusion that they're really worth that much. I mean, if a client calls me up for help and I spend fifteen minutes advising him to go to Small Claims Court, I'm not going to charge him twenty-five dollars for telling him I won't handle his case, but that's what a lot of lawyers do. It's happened many times that I've said to someone, "I really don't take your type of case but I'll send you to another lawyer who does." So the other lawyer visits the client in jail, spends two hours telling him there's nothing he can do for him, and then charges him two hundred dollars.

After finishing law school I stayed with Lila about two years. My God, I can't even remember what they were like. The whole marriage fades into one long totality—it's hard to distinguish those two years from the other twenty. I guess I was just pushing forty-seven, maybe saw the approach of fifty. You know, age coming upon me, my hair turning white.

As a matter of fact, that's nothing new—my hair has been turning white for twenty-five years. But I was overweight and wanted to lose—maybe I thought if I went away from my wife, who's such a good cook, I wouldn't eat so much and I'd lose weight.

Our sex life was probably a once-every-two-weeks thing —it must have gotten to that point. I wasn't doing much dating of other women, I don't know why. I had sort of let things slide there. Maybe having a healthy sex life outside of marriage helps the marriage last, and if I'd encountered frustration on the outside I might have left Lila a lot earlier.

My memory is vague—I guess we were at the kitchen table, that's where we had so many of our conversations— and I said something like "I think I should get my own place." And she said, "I think you're right, maybe that's the best thing." The fact that she felt she could get along without me made me feel, Well, she's not so dependent upon me as I thought, I guess she'll be all right. One of the reasons I'd stayed married to her was I felt she couldn't survive without me, which was a mistake, of course.

At the time my daughter was away at college. My son had just moved back home. He was deeply involved with dope, and that was just horrendous, upset the household terribly, and Lila and I disagreed on the handling of the situation. That's another reason I was happy to leave, to get away from that. After I moved out she got rid of him and rented his room out to a big, brawny college kid who could deal with him when he'd come around in case there was trouble. My son wanted his own way, couldn't take no for an answer and would get violent—he wanted to grow and smoke dope right there at the house. He was also selling—mainly marijuana, but I'm sure he was involved with other things too because of the violence and the paranoid reactions.

Lila and I told him together that we had decided to live apart. He thought it was his fault but we assured him it wasn't. He's living now with a girlfriend. She doesn't have a job and he supports her. He feels sorry for her so he can't kick her out, he can't get rid of her because what's she going to do?

I still have affection for him—for part of him—it makes me feel good to see him. He went through an awkward stage and now he's grown taller. Before he was only five feet ten and I felt bad that he wasn't at least my size—it might affect a boy who doesn't have good feelings about himself if he's not as tall as his father. But now, all of a sudden, he's shot up, grown another couple of inches, and he's my height—six feet two. And he's getting better looking. He used to be very gaunt, with long straggly hair like the hippies of ten years ago. He still doesn't fit in today's world—looks like a doper, acts like a doper, and the cops spot him a mile away.

He has some very naive qualities and in many ways he's sweet and gentle and nice. But there are other parts to his personality too. My happiness at seeing him can be short-lived because he often starts right in with the dope business, rubbing my face in it, and I don't want to be involved with that craziness. He still smokes dope a lot—says he has to sell it in order to afford to use it even though he earns about two hundred a week on his job. He's a kid who's been in trouble a lot with the police, has gotten himself arrested at least two or three times a year, and he says to me, "If I get arrested will you bail me out? If I get arrested would you defend me in court? Would you pay for a lawyer for me?" No, I won't do these things! I tell him, "You're a big boy now, you're twenty-two, and when you get in trouble it's your fault, the police aren't picking on you. If you sell dope and get arrested, that's your responsibility, not mine. Don't smoke dope and don't get in trouble. I don't do criminal work and I couldn't do a proper job of defending you—you'd have to have another lawyer. I can't pay for you not to go to jail and I can't pay for a lawyer—I don't have the money. Besides that, I don't want to pay for you—you pay for your own trouble. If you're ready to sacrifice all that for the dope you smoke, then be ready to do what you have to do. It's your thing."

When my daughter heard about our separation she felt bad, but she accepted it. Then some time passed and we saw each other and she wanted to know all about who the girls were I was taking out and was I making it with a bunch of different girls and how young were they and so forth. She's bright, pretty cool—and she's also very close to her mother.

Sure, she was upset, but not so tragically that it was going to ruin her life or affect her so that she couldn't function. She continued functioning well. What it does to her inside, I don't know. I'm really happy that she likes being away at college. She participates in everything and enjoys whatever she does. She thinks there are no limitations, like she's a rich girl and can do anything she wants to do—which is great!

Lila was agreeable to my leaving, but after I went she felt a terrible loneliness—it was devastating to her. She told me and we talked about it—she wanted me to come back immediately. She wrote me a couple of letters telling me how sorry she was about the way she'd treated me, how wrong she felt about certain things, and if I came home how everything would be different. I acknowledged that I got the letters but I didn't answer them. Then we didn't see each other for almost a year. I'd come by to pick up my mail, but that was it—there were months and months when we didn't talk at all.

When I first moved out I felt physically cheated, moving from a big, big house to a small apartment that could fit into any one of four rooms in my house. And I felt a little lonely at times, coming home to be alone rather than to find someone there. I cooked my own meals, mostly because I couldn't afford to eat out, but I really do enjoy preparing meals—it's a creative expression for me—so it wasn't so bad. I felt good about the freedom, about not having to come home if I didn't want to. I could run out, go to a movie, do anything, not answer to anybody. Just a general good feeling of, I'm free! Basically it's still like that. I have my music, mostly Bach and Mozart, and I watch television and—I have a ball in my little apartment.

Sexually, my life is obviously better now, although during the last couple of years I've gone through periods of doldrums—wouldn't see anybody socially for several weeks at a time, just didn't bother, didn't date. Felt shitty, came home and vegetated. Sometimes I'm lonely, have to eat alone, and I eat too much. When I'm not screwing I'm eating. I'm a sensualist, really enjoy everything I'm doing or seeing or touching. The doldrums can last a couple of weeks but they're not so bad—I always know that tomorrow I'm going to meet someone nice. You find another relationship, call someone and have a good, happy time—meet a girl who laughs when you fuck her—that's great!

Unfortunately I find that most of the women I meet, like most of the men, are dumb. You're lucky if you meet bright women with tastes that go beyond pop music and disco, which is what you get when you take out the young girls— they're in a world of their own. I take out more mature women. Some have traveled, they're bright, I have respect for them. I like them and I also like to go to bed with them. If we can go to bed and be friends too, that's nice. If we just go to bed, that's not so bad either.

Lila and I started dating after I'd been gone about a year. I don't remember how it happened—if I called her or she called me. You know, I liked her all during the marriage, had a great liking for her, but not a love. Now it feels maybe more like love as compared with what I feel toward most of the other women I know, a very special feeling. Of course, after twenty-four years . . . We're relaxed with each other, and I know that she loves me and that's a comfortable feeling. I don't know whether she dates other men but I doubt that she could ever make a real commitment to anyone else—she really has centered her sex life around me. Every once in a while when I'm unhappy or don't know where I am, when I don't have any girlfriends who are interesting or exciting or satisfying, it crosses my mind that the best thing might be to go home. I still think of myself as married, although free. In a way I have the best of all possible worlds. I know that if I were sick I could move back home, or if Lila were sick I would move back to take care of her.

She treats me differently now, defers more to my wishes. And I know I don't have to take any crap from her any more. Sex is better than it used to be—that is, sometimes it's better. At my place it's better, at her place it's not so good. I think that's because the house costs too much to heat so it's cold there, while my little apartment is as warm as can be after five minutes of heating, and you don't need blankets. People can be much freer when it's warm and that makes sex better.

We have a friendly separation—no legalities. For a long time I was giving her all the money I earned, just like I'd done before, and I was living on very little. I mean I didn't have ten dollars at a time. I would have just barely enough to get by eating, and I couldn't even afford to date very much. I've finally cut down a little bit. She's paying the taxes on the house and I'm giving her less cash, keeping more for myself. Lila works, but we have a big house and lots of expenses and my daughter's in college. I'm still giving her more than I would be required to do by a court so that she can afford to stay in the house.

I'd like her to stay there. Coming from a poor family and

not having a tremendous income, I feel that house represents a big accomplishment, and I still think of it as my home. It's the only thing I've ever owned, my basic investment—although I wouldn't mind having half of it right now drawing interest in the bank. I do see myself continuing to support Lila, and I think that sometime, when I run out of . . . when my sex drive lessens . . . if that ever happens, I might go back. You know, in my dotage—I figure maybe when I'm around seventy.

Diana

Diana, while in her mid-thirties, resumed her formal education and is now completing her master's degree in political science. She is forty-four, has been married for twenty-five years, and is the mother of two girls, twenty-one and eighteen. At the time of her interview, plans for separation were in progress; her husband moved out of the house a few days after.

"Andy accepted me as his friend, the mother of his children, and this middle-aged lady who was his wife—but I was rejected a long time ago as a woman."

THERE WERE THREE INCIDENTS in the past few months that should have told me something was going on, but you know, you just don't think about it—you push it out of your mind.

Last fall, friends of ours who have a place in Prescott and a house in town were spending a few days apart in separate places. Andy mentioned it to me and I asked how come? He said, "Oh, he's having problems with his allergies—it's just for a few nights." I said something like, "Fine, if it makes them both happy—if it works for them. . . ." He said, "Yes, evidently it does. They've done it before." Then he looked at me and said, "You know, everybody needs their space. Everybody has to have space." I took this to be an allusion to our friends, but Andy was really talking about himself and I didn't know it at the time.

As for the second incident, the phone rang and I picked it up and there was a wild man on the other end of the line who said to me, "Will you tell your husband to stop fucking my wife?" And I said, "*Whaaaat?*" He said, "Your husband has been fucking my wife for the past six months and I'm sick and tired of it and I don't want it to happen again and the next time I'm going to have some people I know come and take care of him. I have people watching them . . . I have pictures . . . I have everything!" And I said, "Wait a minute. Calm down. Have you discussed this with your wife?" And he said, "No, I'm throwing her out. She's going to be on a plane to Dallas in two hours." And I said, "I think you better talk to her and I think I better talk to my husband." It was a long conversation—it went on for about forty-five minutes, but in the end he was relatively calm and I had convinced him not to throw her out but to sit down and talk with her and that I would talk with Andy. It ended with my saying to him, "Hey, listen, are you busy on Saturday night?" He laughed. This left him in a good frame of mind.

So I proceeded to call Andy and I said, "What the hell's going on here?" Well, he couldn't believe it. He was beside himself. He was *so* upset—so terribly upset he didn't know what to say at first. Then he explained to me who the girl was, who her boyfriend was—they're not married, just living together—that there was no truth whatsoever to what the man had said and that I should please not be upset. I said it was okay, not to worry about it—that I believed him. And then he said something like "The irony of it all is . . ." And I said, "What?" And he said, "Oh, nothing—it's nothing." And I let it go. The irony was, of course, as I later found out, that he *had* somebody else. He had started to say something about it and then caught himself. I didn't think anything of it. Perhaps I've always been rather naive, or perhaps just trusting—or perhaps both. I don't know.

The third thing that happened was that we sat down and had a long conversation about the point at which we were in our lives and where we were going. Andy began to talk about the need for a change, the need for coming to terms with the other half of his life, and I began to see seeds of this midlife crisis business. Shortly after that I read a review of *The Grey Itch* and I cut it out for him. He bought the book and agreed with a lot of it. We had another long talk and he told me that he felt the need for romance—for passion.

At that point I said, "Look, if you really feel the need for it that much, maybe you have to have it. *Do* it. Get it out of your system." I truly felt that I was enough of a person and secure enough in myself that he could go and experiment and do what he had to do—and that if he could get it out of his system perhaps it would help us.

You see, in the last two or three years, what seemed to *me* to be happening to us was more of a coming together—a unified, deeper, more contented and fulfilling relationship. Part of this was due to the success of his business. He had become financially and professionally secure. And there were other factors—our life was comfortable and predictable. The children were doing well, we had a nice home, good friends—we loved each other. In my mind, the feeling of satisfaction and contentment seemed to increase. I have to say that my sense of *myself* had changed. There was for me a certain sense of freedom in becoming forty. Lots of things rolled off my back—previously held conceptions about how I should conduct my life. I was freed by my children being older and more independent, and I was freed by returning to school and discovering that I was a first-rate student. I started to become satisfied with myself as a person—I began to really like myself. So, my sense of well-being was growing and that had a great effect on how I felt about our union. I was wrong. It was *me* that was growing—it wasn't the union. But I didn't know that. I'm just learning that now.

We were sitting in the den—this was just last month—and he brought it up again—this business of finding our own lives. As I said, this was something we would talk about from time to time. He would bring it up, drop it, bring it up, drop it. Just a mild sense of dissatisfaction—that's the way I per-

ceived it. Or sometimes I'd bring it up. I was feeling good
enough about myself to maybe want something more for me.
But this time he brought it up and I really encouraged him
to tell me everything. I said, "Let's not just drop it. Let's talk
it out. What are your feelings?" I told him it wouldn't hurt as
much as he thought it would, that we had to be open with
each other and that I would be as objective and as open as I
could.

So he did. I cannot remember—because we've had so
many talks since then—exactly how it proceeded and what
was said that night. But at any rate he told me not only that
he was seeing somebody, but that he had had a *lot* of sexual
activity in the past. He said that this one—the woman he's
seeing now—is somebody with whom he feels he might be
able to establish a lasting relationship—that the others, except for one or two, were just sexual, getting his rocks off,
fulfilling his ego—whatever. He said that he's been just incredibly active constantly, sometimes two different girls in
one day. I said, "My God, why? Why did you need it?" He
said there was an excitement to it, going from one girl to
another—a sense of conquering, I suppose.

I really think I need to go back to the beginning at this
point because I do want to try to be objective about this—as
objective as possible. I don't want to look at him from the
standpoint of the wronged wife clinging to—you know—to
this Don Juanism of her husband. There's more to it than
that.

I met Andy three weeks before my fifteenth birthday. I
was a real wild Indian as a young teenager, though probably
not by today's standards. I felt guilty about that for years. I
felt guilty as hell about it then too, but I had fun. It felt very
good—gee, all those good, nice feelings. And then I met
Andy and after a while an interesting thing happened. I felt

—ah well, now—he's going to save me from myself. I won't have to do this any more with all these guys. That, in and of itself, may not have boded well for our sexual relationship. It's as if I said, I'm going to be Goody Two Shoes with Andy.

One of the things about him that attracted me was that he was very strong and very independent and very mature for a kid his age. He was seventeen but he could have been much older because of his air of self-reliance and his sense of who he was. I liked that. I also liked the fact that he was one of the few boys I had ever gone out with who I could *talk* to. He wasn't just one of the neighborhood teenagers—he knew what he was about.

So, I was attracted by this independence and self-reliance and reserve and aloofness—and paradoxically these are the very qualities that caused problems in the marriage and also the very qualities that helped to make me strong. I had to become myself—to be my own rock. I've told him that—that I'll always be grateful for the sense of self which he inadvertently gave me.

We knew each other three and a half or four years before we were married. His father died and it was absolutely devastating for Andy. He needed me a lot at that time. Frankly, in the year between his father's death and the time we got married, I wasn't sure I was doing the right thing but I was terrified to do anything about it. If I'd had more strength, if I hadn't been this scared young kid, I might have said, Wait a minute—just a second—what's going on here?

Andy claims now that he has never been satisfied with our sexual relationship. Well, neither have I. You could say a lot of things were wrong with it. We are perhaps not chemically suited to each other. Maybe deep down inside we are two people who are not really physically attracted to each other. And what else is wrong with it is that all these years have gone by and we haven't tried seriously to do anything to make it better.

From time to time there has been pleasure, but not regularly. For the greater part of our married life, when we did get it on, it was really just physical release. It would happen because things would get to the point where I needed somebody's body—and he was handy.

I think it was a real problem that he hadn't had much sexual experience before we were married—and he didn't know how to come to terms with that. He would go off by himself, take care of himself alone because he just didn't know—literally didn't know how to make a sexual thing happen, make it work. Not technically, I don't mean that. He was a great technician, but it was always a mechanical act— emotionally he was cold and removed, and that was almost from the beginning. He would not often make sexual advances—he would rather masturbate than make advances to me—and when he did I didn't like the kind of advances he made. They were simply not satisfying to me, they were not *affectionate*. And I didn't know how to handle it. I had no idea what to do—how to work it out except to be resentful and angry and hurt and unhappy. Nothing positive, nothing constructive—all negative. Everything we did to each other for a long time was negative, and the negativism just grew and grew and grew. . . .

So you could say that for the first few years of the marriage it was a couple of kids not knowing what to do. Then I guess I gave up or gave in or something. I went off and had a few affairs. Interestingly enough, I never felt guilty about that— oh, a couple of times a pang here and there, but I was never consumed with guilt in any way, shape or form. I wasn't getting it at home—it was that simple—I was being rejected at home.

The first time we separated we'd been married for ten years. I instigated that. I asked him to leave because I was very involved with somebody. I thought I was in love—I *thought* I was, but it didn't work out, not at all. Andy and I were separated for nine months. I had my little adventures, and when we got back together again, things improved. It was never great by any means, but things in me changed. I think the experiences I had with other men helped me to become more secure about myself—enabled me to learn and grow, and I thought we could eventually get it together, but I still didn't know how to do it. I still didn't know how to do it right, and I had no idea that because of what he had gone through in the first ten years of our marriage he needed to prove himself. He started on his own adventures during our separation, and that has continued for the past fifteen years. So in many ways, we've never had a chance at a good sexual relationship.

During those first years I think he was in his own mind so sexually insecure—the aloofness and reserve covered that— and so afraid he couldn't attract a woman. As I said, he'd had virtually no experience, so during our breakup he became very active, and it just became a continuing thing where he had to keep going and going. He has certain compulsive traits in his personality and they manifest themselves in different ways.

You put together this slightly compulsive personality with a sense of insecurity about himself sexually—I can see this kind of thing taking place. But I can't for the life of me see it taking place to the degree that it has. That's hard for me to fathom. Maybe there are other guys who do it—I don't know. Oh, I know that men are able to get it on without emotional involvement much easier than women can. That's there, whether it's this need to prove one's masculinity with everybody on the block or to show yourself you can make it with a particular girl, or whether there's some kind of hormonal thing where the sexual release is an end in itself. Still, it's the degree that mystifies me.

Anyway, we got back together after that first breakup and I stopped messing around. At a certain point I decided I was a wife and a mommy and I was going to make something of my marriage and my life as a nice middle-class housewife. I felt that very strongly. It was a compulsion of mine. Maybe this was guilt, I don't know—but I decided I was going to be a good girl.

But when I did this—when I became this nice middle-class wife and mommy—my ego suffered terribly. As I said, things were better for a while but then it was the same old story again, chapter and verse, rejection after rejection after rejection. And when he did come on to me, it was mechanical—he was just doing it to shut me up. I once told him that I have never been able to trust him with my feelings. I always had to keep certain kinds of feelings to myself because if I gave them over to him he would reject me. He just couldn't handle that kind of closeness and emotion because of his nature—because he's so reserved and removed. We discussed it, yes, but negatively. It was a thing of "Why *can't* you . . . ? Why *don't* you . . . ?" "It's been *six* weeks. . . ." God, how we argued! I would cry and carry on and then we'd do it—but, unfortunately, too often as a result of my unhappiness. It was never a positive kind of thing. And I would make terrible accusations. I would accuse him of being homosexual because he wasn't interested in sex with me. I put him down horribly.

It wasn't a question of impotence, although sometimes maintaining an erection during intercourse was a problem—we'd do much better orally. So-called vaginal orgasms, I may have had those only a couple of times with him as a result of intercourse. And I may have thought about that in the past. You know, why couldn't I do that because according to the books I was supposed to be doing it?—but it wasn't a big thing. I had become satisfied with getting it however I could. I had made my bed and I was lying in it.

Anyway, as this wife and mommy I put on weight and became in my own eyes very unattractive. I punished myself a lot—punished myself for my past sins by being unattractive to him, by paying less attention to myself. I felt less and less like a sexual person, although I had the need for it and certainly the need for affection. But meanwhile I had no idea he was having all this activity. I'm just now putting this stuff into place. In the last few weeks I'm putting lots of things into place.

God, how we've punished each other in these twenty-five years—and yet in spite of it, we've had a very close, very deep relationship which I think can be attributed to a real caring for each other—liking, loving each other very much, needing each other, being safe with each other. On one level we're very affectionate. We're the kind of couple who hold hands in the movies, walking down the street. There's a warmth—genuine deep warm tender feelings that I could extend to a sexual relationship, but he has never been able to. With him, it's the warmth and affection of a very deep friendship.

He says that he is not attracted to me—that he is not attracted to me at all, physically. I don't know if that's a justification because of what he's been doing these past fifteen years or if it's really true. I mean, maybe he's needed to justify his activity by not being attracted to his wife—does that make sense? I am mildly attracted to him, although there are parts of his personality that are a turn-off to me sexually. But maybe I see him that way because of the way he sees me? It's so goddam complicated!

Sex isn't the only problem, but it's the main one—it always has been. I don't know how much other factors contributed. He says he's always resented having gotten married at such a young age, resented the responsibility of having children at such a young age. He's never been close to his mother. That may have some effect on his attitude toward me, toward women in general. Then there's his work. After the first ten or so years, his work was not bringing him the satisfaction it had in the beginning.

He was with the same architectural firm for fourteen years, and during the last five or so of those he hadn't gone anywhere—was on a treadmill, just standing still—unhappy with his lot. He bought a car—a racing car—during that period and that was something of a distraction, but he still became more and more discontented with his work. In the last year there he began to talk about leaving. Finally he did, and opened up his own business. It grew quickly—it was very successful and gave him a lot of satisfaction.

Another thing—I had started to come together myself. I'd been taking classes off and on for several years with the thought of eventually getting my bachelor's. I graduated and started to work on my master's. I'm still doing that. During all this we would have discussions from time to time on why our sex life wasn't so hot, but because it never had been, and because I was beginning to be relatively satisfied with myself, it just didn't worry me so much.

There was an incident—more than an "incident"—a little over a year before he went into business for himself. We were on the way home from a vacation and to my absolute bafflement and surprise, Andy expressed a desire to leave me. He explained to me that he just wasn't happy, that he thought he wanted to go on and to look for something else in his life—that there wasn't anybody else, but that he was just dissatisfied. I fell apart. In the car driving home I just fell apart and stayed that way for two days—couldn't do anything. We went to see somebody—a psychologist—three or four times, and he didn't leave. We grew back together—closer together in a way. I guess I simply refused to see that he was as bothered as he said he was. It went away—that feeling of his wanting to leave. Or I thought it went away. He has since brought it up. "Remember the time I wanted to leave? I've not been happy since. . . ." But he didn't leave me. A year later he left his job and went into business for himself.

I've read that the death of a contemporary or someone very close is a factor in the midlife thing, but I really don't think it's applicable in our case. He lost his closest friend but this was several years ago. And then before he went into his own business there was a period where a few people in their late thirties, early forties, died suddenly—three or four in a row —but they weren't close friends. It was a shock but I don't think their deaths had any pronounced effect on Andy. Or maybe they did and he didn't tell me because he didn't connect it with himself.

What has had an effect is that in the last year we've seen a lot of couples separate, people in our age bracket, and that has given him incentive—seeing that this kind of thing goes on and the people involved come out of it relatively secure —not all of them, but some, so far. So there's that and the fact that he's forty-six years old. He's gotten to that point in his life where he's on the other side, and he knows it.

So now he's met this girl with whom he has established a relationship which he feels could become a lasting one—an important one. He's told me a little bit about her. She's been around, has had lots of interesting jobs, is a strong personality, has lived with a couple of guys. She's doing well financially and this is something that attracted him. He sees a way of his not having to work so hard, eventually. She has an income she can share with him and that will make it easier for him.

I think what has happened to both of them is that they simply met each other when they were both ready for it, at points in their lives when it's time for a relationship like this to work. She, at thirty-three, having lived this relatively free, easy life—independent, never been married, no kids— meets this guy who's been fooling around for fifteen years and now decides he wants something more than that.

I said to him, "Don't allow that you're both ready for this to justify how you feel about each other. Try as dispassionately and objectively as possible to judge what you could have together in addition to the readiness." But the truth of the matter is you never know. So many things go into making up why we are attracted to someone. I asked him, "What are her interests? What does she like to do? What is it you have going for each other, not in relation to me, but in relation to the two of you? Do you like to do certain things together? What is making this work besides the fact that you found each other at the right time?"

He says there is a tremendous sexual attraction. There is probably a personality attraction as well, and I don't know if my question "Do you like to do certain things together?" is valid or not. Maybe that's not necessary—maybe that can work itself out.

He's known her a long time, but just as a girl he liked as a person. He started seeing her while I was away last summer. She's broken off with him twice because she's had a hard time dealing with the fact that he's married. He says that for the first six weeks she wouldn't sleep with him. She's been around enough so she didn't have to do that—she wanted to make sure of him before they slept together, so it wasn't until after their second breakup—as much as I can get from the story—that they culminated their relationship. It was after that that he came to me, sat me down and told me about it.

So, there's been a lot of talk, a lot of back and forth—a lot of explosive feelings in the past month. At one point I suggested perhaps going to see somebody, but Andy had no desire to do that. He feels he knows himself—knows the problems, knows what's going on—and he wants out. I thought maybe I should just take him by the hand to the shrink and see if we could work something out, because he is a nice person and we do get along and we do love each other and we have a family and we have twenty-five years. If we went to the shrink, maybe we could do something about it and to hell with his girl—I'm his *wife*. But on the other hand, we've done so much damage to each other, and I don't know if the shrink could erase that. So, I said, "Yes, I understand. I might need that too—to move on—but let's hold off, let's wait till Jennifer graduates, and let's wait until I finish my research project. I don't know that I could carry on and complete my paper while going through this at home—and let's discuss it further." I was putting it off, that's what I was doing.

And another thing I did—I gave him permission to see his friend if we could continue the way it had been. His friend was pressuring him. It was hard for her to maintain a relationship with a married man. But when I gave him permission, when I gave him his freedom with my blessing, what happened was he took his freedom and he went. And that's not how I perceived it would be. We perceived it in two different ways and he's no more at fault than I was. I saw it as, Okay, you can see your friend—and in my mind that meant a couple of nights a week—but the rest of the week you are here, husband, father and everything else. That was stupid of me, and that's not how he perceived it at all. He saw it as, Diana understands, and now I can be with my girl, which meant a couple of weekends away almost immediately, and several nights a week besides.

I realized, Hey, this isn't what I meant—I didn't mean this at all. I cannot live this way. I cannot live with him away most of the time and pretend we have a life together. And the pretense makes it hard for him too. Actually he's just living at home as a boarding place until he can go, and that's not what I had in mind. I suppose what I meant was trying to work it out—maybe.

It was just this last weekend I realized I couldn't go on like this—with him away and me marking time. I felt like I was in limbo or vegetating in the closet—it was a "closet" separation. I couldn't get on with my social life, couldn't bring it out in the open with my friends. There was nothing

I could do with my life, and if indeed this thing was going to happen to me, I had to get on with it. I'd had a couple of bad days envisioning what life was going to be like alone. I haven't been utterly devastated, but I've gone through periods of depression, periods of crying. Anticipation of loneliness had a great deal to do with that. But I'm at an emotional point where I recognize that I cannot live with the situation as it is. If I'm to get on with me, then he's got to go. It's masochistic to have him around. I would anticipate his coming home—it would get to be ten, ten-thirty, a quarter of eleven. I'd know where he was—that he was with his girl—but in my mind I'm thinking, Where is he? How come he's so late? I want to see him. I want to tell him what I've done today. . . . And then I'd say to myself, Stop that. He's not going to be around any more!

And I know what's in the future. After I'm alone every night for twenty-one nights in a row I'm going to go right downhill, but I want to get to that point and I want to get over it—I want to reach the other side of the hill.

So I told him I couldn't go on this way and I'd done some thinking and I was going to call the psychiatrist and talk to him and I thought we should see him for some help in how to deal with the girls— and maybe I should even see an attorney. That shook him. He said, "You're throwing me out."

And that's where we are. That's what's happening. Andy's looking for an apartment—and we did see the doctor. I told Jen last night and Andy's talking with her now. What I expressed to Jen was a desire for change on both our parts—mainly on Andy's—that he's at a point in his life where he wants to see if there are other kinds of solutions for what he's been going through and that I support his need for a change and I understand it—that I have felt a little of that need in myself. I said this doesn't mean he doesn't love us. I said that he *does* love us—that he will be seeing us from time to time, that we'll be able to have dinner together, that I don't know if it's permanent—that it may be and it may not be—that he won't be living too far away. . . .

At one point Jennifer said she would like to cry, and she did. She said that it might be best for all of us in the long run and that she wants what makes both of us the happiest. That was the essence of it. We haven't told Evie. She's at school and I don't want to tell her on the phone. I was hoping she could come down this weekend. Maybe we'll go up there and talk to her. I just don't know yet how we're going to work it out.

But meanwhile I must get on with my life and that means finishing my research project, completing my master's—it means letting my friends know, and it means little things like putting the garden together, cleaning out one of the rooms and putting that together, and dealing with things day to day. No big plans—I think that's wrong. One change at a time. Looking at it from a selfish point of view, which I must do in order to retain my sanity, I want to stay where I am for as long as I can. I'm in a relatively good position. I am not forced to look for work. I am not forced to move. If I had to consider at this point not only his leaving but the necessity to move from here because I couldn't afford it, or the immediate need to take a job because I didn't have an income, I'd be in a mess.

Also, I want to get out, see people, make new friends. There are some women who are able to simply pick up the telephone and put themselves into situations without a thought but that's not easy for me—it's just not easy. I've always been independent, but I'm shy too and I know I'm going to have to overcome that if I want to have any kind of social life. It's a balancing thing here—loneliness versus my personality. I'll have to overcome the shyness because the threat of loneliness is just too devastating. Oh, I can be alone and I can be busy and productive alone, but that can go on for just so long.

It isn't that I look at going out with men as an exciting adventure. I look at the whole thing as a need for companionship. I don't feel the need to find a guy every other night of the week. I don't feel that need—but that's right now. I can't tell what I'm going to be like a couple of months from now. I can't even think too far in the future, and I think that would be a huge mistake at this point. The thought of spending the rest of my life alone does not appeal to me. I would hope that doesn't happen, but I can't even think about that now. You see—something like this brings out your insecurities even if you think you've got it all together. But I *am* a person—a real person, and goddam it, I can make a life for myself even if I do have to spend it alone. And yes, even if I do go downhill for a while, I think enough of myself—I like myself enough, I have enough going for me—that I can get back together again. I'm sure—I'm pretty sure.

I think it's the insecure parts of me, the weak spots, that cause me to want him to stay. Because when I put those insecurities away, deep down inside I'd rather not have him back.

It's so confusing. I want things to work out for him. I have such a dear feeling for him. What made Jen cry last night—and me too—was when she said, "I'll miss certain things about Dad even though he's not around that much. When I get up in the morning I hear him puttering around in the kitchen or in his den. I hear him clunking around and I just know he's there—and he won't be there. . . ." That made us cry. But the point is, in a sense he hasn't been there. Should I be satisfied with a life with him where he's just a clunking presence? Satisfied with the safety of the sound of him moving around in his slippers, the safety of the dinners and the movies and the friends, the safety of the things we do together?

The presence—the slippers, the warmth of our relationship—is good. It means a lot. It has filled my life—but it has filled the *exterior*. There's been an emptiness inside that I'm just now admitting. What made Jennifer and me cry was the thought of missing the presence—the person who's always been there. It was like a mourning—it was almost like he had died when Jen started to talk about it. I know about great expectations and how foolish they are—that's why I've settled for the life I have. What would make me continue to settle is my fear of the unknown, of the future without him —fear of letting go what is safe. I think I can overcome that.

His girl—my feelings about her are changing. In the beginning I didn't think of her as an individual—she was part of the whole picture, of the process—but now I'm letting her become more of an individual. I still don't know her name and I'm not ready for that. When I told Andy I would want him to come for dinner with Jen and me, he said she might not like that. And I said, "So bring her along." And I could do that. It's not altruistic, believe me, far from it—it's a way of my being accepted by him. If I have her to dinner and we're all one big happy family, then I am not rejected. That may be a little crazy.

I don't consider her my enemy. I don't feel competitive with her. I don't know, maybe it's because of my own experiences. I understand this side of human nature—I understand that people do get involved with other people. I don't feel that he's rejected me for her. I don't feel he's made a choice of her over me—we're way past that. There's the overwhelming reality of his going from lady to lady to lady for the past fifteen years—He's been doing this for so *long!* This is a culmination—and maybe it is a real relationship and perhaps I don't let that possibility intrude much on my thoughts—perhaps I protect myself. But I honestly don't look at his thing with her as a reflection on me. I've had too much shit and have been rejected too much for too many years. This isn't a rejection—the rejection was in all the stuff that has gone before.

Andy accepted me as his friend, the mother of his children and this middle-aged lady who was his wife—but I was rejected a long time ago as a woman, as a sexual being. So I protected myself by being a wife and a mommy, and it wasn't until the last few years that I started rejecting that. I am a woman, I am attractive, I am pretty—I am me.

Maybe we are two people who should never have gotten together in the first place. I belabor this because I'm trying to understand it. Our needs are so different. I need *expressions* of affection, the words and the music—making *love*— not just making a set of muscles go into spasm. He needs a lot of different kinds of sexual activity. He says he's done it every way there is to do it, that he has to have that . . . infinite variety. He said, "I've done it in every position, every conceivable way—you name it, I've done it."

We've talked about this from time to time. I'd say, "Okay, okay, what do you want? Tell me, tell me—let's do it!" And he'd say, "If you don't know, I can't tell you. I can't tell you how to push my buttons—you have to know how to do this and how to do that. . . ." But, you see, I probably didn't *want* to push his buttons because I wasn't getting what I wanted.

Here I am, wanting a lot of holding, a lot of warmth, loving, touching—lots of touching. And there he is—the more positions and the more different kinds of things you can do, the better it is. But I don't see the rest of my life hanging from the ceiling on a swing—I just don't! Maybe I could hang from the ceiling on a swing if I got a lot of touching as well. Maybe that would work.

When he got the attachment for the TV, he brought home some porno movies. Neither of us had ever seen any of that stuff and they were a turn-on to a degree. They're fine—you can really get it on and really get excited and carry it off beautifully. But it isn't a substitute for all the other—for the affection and the tenderness and the gentleness and the caring.

He devoured *The Hite Report* because he wanted to know how to give pleasure to women. It's important to him to give pleasure. Okay, you can read these books and find out that somebody likes her clitoris done this way and somebody else likes it done a little more to the left. Yes, that *is* giving pleasure to a person and making her feel good—but is it loving? Is that being loving? I think he reads those things so he can be *good* at it. . . .

And maybe all that I'm saying is just a defense on my part, a justification. He would tell you that he *is* warm and affectionate, and he *is* in many ways—but he is not warm and affectionate and loving sexually with me. Maybe that's as much of a statement as I have a right to make. I have never felt that Andy was giving himself to me sexually—never. Giving yourself over lovingly and affectionately means just unzipping the zipper and opening yourself up from head to toe—revealing everything. When you do that in a sexual relationship you have totally exposed yourself. There are some people who can't do that, and I suspect he may be one of them. It's a total trusting. It may be that you have to be so sure of yourself that this act of total trust and total giving and total exposure has no fear in it. You can do it without expectation because you care enough about yourself. You *give*— nothing is taken from you. What you're doing is giving love. You are reinforcing and renewing someone else—and if you're lucky and you've got somebody who's as sure of himself or herself as you are—then they're doing the same thing. I've had that. I'd like to have it again.

But right now it's one thing at a time. I know that soon I'm going to have to take stock of things and decide what I'm going to do with myself. Unknown things are scary. Everyday things, practical things, that doesn't bother me. Investing my money wisely, that doesn't scare me—that's just getting the right kind of advice and following it correctly. There may be things I haven't thought of. I don't know how to do the taxes, I'll have to find out about the insurance—those are the only things I don't know how to do on the financial side. But that's easy. It's the human things that concern me. I hope my girls aren't too shaken by this experience as far as their own relationships go. I hope we're doing the right thing.

The money . . . support . . . ah, yes, the money. We have been very calm and cool and collected about the money. I suspect it will not remain that way because I don't think it ever does. When you're calm and cool and collected about your entire situation, and everybody loves everybody, when the shit hits the fan it's because of the money. That's where you get all your hostilities and all your baddies out. So far we've been just splendid. We'll just split everything down the middle and because we've been married as long as we have, I'll probably get decent support for a certain amount of time. At this moment, nobody's arguing about anything. He will support me and take care of the children. He has expressed that and I have told him that's all well and good to say and that I believe him, but because of the position I'll be in and because he can afford it, I have every intention of protecting myself. I will try to get as much as I can. Even though he'll have to split everything in half, he will continue to have a very large income, of which I will get a very small percentage.

I have no guilt feelings about it at all—none whatever. If there's any vengeance that I'm not taking out on the situation as it exists, I will probably take it out over money. But on the practical side, I do want to insure I have as much of an income as possible for as long as possible—and he can be very tough. He isn't, right now, because of his guilt, but it'll come. I can be tough too.

I've had the benefit of the advice of a couple of dear old friends. They are wives of men who have made it very big, and they are treated royally. They're the "buy me, take me, bring me, show me" ladies, and they say, "Don't be a nice girl for anything. Get everything that's coming to you. Look what's happened to you. You deserve every goddam penny and more." I trust him, yes, and I love him, yes, but I'm going to look out for myself.

You look at the end of an old marriage, and no matter what, it's all so confusing, full of rationalizations, trying to justify this and to understand that. But it's nothing that happened, no one thing—not in the last seven months or the last two or three years or the last ten years—it's what has taken place and has not taken place for twenty-five years.

The last two or three years have brought a sense of self, an inward strength and a feeling of independence so that in spite of everything I am content with me. And I think this is true for Andy too—that he feels relatively independent and strong about himself. So perhaps *now* the twenty-five years can be put in their proper place and we can go on with our lives—with who we are now.

In spite of what we've done to each other, we've managed to grow and to grow rather well. Forty—trying to find out about yourself at forty isn't a coincidence—it *is* a midlife crisis or syndrome of a sort. You're on the other side of life —you *do* realize that there's only so much time left, and you say to yourself at some point, "Look, either put up or shut up."

It's a time of renewal—of reaffirmation of one's self. This is not to say that you can't accomplish the same thing within the marriage, because I feel we *could* do it—and who knows, perhaps we will. What I do know is that—either way—I will make it.

Max

After twenty-two years of marriage, Max and his wife were doing well enough financially to realize their long-held dream of buying a place in the country. But his work as a film editor required him to spend extended periods of time away from their ranch, and these separations, with other pressures, intensified the ancient and unresolved problems that finally ended their marriage. Max is forty-four and has one grown daughter. He was interviewed thirteen months after the breakup.

"People live in situations that are very strange, and I don't think they're happy, they just go on. That's what we did. . . . It's more comfortable than the alternative you contemplate. I guess when it isn't any more, that's when you do something about it."

OFF AND ON over a period of maybe ten years Irene and I had talked about moving from Los Angeles into a rural area. Then we took a vacation to Siskiyou County and fell in love with the countryside. We wanted to buy a house and move up there but the problem was that I work in the motion-picture industry and that's Los Angeles. But I'd had three or four really good years—saved a lot, had no money problems at all—and the money we'd saved made us feel more capable of making a move. Then, too, I hoped to do some freelance still photography and wildlife projects up north. So we looked for some property. A tremendous amount of energy went into the whole thing—it took a year and a half of working our butts off to get up there—a lot of energy, everything focused around that. It was a major move—we altered our lives drastically. Friends have asked me, "Don't you think it was moving, really, that broke it up?" But I can't say that. Who knows? Maybe if we'd stayed in L.A. we might have been divorced a year sooner.

So in 1975 we found a thirty-two-acre ranch with house and barn and we bought it. It took us five days of traveling. We drove up in a van with our numerous animals—it was like the Joad family moving. We unloaded the van and I turned around and came back to Los Angeles to work for three weeks. So Irene was on her own for the first three weeks—totally alone in a strange place, a big old house. After that I commuted; I continued to work in L.A. It was hard on both of us, those last few years—unlike anything we'd ever experienced. We'd never been apart on a regular basis before and I think that was a factor somehow. It was, for me.

For one thing, I realized that I could function being alone and I don't think I was sure I could do that before. I was very dependent on the relationship, even the unpleasant aspects of it, even the fighting. Also, there was a great deal of pressure on both of us and we never came to grips with what the situation really was—having to draw income from an area other than where we were living and the separation this necessitated. We hadn't anticipated those long periods apart. I'd overestimated how much I could earn up north and underestimated the amount of money needed to support what we were doing. We did *not* move to the country and live in a tepee. It was a ranch, a home with a good-sized mortgage, and it was not self-supporting. Even growing your own food takes a lot of effort, a lot of work, and we were the only two people doing it all.

So I had to be away in order to work to pay the mortgage and I was frustrated at not being able to share in all that was going on at the ranch. I resented it—I mean I resented Irene's talking about it, her saying, "Oh, you should have seen such and such, it was terrific!" She didn't offer this up in a baiting way or in a way to try to make me mad, but that would be my response—resentment. On top of that, by being away I couldn't do all the things that needed doing. I'm in L.A. working but meanwhile the porch is sagging and has to be shored up, and Irene is there alone, with no help, and she walks on the sagging porch every day. So her outlet was to get on the phone at night and tell me the porch was sagging, which irritated the hell out of me. I'd say, "What the devil do you think I can do about a sagging porch from five hundred miles away? It's going to have to wait till I come back." And she'd say, "When are you coming back?" And I'd say, "Well, I thought it was going to be Wednesday but now I don't think I can get away before Friday."

On her part, Irene felt left alone, and no matter how noble the cause she still literally *was* being left alone to take care of an enormous amount of work. All of those things were stressful and we never really worked them out. We kept having the same kind of antagonism and toward the end of the marriage, during the last few months, I'd come home and we'd spend three or four days fighting and then I'd turn around and leave and go back to work. The number one source of irritation in all marriages is money—the thing people say they fight about most. That was true of our marriage. I don't think it was the number one problem but it was the number one thing we fought about—the management, not having enough, the need for me to be away in order to get it —which was a vicious circle. And the circumstances under which we were living compounded some problems which were already there.

We were married very young—she was eighteen and I was twenty. Neither of us had brothers or sisters. My parents were divorced and Irene's parents almost supplanted my family. Her father actually replaced mine, who was an alcoholic—our relationship wasn't belligerent, it was just kind of nonexistent. So Irene's father filled the role for me, but there was a price for that. He's very volatile and emotional so there were lots of family blowups and fights and we got involved in their domestic disputes. The pyrotechnics that would go on were unbelievable! Irene's mother was a steady person, a presence and a force, always there taking care of things. The non-Jewish Jewish mother—we were and always would be "the kids." We spent a lot of time with them, were very close —with both the good and the bad aspects of that—and when we'd have problems, which we did over the years, her parents would step in, mediating. And when they had problems we would end up mediating. It was a closed little clique, terribly intense, and as long as we did things in certain ways —they had some very rigid concepts—everything was fine. I think we influenced each others' lives a tremendous amount. My feeling later in life was that I didn't really exist outside of this tight little family ship, either in Irene's eyes or in her parents' eyes. And I saw her in about the same way. It was as if we had lost sight of each other as individuals—if we ever really had considered ourselves as individuals—and that everything we did and said to each other was a playback of the same old tapes. We hadn't grown very much. In the last six months of our marriage I clearly realized I did not like Irene, and it scared the hell out of me because we'd been married so long and I had a lifetime involvement with her and she was the only woman I related to romantically— sexually—even though sex was always a problem for us. It was a continuing problem, and during the last few years it was *terrible*.

We'd gone through a very rough period when we'd been married about two years—our daughter Jessie was a year old. It was in the middle of intercourse and out of the blue Irene said, "I don't feel anything." That destroyed me. I couldn't deal with it. We were twenty-three and twenty-one and our dealings with each other and with most things were fraught with high trauma at all times—a crisis to be approached in great frenzy. And I think being married young, having had little experience with other girls, I wasn't very sure of myself even though we'd been married a couple of years. So when she said she didn't feel anything, that upset me so badly. What I could never deal with was that in later years she never remembered saying it, denied saying it: "It never happened—I didn't say that." That was one of our problems, recalling incidents differently. I mean, I don't think it is the sort of thing a person would just toss out—not something you would say lightly.

The first two years had been terrific, and I remembered that and said, "What? There's never been a problem—we've never talked about it. I'm not *that* insensitive—I'd have been aware of discomfort or boredom or something!" That's why I thought, My God, has she been *faking* for two years? I can't believe it!

From that moment, I approached our sex life with extreme timidity. You know—Is this doing anything for you? Is this right? How about this? Which of course was absolutely the wrong thing to do. The point is that I became impotent for about two years. Struggle, struggle, *ohhhh*, man, it was terrible! Very painful for both of us, horrible. She would get angry, which of course made it worse—and it just kept getting worse because of the fear of failure. I mean, it had all the fun of being buried in the sand up to your neck and having the fire ants eat your eyes out. It was terrific. You want to have sex? No, I think I'd rather amputate my left hand.

Oh God, the fights we had over it—middle of the night, three, four, five o'clock in the morning. Daylight would come up and she'd be saying, "I can't live like this, I don't know what I'm going to do," and I'd be saying, "I'm sorry ... I know ... we'll have to work it out" ... on and on. It was madness. Finally, in all fairness, Irene stopped getting angry, which was a tremendous help. She'd say, "Hey, relax, it's okay." No one was saying "Listen, get hard, you son of a bitch, what's the matter with you?" and the problem ceased.

From the time of the impotence on for about eight years, Irene would always have to make pretty broad hints and gestures, would have to initiate, really acknowledge that yes, she wanted to have sex. Because otherwise I wouldn't risk it.

I'd been burned once. So our sex life—instead of being a natural part, an extension of the relationship—became a big deal, fraught with import—the center of great struggle and frustration and sadness.

Affection wasn't a problem—we're both affectionate people. And Irene is a physical person, not inhibited—God, "frigid" is the last word you would use for her. When we had sex it was good, but we just couldn't make it a normal part of our lives. There was something about it that was uncomfortable for Irene. The positive emotions of sex and the aftermath and the afterglow would disappear with the morning light, would be gone and forgotten. And that was one of the things that puzzled the hell out of me. I said, There's no continuity—it's like we've got to do it *all* over again and start over again learning how each time. What the hell is this? We did it real good, all the parts worked, all the functions, and physically and mentally we were happy, but *now* do we have to wait eight months to do that again? I don't know. I'll never know.

In between times nothing happened—*nothing!* We didn't have sex for long periods, sometimes weeks, sometimes months. Sometimes three months would go by—which is unbearable, really. I don't mean that I'm running in the streets screaming, "I gotta have sex, I gotta have sex!" because that's bullshit. I don't believe for one minute that sex is physiologically or psychologically a necessity. But if two people are living together, then it *is*. It would be okay if it's totally comfortable for both people, if both of them say, Hey, I don't want sex more than every three months because that's what I like and I have no desire—something that's spoken, acknowledged. With us it was unspoken and unacknowledged.

I went through some therapy in 1962 and that helped a little and I went back in '67. We had problems in '62. Irene had a problem—seemingly, she had a nervous breakdown.

One day she said, "I just can't handle things." We had a friend who was a psychologist and he recommended a psychiatrist, and Irene started to see him. That was a shaky period at first because she didn't know if she wanted to stay married or not and had to work it out in therapy. I felt guilty, felt I had driven her to whatever it was that was going on. And she herself expressed that—that it was me. This was after the impotent time, but we were having some off-and-on trouble. Then her psychiatrist decided that she didn't really have a problem so I said, "Well, I think I should go," because it was my doing anyway more or less. Something in my behavior was screwing things up and giving her a nervous breakdown.

I didn't do well in therapy—I got a C minus in therapy. I went to a guy who was a good doctor but he was just starting out in practice and maybe he'd have been good for someone else but he wasn't too good for me. My thinking was that you got graded on it and you had to do good and he had to like you—it was real important that everybody like you—and that you keep talking all the time because you got to keep the ball rolling. I mean, it's up to you, you go in there and you got to keep talking for fifty minutes no matter what, because he didn't talk. So I would verbalize a lot of meaningless crap which he would listen to. What I should have had was some older cocker who'd say, "Hey, sonny, if you want to come in here and babble away about all this shit and not say anything about what you really feel, that's terrific. But I'm going to put a tape recorder in here and I'm not going to come and listen to it!"

Another thing that happened at that time—Irene had an affair with the psychiatrist, the one she had gone to, and she didn't tell me about it till later. She told me about it one night and I was angry, terribly mad. But I couldn't express that anger because I felt responsible for all the problems we'd had and would have periodically. That's what's known as the Big P—Provider—the guy who's responsible for *everything,* for all the crap as well as all the good things. That's taking a lot on yourself and being super-egotistical and totally unreal. And the fact was that our sex life was still shitty. We never got it down to where it was just a casual thing, an expression of niceness. It was always fraught. Oh, every once in a while we'd say, "Hey! This is silly, what's the big deal? There's no problem—we just had a terrific fuck here, we loved and everything was fine. We pleased each other, so why can't we do this all the time?" It was like a Sid Caesar routine. And then, six weeks would go by. I'd try to start things but the moment there was a little rebuff, you know, I'd stop immediately. And we did not talk about it. Embarrassing, for both of us. I could not confront it. There was too much tied up with ego and macho. So I would not discuss it and that also became a bone of contention between us.

In retrospect I could analyze it to death, but whatever Irene's needs were I wasn't meeting them. If she wanted to be forcibly taken or swept off her feet or cajoled or whatever it was—I was not doing that. And what I needed was, "You crazy wild beast, I just can't get enough of you"—which she wasn't doing for me.

In 1967 I became interested in someone. I didn't have an affair—it was a pseudo-affair, not consummated—but I did spend time seeing a girl after work. I wanted to have an affair but I couldn't do it—I was frightened. I didn't want to break up the marriage and I wasn't sure what would happen, but I wanted to—to have both. I did it badly, acted like an ass— put Irene through a lot of crap, mentally mistreated her, and she never really forgave me for it. The resolution was long and painful. Irene and I were both drinking a lot and being violent with each other—physically battling, in rages, punching one another. It took six months to get it worked out where we were on an even keel—perhaps longer than that —a time of penance to be done. Difficult. And it continued to be referred to—it was like a club you hit somebody over the head with when you need some extra ammunition. I think now that much too much was made of it, and if we hadn't had other problems, especially sexual ones, it wouldn't have happened at all.

There were a couple of other things too. In 1971 I went to New York to work. I was on call constantly and had only one day off in the six weeks before Irene joined me. I told her beforehand, "You know, I want you here but it's going to be difficult. I eat, so we'll have dinner together, but then I may have to go back to the office." They were previewing a picture that I'd edited, and the cast and the people involved with that picture were there, and I said, "You can be with these people and go around and see the sights, or go out on your own—you know, go and see all the things I wish I'd seen here in six weeks and tell me about them. And whatever time we have is what we have and we'll adjust." But she could not do that. Consequently she made herself extremely miserable and me too. She'd say, "Oh, God, do you have to work again tonight?" like it was news. Now this is the crazy thing—when we got back to L.A. she told me that she'd had an affair with the guy who was the lead in the movie I'd edited—and I knew they had spent some time together in New York. She let me believe that for a *whole year* and then told me it wasn't true! I was awfully upset—couldn't believe that she'd lied, didn't want to believe that—would rather have believed she'd had the affair. I said, "I can't grasp that you'd allow me to think something like that which wasn't true for a *year!* Why would you do that?" And she said, "Well, when we went to the office to say goodbye to everyone the secretary looked like she had a crush on you, and I thought you'd had an affair." I mean, it just wasn't true.

And there was another time, a couple years later. I hired a girl—Cindy—to work for me on a special account. She was good at bookkeeping and film editing as well. She was sort of an offensive person, especially to Irene, a kind of nut, whacko off-the-wall Hollywood character, but she did her work very well. She had a boyfriend, there was no fooling around, but she projected this image of the femme fatale which was her coloration, and obviously we were spending a lot of time together, working together all day. It was not like the pseudo-affair in 1967 which I used just to get even with Irene for her past affair. But Irene found Cindy a threat because I think a sexual relationship as fluctuating as ours can't help but leave room for doubt. So Irene became adamant that Cindy had to go. She'd say, "Fire her," and I'd say, "I can't do that. Look, we've got to be trusting with each other, and I can't account for every minute that I'm not with you. If I say I'm going to be home at six-ten and I get here at six-twenty it doesn't mean I've been fooling around. You can't work at any job under such constrictions, and certainly not in this crazy business where people always say they'll be with you in a minute and that means three hours."

That was another point when I wanted to sit down and get something resolved with Irene and we didn't resolve it—again we didn't. All the effort and energy put into negative feelings was saying *trouble* but we didn't deal with that, didn't accomplish anything. Actually, the marriage had to break down—there was a leaky valve someplace. There were things Irene said to me during the last years—for instance, that outside of the marriage I would wind up on skid row, be a bum—or I'd be another statistic of a broken marriage, one of the people who commit suicide or lead lives of quiet desperation. It was terribly depressing and I didn't buy it. I'd say, "See, there you go, you're trying to program. You give me a choice—either I'm going to be a Hollywood swinger or else I'm going to be destitute on Fifth and Mission. It doesn't have to be either one of those things. If you sincerely like me as a person, then you would hope I would have some wherewithal—would be able to function. If I imagine myself being killed in a plane crash flying to Los Angeles on one of those trips, I don't want to think of you just ceasing to exist or withering up or falling down and saying you can't go on. You're a person, and difficult as it is, you maintain yourself—you *do* something."

People live in situations that are very strange, and I don't think they're happy, they just go on. That's what we did. In the bad times, going along becomes the norm—I mean, it's more comfortable than the alternative you contemplate. I guess when it isn't any more, that's when you do something about it. Apparently it's happening a lot to men around my age, in the mid-forties, for whatever reasons. Maybe you act at some moment on the biological clock. I wasn't telling myself, Listen, aren't you afraid that you might kick tomorrow, so you want to get it all in early? No—there was nothing that dramatic in my thinking. I don't know why it hit me in 1977 and not 1965, I really don't. There was certainly plenty of provocation in the past, but I couldn't do it then. Off and on for a long time I'd felt very strongly that we had stopped liking each other a *whole lot* and we hadn't dealt with those feelings, because it was too hard to handle. So instead we would patch it up, make it up in some way, or find another focal point for our arguments—money or sex or the raising of our daughter, whatever. And we didn't confront the basic problem, never did confront it—and I'm quite sure that when we split up she still didn't understand it at all. She simply preferred to terminate the marriage without working anything out or looking beyond the framework of the ways we had done things in the past.

I myself wanted to examine the relationship—wanted to sit down and discuss our attitudes toward each other, how we saw each other, how we felt about each other. I wanted

to find out whether in fact we did like each other or not—
what we expected of each other, perhaps. Irene's mother had
told her I was in the male menopause. I think Irene believed
that too and her premise was "Stop acting like a jerk and quit
talking about these things, and don't you realize that this is
only the midlife crisis and this is dumb. Take a cold shower
and it'll go away and don't worry about it—I mean, look, stop
being a baby, we're going to all sit down now and eat something and you'll feel better."

I hate terms like "midlife crisis." When Irene's mother
said, "What's the matter with him, doesn't he know it's just
the male menopause?" I thought, *Shit*, now you're both
going to agree that Max has just gone around the bend mo-
mentarily and if we just lock him in the henhouse for a couple of weeks he'll get over it. That's so simplistic. I don't
believe you have to pick up Gail Sheehy's *Passages* and carry
it around with you like a Torah! It's just that at some point I
started to feel, Hey! I don't want to do this any more! I don't
want to do it this way any more! I was just aware of a change
in myself that said, as scary as the alternative might be, "This
marriage is terrifying—this is not livable!"

I told Irene I thought we had some serious problems that
needed attention because I was not happy. I said, "I don't
want to indulge in mind raping, but I don't think you're
happy either. We're just pushing aside something that needs
to be dealt with and it's at a point where I *have* to deal with
it—I *can't* just forget it. Because when I'm home we are
always fighting, usually about practical things—the day-to-
day kind of business—but there's an atmosphere of hostility,
a constant underlying theme of Max against Irene. And now
here we are, living in a supposedly idyllic setting on this
marvelous ranch, a marvelous showplace, and it's a success
only in the cosmetic sense. We're devoting tremendous
amounts of energy to a *place* and meanwhile the human relationship is not good. We're not working together, we're

sniping at each other all the time, taking shots and treating each other badly, which doesn't fit with the face we're presenting to everybody else—the friends and relatives who think, 'Oh, isn't everything terrific!' Well, no, this is *not* terrific, and I'm working my butt off to maintain this place, and for what, if the human relationship isn't working? I don't want to do this. I'd rather be uncomfortable in an environmental sense with a good human relationship. I don't want to give this up but I want both—I don't want to go on living with this relationship the way it is in the best of all possible places. It's not enough. It doesn't work. You know, the tail is wagging the dog."

There were some things that were bothering the hell out of me. Drinking was one of them and we did not talk about it, we did not say, "There's a drinking problem going on here." Not only did I not confront the problem but I participated in it, in all the drinking and the mild little efforts to limit it which were so ineffectual. It's like somebody saying, "I'm going to stop smoking. I smoke three packs and I'm going to stop by smoking only fifty-nine cigarettes today and I'll smoke fifty-nine cigarettes a day for the next two years and then I'll go down to fifty-seven and really kick the habit." That's what we'd do. You make the martinis in a pitcher instead of pouring them over the rocks so you won't drink so much, and you end up making three pitchers. I was responsible for that too, because I didn't say—"This is bad, this is affecting me."

We started off all our discussions on the wrong foot, with Irene drinking and me drinking with her. Wrong. Bad. Irene liked to have someone drink with her and it would anger her if I wouldn't have a drink or if I'd have wine instead of vodka. She'd think I was trying to put her down or make her look like an alcoholic by not drinking: "Oh, you're gonna be a good guy, you're not gonna drink." She was into the sauce pretty good and I drank drink for drink with her, and you just can't deal with problems when you have a load of alcohol under your belt. The discussion would break down after about twenty minutes and we had some very strange evenings while we were hashing all of this out.

I remember one night when our talk started out very sensibly and rationally. Then it cruised back and forth and finally it got totally bizarre and emotional—by emotional I mean raging anger, fits of rage from both of us. We would do that to each other. One of us would say something that triggered the other and we'd go off on a tangent pursuing that—the kind of fight that dissipates into some minuscule wrangle of "Remember the time when . . ." until we'd settle back down again and say, "This is dumb."

Sometimes we talked way into the night and went to bed angry and exhausted. After a few weeks of this Irene stopped drinking—I'd already pretty well stopped, and we both knew we were drinking too much—and then we communicated better but only in the sense of not going into the rages. It just wasn't a situation in which we could say, "Listen, we'll go back to the solution we used in 1963 because we had two good years after that." This wasn't something just to be patched up.

There had been other times when we'd had disagreements that were resolved in ways that weren't satisfactory to me—when I felt I'd copped out on something. We'd make up, but I hadn't really felt that I was at fault or wrong, just that it was better to patch it up. Then later I'd think, Wait a minute—you made me the heavy when I wasn't, you went along with that, and it was good for you but it was shitty for me! Those sores don't heal all the way—they're still festering.

I told Irene, and I meant it, "I'm not making you happy. How in the hell can you be happy? I don't treat you as if I like you. Your behavior irritates me and we don't, we can't discuss it. Instead I put you down in front of somebody or take a cheap shot. We have all these ways we've rehearsed

for twenty years, we're real good at it. And physically—I
don't know about you, but I have to say, *My God*, there's got
to be more than that. We've had a twenty-year-plus shot at it
and we don't have it right yet. I mean, how much rehearsal
time do you need? Christ, you can't play Boston forever—
you've got to move on to Broadway sometime, gang, and
we're overdue—we're way overdue. We're acting out the
same roles we were doing twenty years ago, which was ex-
cusable then because we were naive. But not any longer."

She said, "Well, what do you want to do?" I said, "Hell, I
don't know what I want to do. All I know is there's something
wrong—major surgery is needed. We can't just say, Okay, go
to sleep, have some chicken soup and it'll be over tomorrow."

"But what do you want to *do?* You want to break up? You
want to go on living here? You want to . . . ?"

I said, I don't *know!* I'm delineating the problem. Like
Eric Sevareid, I'm going to tell you what's wrong with the
world. I'm not telling you how to fix it—I'm not paid to do
that, right? If I knew how to fix it, for Christ's sake, I would
have proposed a solution. I don't have any solution—I'm just
unhappy and I think *you're* unhappy. You express this to me
by screaming at me for three solid days. That is not the mark
of a happy person. And we've gone about it in the wrong way
for so many years I don't know if we *can* fix it!"

She said, "Well, that's pessimistic, and if you're going to
be pessimistic we're never going to fix it."

So that was one of the reasons why we didn't stay together
and try to work something out—because I wouldn't say that
it could be worked out. Because I didn't know that it *could*
be worked out—I didn't know what the answer was.

So finally she said, "What are you going to do?" I said, "I
don't know." That was a Friday night. The next morning she
got up and said, "I've made up my mind. I'm going up north
—I've got to get out of here. I have to think and I can't do it
here." I said, "Okay, that's a good idea."

We boarded the dogs and I arranged for someone to come in and feed the other animals. She went to her parents and I went to a motel in San Francisco. I didn't know what the hell we were going to do—I really didn't at that point. I didn't bring up the idea of separation, but if I'd been willing to go along with things as they were, if I hadn't forced the issue, I think we would have stayed together.

She called me at work on Thursday and said, "Well, have you made up your mind what you're going to do?" I said, "Nothing has changed—I don't have any solutions." And she said, "Well, I'm going to file for divorce." We saw each other a few times after that—it was rugged.

I felt the decision was scary, terrible. But I also felt that it was important, because nothing in our conversation had convinced me otherwise—nothing had been said about dealing with our problems differently. It was going to be a repetition of the solutions or non-solutions that had been provided in the past. I was more afraid of that happening than I was of divorce.

I continued to live at the motel for a while and then moved into an apartment. I was finishing a movie for a company that was paying me per diem and I figured that one per diem would pay the rent on the apartment for a week, which was better than putting out that much each day—Irene and I had agreed on interim support. I felt fragmented, peculiar—but frankly, being alone was not that unusual, and the respite from the fighting and haranguing back and forth was good. And not knowing what I was going to do—not making those kinds of decisions was okay too. I knew I had a job for a while. I had a possibility of going to Paris to work and I was looking forward to that. There were a couple of bright distractions, doing things I hadn't done before, and I wasn't really thinking much beyond that.

When we split up I don't think Irene believed there was another woman—that I was seeing someone else. I think she thought I had just kind of gone whacko—that it was indeed male menopause, that I had a hormone imbalance and I'd wake up six weeks later being sorry as hell.

I was the one who told Jessie, our daughter. She reacted very sensibly, incredibly mature—which I don't think was all that great, because it wasn't realistic. She was too under-standing. I'd done the same with my own parents when they told me they were getting a divorce. I'd said, "That's okay. I understand—you're two normal people and if you don't get along, you break up." You know, who cares? Like I was some damn counselor instead of their eighteen-year-old son, and of course I cared! They were my mother and father, I'd grown up with them, and now they were divorced. I mean, I understood but I *didn't* understand. There was anger there, and guilt. If I'd been a better kid they would have stayed together—all that shit. It isn't only a lot of analyst's jargon, there's substance to it, and I had those kinds of feelings as a child. And if I'd been a better kid my dad wouldn't have been an alcoholic. You know, things like that. So Jessie was very sensible, and at the moment I was gratified because it made it much easier for me to deal with. I think she was objective—she had some good suggestions, and she didn't castigate either one of us. She doesn't have as good a rela-tionship with Irene as I would hope for both of them, but I think it will get better. Jessie is very volatile and Irene is, too, in her way—they're still carrying on in the way I said I couldn't handle any more; that is, they'll be talking to each other on the phone and one of them gets pissed and hangs up. Then they don't talk for a period of time. But they know each other well, and Jessie says, Well, that's Mom, so the next time I call her I won't bring up politics or whatever. Jessie doesn't have to have these confrontations any more or say, "I gotta make her know I'm right or else."

When I told Jessie about the divorce she was very good about it, as I said, but a couple of months later she called me at one in the morning and she was terribly distraught. She said, "Dad, I've got to talk to you!" She wasn't incoherent but she didn't make a whole lot of sense. The conversation centered around some trouble she was having with her husband, but I had the feeling that at least part of the turmoil she was going through had to do with the fact that her parents were divorced—that something she had taken for granted in her life had been changed. Like "I've got a husband and these problems over here and you guys used to be over there for me and now you aren't there any more. You used to be a couple there and now you've split off—like protozoa—and that's difficult."

I said to her, "You can be real mad at me and tell me so, and that's all right, it won't hurt a thing—you can get angry at me and yell at me, and if you feel like doing it you should. It's all right because I complicated your life, if nothing else." She said, "I know, but it still upsets me." We didn't talk about it for some time after that and she never has gotten mad at me. I've never come out and asked her directly "What do you feel about that?" Somehow it seems to me as if it would be a forced question, out of the blue. I figure she'll talk about it when she can and if she can. Either she's relatively comfortable with her feelings about the divorce or else she's avoiding them. Jessie and I don't talk much about serious feelings—I'm kind of at a loss to know them.

In September, while I was in San Francisco, I had a date with Michelle—she was a friend of the wife of a producer I'd worked with, and she lived in the apartment next door to them. We went out and I started dating her fairly regularly, and by November we were dating exclusively. So after separating from Irene I only spent about a month alone. Then in February I was offered a job in Arizona that was to last three months and Michelle said, "I want to go with you because I don't want us to be apart for that long." And I said, "Good, I'm glad." I hadn't known how she'd feel about leaving her job but it turned out she didn't like her job that much anyway

—she'd been a lab technician for about eight years. Now we're living together.

My relationship with Michelle is very relaxed, whereas Irene is a very intense person, very dramatic and emotionally mercurial. With her there are blacks and whites, no grays. That intensity was invested in everything she did, which in some areas was good—it carried a certain brilliance—but it was applied to everything and I found it ultimately hard to live with. For instance, she was a great cook—*is* a great cook —excuse me, she's not deceased, just divorced. When she cooks, everything has to be done right—she can't make a lunch without it being fit to go on the cover of *Gourmet* magazine. Even if it's sandwiches it's terrific—a heaping platter, mounds of sandwiches. People would stop by and she'd say, Can you stay for lunch? and they'd end up gorging themselves. But what I'm saying is that in comparison to being with Michelle, there was nothing I could do to help. Irene would say, "You can help by sitting here and talking to me." The inference was, You can't help, you can't participate because you're just a clumsy man. Which I find reverse sexism. I mean, I did boys' cooking in junior high school. I know how to do these things. When we parted she gave me a vegetable peeler and said, "You probably don't know how to use this." Christ, a chimp could use it. What do you mean, I don't know how to use it? Seriously, I would have done more. I did do dishes and clean up, but she slaved in the kitchen— she liked doing it, it was an avocation. Also putting up food —it was all part of living on a ranch, you did this. But it was totally consuming and there was little I could do to help. I objected to that. It was important to me and I didn't understand why it wasn't important to her too.

When we moved up there, time was always important to her. "Okay, now it's lunchtime." What was important to me was going out and just being there and experiencing. If you go for a walk in the woods, why does it have to be twenty minutes? What if you go out and decide to spend the day? "Oh, I can't, I gotta get back because it's gloomph time," or something. We got into a few arguments about this, about time and about being here and being there and I said I didn't move to the country to punch a goddam time clock. That was the last thing I wanted, because there you go down to get the mail and wind up bullshitting for half an hour with Rosie at the post office and that's part of the charm of the place. I think Irene understood that, but there was too much of the other in her. Once I went for a walk with a man who lived down the road and Irene thought we'd be back for lunch, although we hadn't said we would, and when I came back at one-fifteen she was furious: "I had lunch and where were you?" I said, "This is not important." It *was* important to her because she'd put all her focus on it.

By contrast, Michelle is completely the other way—she isn't concerned about restrictions on time. You do what you want, within reason. And neither of us has such a total passion for one thing that it excludes all others. I mean, it's not like sitting down with a Nobel physicist. If there's something she's interested in, she can communicate and I can hear about it and share with her in areas I may not have been exposed to before. And in a casual way, an offhand way, we're very open and honest about feelings. We don't have to make self-conscious announcements about them: *And now I'm going to say this.* I've found it very easy to be honest with Michelle and she's terribly truthful about herself and her feelings. Irene didn't deal with truth—she created her own conception of what was real, and in some cases that had become her reality—was real as hell for her. I'm not talking about embellishing stories to make them better, I mean she'd describe events to people and it just wasn't the way it happened. The stories would begin close to what had happened, and pretty soon what was true and her construction of it would get mixed up in her head, and as time went on I think she didn't remember any more, she believed that was what actually had happened. And this was strange because when we were first married she could remember anything, like what you were wearing four years ago on a Wednesday night when couple X came to dinner, and she was invariably right. Maybe what she did was self-protective, to make herself look good or portray herself in a certain way in memory. After we broke up she said some things about me which were terrible distortions—that I beat her—that I beat the dogs.

Irene is pretty strong. She was determined to look out for herself. She wasn't broken up or destitute at all, and she got right back in there dating. She's attractive, has a lot going for her, and as soon as she was available she had a lot of men coming around asking her out. She's living with another guy now—that's why I'm not supporting her totally. They plan to get married.

We had settled on a thousand dollars a month as interim support, which to me was excessive but I was willing to do it initially because she'd never worked before, wasn't really equipped—had spent her whole life taking care of the home and cooking and doing those things that don't bring in any money on the open market. She thought she was going to get more, but I said "Look, I'm only making twenty-nine thousand. If I give you a thousand dollars a month that's over half my net and I can't do more than that—no way." It wasn't until later that we sat down with lawyers and she finally realized that. My lawyer told me that the important thing when it came to court was to get a termination on support because in my situation it could go on for a long time, as we were married twenty-two years and Irene didn't work and wasn't educated for a special skill. He said, "It's important that you have a set time when it's off, because as amicable as the separation may be, as generous as you're feeling, two years from now you're going to ask yourself, What the hell am I doing working so hard to crank out all this money? Your feelings will change, particularly if you remarry. You have to think of that."

I feel the agreement we have is fair and I can afford to pay it, but I'll be glad when it ends because I'll have that money, and hopefully she won't need it—she'll have remarried. It's a natural bent for her. She's used to having a provider and it's very difficult to alter your life markedly after being married that length of time.

A natural bent for both of us—that concerned me a lot with Michelle those first few months—getting immediately involved with another woman. It worried me that it might be I need a bed . . . I need somebody to take care of me . . . shelter, sustenance . . . I don't want to be alone . . . any port in a storm, kids. You know, simply trying to find another wife. Michelle and I talked about it. Finally I gave it up as wasted energy, decided that what mattered to me was how I felt on a day-to-day basis about myself and her—whether I was happier, more satisfied, and she as well. I guess what I'm saying is that an issue only has significance if it is significant—if that makes any sense. If an issue doesn't really have any bearing, who cares? Who cares if you're married for twenty-two years or forty-three years or three minutes—numbers cease to be relevant. What's important is how you're getting along with the person. As far as marrying again —I don't know. One of the problems is that Michelle is thirty-two, young enough to have children, but I don't want any more children. She's iffy on that, a bit ambivalent. I think she would like to, but it's not a major goal in her life and she's considered not having children at all. There's some appeal for me in the idea of having a child with Michelle but the practical aspects of it are not real—I have grave reservations.

With Michelle and me, sex is just part of our relationship. It's just—there. Something we can enjoy and discuss or not discuss. It's mutually satisfactory—fine. I'm enjoying every day. I like the work I do. I'm having a good time and I'm comfortable—lots of creature comforts as well as very good health and a lovely woman. You don't ask for a whole lot more than that. I'm not much concerned with making long-range plans. When we bought the ranch I felt I'd arrived at the ultimate and made a lot of statements like "Bury me right here, boy, I ain't movin'." Then I found out that such goals aren't hard and fast. I'd like to spend more time at leisure and travel. I'd also like to direct a picture but I'm kind of torn about this because it would mean spending long hours on the job—a terrific commitment of time.

In the past when the specter of divorce would pop up in our marriage—usually as a threat—I was terrified, because my parents were divorced and I thought of it as a black mark, a failure. Like—You *failed,* you *failed!* Hell, I was married twenty-two years—that's a failure? For me the divorce is a success because I'm a happier person and I hope it's a success for Irene too. I think she has the capability for being happier with another man than she was with me. The marriage itself—our marriage—it wasn't a success or a failure, but some of both. You can't say it was a failure, because that negates anything that was good in the entire relationship—and I say that not only because no one likes to negate twenty-two years of their life but also because it just flat out isn't true. It wasn't twenty-two years of hell—it wasn't that. We did some terrific things together, had some marvelous experiences. And the achievements, the move up north—going out and sitting on the porch in the evening after working all day—it was a great feeling, a fantastic feeling! I was very happy with the ranch—it was something Irene and I could share and there was a lot of enjoyment in that. It just wasn't . . . enough.

Afterthoughts

We asked in the final lines of our first chapter: What caused these old marriages to come apart? And what held them together, albeit by increasingly frayed and tangled threads, for so many years?

At least part of the answer to both questions can be found in the contrast between past and present attitudes toward marriage. Twenty years ago, when the unions described here were young, there was a heavy stigma attached to divorce, and marriage was entered into as a lifetime commitment. No, it did not always last, but the expectation was an integral part of the contract. One did not rush off to a lawyer because "We can't communicate on an emotional level," or because "I'm not having any fun in bed." One did not promise to love, honor and cherish, and then hedge with the postscript ". . . unless of course we don't get along." Divorce was humiliating, personally and socially degrading—it just wasn't done.

These old marriages were conceived and reared on the concept of "hanging in there." In another psychological climate they might not have weathered more than two seasons —who knows? But they came of age, or approached it, in the midst of a revolution that took deadly aim at many of the traditional values that sustained them. Since people are shaped and molded by the times in which they live, by what their state and their peers regard as right and proper, or at least allowable, certainly it is easier in almost every respect to end a marriage today than it was twenty or even ten years ago. Diana remarked, ". . . in the last year we've seen a lot of couples separate, people in our age bracket, and that has given him incentive." And from William, "Oh, sure, that makes sense, why not? That's the way you do it these days."

It is easier, yes. But easy? None of the marriages witnessed in the preceding interviews was ended easily. The process, in each case, was long and painful, full of guilt, regret, hesitation and great sadness.

In our sample, regardless of the complex circumstances building to separation, it was the man who did the leaving. But for many years the ties that held the men in the marriages were very strong. Each man mentioned that he had positive feelings for his wife during much, if not all, of their time together. This must certainly have been a factor in the longevity of these partnerships. Roger comments, "I liked her all during the marriage, had a great liking for her," and Gabriel says, "We liked each other and wanted to get along, yet somehow we were blocked." Guilt about abandoning a pregnant wife or young children was also a potent binding force. Stefan puts it clearly, "There's a lot of guilt in leaving a family and you don't easily get up and walk out when you have young children." Half of the men spoke of the feelings of security the marriage gave them. Max, for example: "I was very dependent on the relationship, even the unpleasant aspects of it, even the fighting."

But finally, all of them wanted out. Their frustrated exit lines read, "I just couldn't live that way any more . . . I absolutely did not want to go on like that . . . I want to do something else . . . I don't want to do this any more!" Why? Why later and not sooner? To appreciate some of the causes unique to midlife divorce, it is helpful to turn to the research of Dr. Daniel Levinson and his colleagues at Yale University. Dr. Levinson's theories are highly regarded and widely quoted and his is a most esteemed heritage: Erikson out of Jung out of Freud out of Shakespeare, who observed through Jacques, his melancholy cynic in *As You Like It,* that "... one man in his time plays many parts/his acts being seven ages." Levinson proposes four major developmental "ages," discrete stages in a man's life, each with its own concerns and conflicts. The time that concerns us here is called "Midlife Transition," which is seen as occurring between forty and forty-five and is defined as a period of moderate to severe crisis. It is a time of uncompromising reappraisal of all aspects of a man's life, "arising in part from a heightened awareness of his mortality and a desire to use the remaining time more wisely."

The awareness of mortality was a highly significant factor for the men in our study. The physical events that occur around forty—the normal waning of youthful vitality, personal illness, the death of a close relative, friend or fellow worker—are *mortality messages.* Upon receipt of the message, the future shrinks markedly and takes on priceless value; it becomes an urgent concern that priorities in a man's work and his personal life be reevaluated and determined before it is too late.

Four of the six men interviewed had ominous experiences with illness and/or death, and they were explicit in their concerns about time running out and the approach of old age. William provides a full-blown example: Around the time he turned forty, his father, his sister, and his best friend died, all after lingering illnesses. He had surgery for cancer and shortly after for a ruptured disc. Add to the injuries of death, illness and disability, the insult of losing his private practice, and it might be said that William was delivered a grossly unfair overdose of the mortality message. "It's like the future became very short and unwelcome. I thought about how I only have so much life left—I'm on the downhill part and what do I want to do for the end?"

Levinson states that "Many men are able to consider seriously in their late thirties and early forties marital problems that they previously ignored or only dimly acknowledged. . . . The flaws that were present in the marriage at the start, plus other problems that entered over the course of time, become unbearable to one of the partners. The other partner, while actually having many grievances, denies them and clings to the status quo."

And this indeed appears to be what happened in the marriages we examined. The men, beset with a new, sharpened and sometimes terrifying awareness of the finiteness of time, took a long, hard look at the past, present and future. What had previously been accepted as the norm became intolerable. The women had many grievances, but they clung to the status quo.

Sex was viewed by all eleven people as a serious flaw in the marital fabric. Both men and women expressed dissatisfaction with various aspects of the sexual relationship. Kate tells us, "I think that distance in bed leads to and feeds other kinds of distance. I know sex isn't everything but it sure can mess up everything if it's in bad trouble."

In each of the marriages, sex was "in bad trouble," certainly toward the end, and also at different points along the way. Problems arose around pregnancy, infrequency, abstinence, physical attraction, orgasm, impotence, intimacy, affection and infidelity. An impressive list. And throughout there is an underlying sense of helplessness about not being able to improve the situation. In most cases a shroud of embarrassed silence eventually dropped over the whole painful issue. As Max said, ". . . we did not talk about it . . . embarrassing for both of us." And Stefan: "There was none of the openness between us necessary for a discusssion of it." The most extreme example of the incapacity to deal with sexual problems comes from Kate: "We did not have intercourse for a little over three years and as unbelievable as it sounds, it was *never* mentioned." *We could not discuss it!* A recurring theme. The lyrics vary, but the melody is hauntingly familiar.

But—in all fairness—if you take men and women who walked down the aisle relatively inexperienced and naive in sexual matters, mix in the debilitating myths of the day from "vaginal orgasm" to "the male fucking machine," add a dollop of Hollywood fantasy where the handsome hero and his lady fair disappear into the sunset but never the bedroom to make the babies that are instant dampeners to ardor and romance, then finally sprinkle generously with the heritage of inhibition about bodily function—it is a wonder that any of the marriages made in the fifties are alive and well today.

As is all too evident, the inability to communicate was not limited to sexual concerns—it extended to and eroded those areas we think of as deeply personal—places where we hide ourselves, where we store our misgivings about who we are, how we look, what we do, what we dream of doing—and not the least, what we are afraid of. Ellen said that over the years she had learned she could not discuss her unhappiness with Stefan. Diana said, "I always had to keep certain kinds of feelings to myself." And Kate observed, somewhat wistfully, that she and William began to assume a lot about what "the other felt, or wanted, or needed instead of going through the pain of finding out what really was going on." The men described how their signals were blocked or weakened, as with Roger, who confesses he is unable to communicate on the feeling level, and Stefan, who says, "I have a terrible time expressing angry feelings." Or, when a message was transmitted, there was no one tuned in on the other end of the line. Stan says, "After you say it three times why say it again? It's not being listened to even if it's being heard." William, early in his marriage, complained to Kate about "a few things and it seemed to make her so mean I decided it wasn't worth it." At times the entire connection was obscured by static. As Gabriel says, "Really good talk was rare."

The personal exposure required in a truly intimate relationship involves tremendous risk to our poor, fragile egos. Diana speaks of "opening yourself up from head to toe . . . revealing everything," and that "it may be you have to be so sure of yourself that this act of total trust and total giving and total exposure has no fear in it."

None of these marriages achieved the level of assurance and openness that Diana describes. They were tragically flawed in terms of sexual expectation and the sharing of that vast emotional interior we have come to call good communication. Even so, they labored, tongue-tied and hamstrung into and beyond the twentieth year.

Each man expressed some form of dissatisfaction with his work. The death of Roger's father prompted him to go to law school because "he would rather be an old lawyer than an old salesman." Stan felt he had "never been a major hit at anything." Stefan was "under a great deal of stress at the office and could only continue on in the same way, working harder and harder and putting in more hours." Gabriel sensed something "nagging" at him and questioned his lack of ambition. Max was "working my butt off," and William, ironically the most highly educated of the men interviewed, was the most disparaging of his own achievement: "I'm just a hack."

Discontent with work was compounded by feeling unappreciated and taken for granted at home. Gabriel, in his efforts to find a new outlet for his creativity, felt "misunderstood by Julia." Stan became increasingly resentful about the domestic chores he was expected to do on weekends. Stefan complained that Ellen made him feel that what he said was "not worth listening to." William thought Kate was just waiting to get rid of him, and Max came to believe that Irene "did not like me as a person." Again, these grievances were not resolved—they were stored away and brooded upon.

Four of the marriages were strongly affected by the drinking of either one or both partners. William felt that Kate's drinking reflected on him, that it meant he "wasn't being good to her, wasn't making her happy," whereas Kate saw it as a reaction to her mother's death. Stefan, a reformed alcoholic, observed, "Ellen is two distinct personalities and she changes suddenly from one to the other when she drinks." Stan states that his wife's drinking was finally the cause of his leaving, that he "just couldn't handle it any more." But it is Max, as it often is, who sums up the practical aspects of the issue: "You just can't deal with problems when you have a load of alcohol under your belt."

As was noted earlier, the presence of young children can keep a disintegrating marriage superficially intact. However, the growing independence and self-sufficiency of adolescents liberates parents from many nurturing duties, and can reduce the amount of guilt involved in leaving. William remembered thinking he was not going to do as his father did, "not going to get a divorce, at least until the kids are grown up." And in some cases, the nuisance value of an older child makes a contribution to the breakup. Roger felt his inability to cope with his son was "another reason I was happy to leave."

A yearning for romance, for passion, often reasserts itself during the middle years and can provide the impetus to end a troubled marriage. Gabriel said that when he "got into bed with Margot, it was like a revolution shook me," and he thought, "God—that whole marriage was a waste." And William recalled thinking, "[That's] what life's all about—to have some kind of fancy love affair."

Consider: A man's recognition that there is more time in his past than there is in his future; that he has not achieved what he set out to achieve, or worse that he has and found it hollow; that he feels unappreciated, isolated, devalued and sexually frustrated at home—and the result is tremendous resentment against all the family responsibilities he is carrying, and has been carrying for twenty years. He begins to feel and hope and demand that there must be more to life than hard work and obligation; that there must be some pleasures and rewards for himself. It seemed to William that all the things he'd done had "been for other people," and Stan felt he was "responsible for the whole fucking world!" All the men cried out for change, but these were silent shouts, or awkward, hostile, bewildered efforts that went unrecognized for what they were.

Given the circumstances outlined, it is only a few short steps to the door and the outburst, "*I don't want to do this any more!*" The scene—twenty long years in the making— is set for separation.

But what of the women, "clinging to the status quo," unaware of or denying how desperate the situation has become. It is significant that the women who here tell their stories have certain background elements in common. All are attractive, middle-aged, Caucasian, middle to upper-middle class in terms of education, and/or social and financial status. All worked outside the home before the birth of the first child, but none had what she regarded as a career. All viewed their positions as wife and mother not just as a job, but as a way of life. Julia and Kate had conflicts about career versus family, but these were resolved early on in favor of the latter. In short, these women are highly representative of an old American tradition: Go to school, fall in love, get married, raise a family, live happily ever after.

While none was emotionally prepared for the loss of her marriage, each had nevertheless begun to broaden her horizons in terms of returning to school, work, or other time- and energy-consuming activities outside the home in the years prior to separation, and these changes corresponded to the emerging independence of her children. Women, particularly women who become mothers, do not develop in the same way as men. They take time off for motherhood. Concerns about "Who Am I?" and "Where Am I Going?" take a back seat for several years to the engulfing experience of bearing and nurturing children, running a home, caring for the family. In their late thirties and early forties, with diminishing responsibilities, many women take up where they had left off earlier in self-fulfillment. Depending on how it is approached and how it is viewed by both partners, this kind of personal expansion can have either favorable or disastrous effects on the marriage. In these marriages, it was seen by both men and women—in retrospect—as one of the ways in which the marital gap was widened.

Paradoxically, four of the five women express a feeling of well-being for some time prior to the separation; they had distanced themselves emotionally and intellectually from their marriages, and were finding increasing personal satisfaction in their own activities. They were all, like Kate, "having a love affair with my brain." Kate, Julia and Diana had returned to school, Fran went into business, and Ellen was investing herself happily in community work. Men and women alike echo in some fashion Roger's statement, "We were each living our own lives." But with the women, there was a contented ring to the words, like those from Julia: "I was becoming more independent . . . I was getting stronger . . . stronger and happier with myself," and then Diana's in-

sight during the aftermath that ". . . it was me that was growing—it wasn't the union."

Like their husbands, the women had serious grievances,
but for reasons that are unclear—to them and to us—all had
come to a decision to remain in the marriage. It may be, as
Julia says, because "I thought that was the way marriage was
supposed to be." Even when faced with the reality of separation, the earliest reaction was a desire, and in some cases
desperate attempts, to keep the men from leaving. Kate acknowledges that "this may have to do with a lot of things:
not wanting to be alone, fear of being old, loss of self-esteem,
rejection, habit—a whole lot of complex things." All of the
women emphasize the *length* of the marriage as a factor, and
they view with dismay the loss of such a long investment in
time. Listen to Fran: "If our marriage had been five years or
even ten years I think I could have accepted it a lot easier—
but twenty-two years? That's almost half my life." What goes
unsaid and lies very close to the center of the issue is, "I am
not young any more. It's too late to start over. How will I live
without the only life I know? and I am afraid—I am scared
to death!"

Regardless of the nature of the marriage—marvelous or
miserable—it is apparent that the mere state of it often provides emotional, social and financial security that the partners, particularly women basically ill-prepared for
independence, are reluctant to give up. Even Diana, who
sees herself as strong and competent, has reservations: "I
think it's the insecure parts of me—the weak spots—that
cause me to want him to stay."

It is also pertinent that these women have been caught in
a cultural crossfire that bombards them with conflicting information about the intrinsic value of the way in which they
have spent such a large part of their lives. They entered their
marriages when the traditional housewife was a highly respected member of society, and they ended them harshly

instructed by some of their liberated sisters that they had enjoyed a twenty-year free ride.

Paradoxes, irony, confusion. None of the women has formed a clear-cut explanation for the failure of her marriage. All have sifted through the rubble again and again, coming up with clues which they often preface with "perhaps" and "maybe." Even Julia, with her view from the bridge of five years, concludes wearily, "Midlife crisis? Women's lib? Mother figure . . . father figure . . . craziness . . . ? What's the difference now?" And Kate, still sifting, asks with a touch of fey humor, "Will the real way I feel about this please stand up?"

Still, they all willingly assume a full share of the responsibility for a foundered enterprise, and they express positive and charitable feelings about the former mate. This is also true of the men. Sociologist Robert Weiss speaks of a "persistent marital bond." In his work he finds that many people continue to be drawn to their ex-spouses. He compares this bonding to the attachment children experience toward their parents, and suggests that while most of the components of love are reversible, *attachment* "once developed can be sustained by proximity alone and fades only slowly in response to absence." Stefan illustrates this concept when he says of Ellen, ". . . there are strong feelings for her. One does not live with a person for all those years and suddenly cut it off. I can't live with her any more, but I do love her very much."

To return to the first of the original questions—What caused these old marriages to come apart?—we have outlined the causes as they were seen by the speakers themselves: societal permission, midlife mortality messages and reappraisal on the part of the men, long-standing and unresolved problems centering around sex and communication, drinking, grievance stockpiling, emotional and intellectual distancing—all validating Diana's observation, "It's nothing that happened, no one thing—not in the last seven months or the last two or three years or the last ten years—it's what has taken place and has not taken place for twenty-five years."

And the second question—What held these couples together? They have told us that their marriages were sustained by fear of social stigma, feelings of guilt, responsibility, dependence, security, lethargy and—in many cases—genuine respect, liking and love.

We can speculate that over the years of a long marriage the partners either consciously or unconsciously come to terms with the union, regardless of its quality. Even though both are aware of serious shortcomings, the marital bond becomes so firmly sealed, so well known, so much a part of habit, it becomes fixed. A feeling of family settles in and the mate is the person one automatically lists as *next of kin.* "In case of death, accident, or madness, please notify . . ." A powerful and enduring bond.

And so . . . they did not all live happily ever after. But then, these are not fairy tales. It is evident from the interviews that some of the men and women have found more satisfaction than others in a new way of life; some are still searching for it, and some are still sorting through the pieces of the old one. The adjustment was, and is, in many ways more difficult for the women than for the men. It may be that this is more a function of "being left"—a severe shock to the healthiest sense of self-regard—than of gender. Further, except in the case of Ellen, "another woman" was involved at the time of the separation. Most women can more readily cope with the loss of a husband who leaves her to do great work, become a starving artist, join a monastery, or even to die, than she can accept his preference for another woman. The green-eyed monster that lives in all of us is unleashed and rages forth in statements like "What I really want to do is kill her."

All of the women experienced the profound depression, ambivalence and feelings of loneliness that are a natural reaction to loss. "It takes time" is accepted on an intellectual level, but for a period it is impossible to believe one will ever be whole again. Julia says it was two years before she recovered, and Fran reports a year and a half of mourning.

Establishing new relationships with the opposite sex was also easier—though by no means a simple matter—for the men than for the women. Both Roger and Stan had a long history of extramarital activity, but even they encountered many unsatisfactory liaisons after separation. William and Gabriel left their wives for other women, but each described frustration and disillusion at the end of that romantic rainbow. It is interesting that the two men who entered into what they regard as a satisfying relationship with a woman came to it without the extra burden of infidelity. Stefan and Max each made a clean break with one woman—with the marriage itself—before beginning a relationship with another. Both of these men also express contentment with their work. Max sums up "the good life": "I'm enjoying every day. I like the work I do. I'm having a good time and I'm comfortable —lots of creature comforts as well as very good health and a lovely woman. You don't ask for a whole lot more than that."

The middle-aged woman who enters singledom often has to make more drastic revisions in her self-image than does the middle-aged man, especially if she sees herself as a matron far more at home at a dinner party with friends or on a family camping trip than whooping it up at the local disco. The words "date" and "boyfriend" stick in her throat, and it may require urging from friends, several shopping trips, a course at the gym, psychotherapy, a visit to the plastic surgeon, or all of the above before she is ready, in the words of Kate's son, to go "out and see the world." Most seem to need a period of recovery before they are willing to risk it, but sooner or later they do.

Julia has remarried, is teaching and performing and is "100 percent" happier. Fran, after three years, is seeing a man she is "very, very fond of," but right now just wants "to be able to support myself, to be available to my kids while they still need me, and to have fun." Ellen, a year following separation, experienced an emotional setback when she learned that Stefan was living with Ruth. The reaction was severe but brief, and in a matter of months she was again receiving great satisfaction from her work. Her religious convictions restrain her from active interest in the opposite sex, but she would "like to have a male friend." Kate, alone of the women, attempted to cure her wounded self-esteem by "proving I was still desirable to men" by "leaping into bed." In addition, a week following separation, she and William began a sexual relationship that has continued up to the time of their interviews nine months later. As was observed earlier, Kate is "still sifting through the rubble." Diana, the only one of the women interviewed who had extramarital affairs earlier in her marriage, saw this as a factor in her relatively mild reaction to "the other woman." "Maybe it's because of my own experiences. I understand that people do get involved with other people." She acknowledges a need for companionship, but more important, she wants to "get on with my life . . . one change at a time."

All share Diana's desire to get on with their lives and at the same time they recognize that they carry with them the memorabilia of the past: long years of shared experience, and children jointly conceived and loved—the community property of their immortality. They express positive feelings about the future, some more couched in caution or confusion than others. But none of these people is standing still; all have moved on, taking with them new awareness and new ways of dealing with themselves and the world.

Diana says, "Perhaps *now* the twenty-five years can be put in their proper place and we can go on with our lives—with who we are now." We sincerely hope these wishes are realized by all eleven of "our" people—people we have come to know so well, and to care about so much.